JACK IN THE BOX

A TV
COMMENTATOR'S
DIARY OF
ENGLAND
V
WEST INDIES

JACK IN THE BOX

A TV
COMMENTATOR'S
DIARY OF
ENGLAND
V
WEST INDIES

JACK BANNISTER

Macdonald
Queen Anne Press

A QUEEN ANNE PRESS BOOK

© Jack Bannister 1992

First published in Great Britain in 1992 by
Queen Anne Press, a division of
Macdonald & Co (Publishers) Ltd
165 Great Dover Street
London SE1 4YA

Scorecards: Malcolm Ashton

Design: Peter Champion

Cover Photographs: Front – Hugh Morris evades a bouncer from Curtly Ambrose
at the Oval (*Allsport/Adrian Murrell*); front inset – Jack Bannister in the commentary
box at Lord's (*Allsport/Adrian Murrell*); back – Graham Gooch and Viv Richards
(*Graham Morris*); wraparound – The Oval (*Allsport/Adrian Murrell*)

A CIP catalogue record for this book is available from the British Library

ISBN 0–356–20771–4

Typeset by August Filmsetting, Haydock, St Helens
Printed and bound in Great Britain by
BPCC Hazells Ltd
Member of BPCC Ltd

CONTENTS

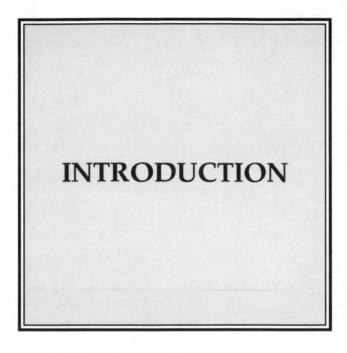

INTRODUCTION

This account of what was only the second Test series in England this century to finish 2–2 is my re-creation of the immediacy of the magnificent summer of 1991, as seen from the BBC television commentary box.

It is not a reflective look at a series which ebbed and flowed – or flowed, ebbed and flowed again for Graham Gooch and England – because a diary format which also features the views and opinions of distinguished former Test captains like Richie Benaud, Ray Illingworth and Tony Lewis, together with two leading former England batsmen, Geoffrey Boycott and Tom Graveney, carries more weight if put to paper as said at the time.

Not quite warts and all, although there are remarkably few warts considering the claustrophobic conditions under which five of us spend nearly a week of our lives during each Test match. Except at Lord's, the commentary boxes at the other five Test grounds in England are so tiny that working at the front-line desk, at which are seated a scorer, commentator and summariser, requires an ability to maintain unblinking concentration in spite of almost every distraction that man can muster.

There are also six television monitors in the box, including the one used for telestrating explanatory points to the viewer by 'drawing' on the TV picture, as well as the lifeline for the commentator and summariser – the two consoles into which are plugged our earpieces which connect us to the scanner van, usually sited at the rear of the pavilion. Each console comprises a switch which either takes us 'live' to the world, or to the producer, and other controls for volume and programme sounds from either channel. Add in sponge mats for our microphones, and there is little room for scorecards or the notes we have prepared on the players. The chairs are almost inevitably designed to cause maximum discomfort – again Lord's is the exception – and the windows are either impossible to open, or offer only the fiercest possible natural air-conditioning which can soon reshuffle the carefully prepared piles of records of our omniscient scorer, Malcolm Ashton.

If commentating is a form of rabbiting, it takes place in a hutch which, at Trent Bridge for example, is less than 70 square feet in area. However, where Lord's loses out is in the position of its commentary box, where we sit at an angle of 45 degrees to the wicket, unlike the other five grounds where we view events from behind the bowler's arm.

England's epic struggle against the West Indies in 1991 was my fourth summer as co-commentator with Richie and Tony, and the gripping cricket played made it my most enjoyable yet.

As a series, it had everything. There were unexpected home wins at the beginning at Headingley and at the end at the Oval. The first Test defied the arctic weather to produce only the fifth Test match in England since 1912 in which 40 wickets were taken for a match aggregate of fewer than 800 runs and although, because of poor pitches, such a statistic was more common in the first 30 years of Test cricket in England, it was still only the 13th instance in 339 Tests.

Where it failed at Headingley, the rain won at Lord's, but the weather gods then gave up the struggle and blessed the games at Trent Bridge, Edgbaston and the Oval with blazing sunshine to match the blazing cricket. Full houses were recorded half a dozen times, with Sunday play proving an outstanding success at Edgbaston and the Oval.

Gooch's wonderful unbeaten 154 in the first Test was one of the few innings in Test history which could be said to be a match-winning one. Throughout the rest of the series, his massive contribution, as batsman and captain, held together a side which only ever functioned on half power. Fears about the vulnerability of Graeme Hick were only too well-founded, and Allan Lamb and Michael Atherton also suffered so badly that Derek Pringle comfortably outscored all three with 128 from seven innings. Furthermore, the 540 deliveries he faced – exactly 90 overs – were more than those faced by any combined two of those three. Robin Smith leaped from tenth to second in the Coopers Deloitte World Ratings, but only Mark Ramprakash, of the other batsmen tried, performed adequately.

It was the same in the bowling department, with Pringle and Phillip DeFreitas carrying the side through the first four Tests, and it says much for the resilience of Gooch that he was able to halve the series with half a side. He is one of the few England captains in history to have a better batting average as captain than as a player. Douglas Jardine was nearly six points better (50·00 compared with 44·60), with Mike Denness (42·14 compared with 34·78), Ted Dexter (53·93 from 42·34) and Peter May (54·03 from 36·42) the next most improved before Gooch. His difference is staggering, considering he once gave up the Essex captaincy because of the strain involved. At the end of the 1991 summer, his 2508 runs from 36 completed innings as captain gave him an average of 69·66, whereas previously he scored 4520 in 124 completed innings at an average of 36·45.

The West Indies were more consistent, with only Phil Simmons failing to contribute a major performance. Batting comparisons between the two sides reveal the lopsided nature of the series. England scored 2323 runs in the five games, including three centuries and six fifties. The West Indies scored 2288 runs and also had three hundreds, but 15 half-centuries.

The one blight on the summer was the turgid over-rate, with England's overall hourly rate of 13·86 putting them three balls every 60 minutes of play ahead of the tourists, whose average was 13·34. If the new International Cricket Council's swingeing new finings system fails, the game is headed inexorably in the wrong direction.

All of these, and many other topics, were debated over the air by an Australian, a Welshman, two Yorkshiremen, a man from the West and a Wulfrunian – not a Brummie, as many people incorrectly label me.

This book features many examples of the wit, wisdom and technical brilliance of the Aussie, the soft, descriptive powers of the man from the Valleys, the no-nonsense, down-to-earth analysis by the pair of Tykes, and the smooth, never unkindly observations from the man of Gloucestershire. Reference to a textbook on the grape gives a variety which might have been grown especially for our team:

RICHIE – *Muscadet*: Makes very dry wine. Should not be sharp – which he isn't – but faintly salty, savoury and refreshing.
TONY – *Gamay Beaujolais*: Light and fragrant.
RAYMOND – *Barbera (in Italy)*: Dark, often sharp wine.
GEOFFREY – *Cabernet Sauvignon*: Grape of great character. Spicy, herby and tannic. Its red wine always needs ageing and usually blending.
TOM – *Verdeso of Rueda (in Castile)*: Potentially fine and long-lived.

And me? Middle-of-the-road house plonk. As the only member of the team who never played Test cricket, it is difficult for me to forget that in our main team of Richie, Tony, Tom, Ray and Geoff, there is a combined count of 320 Test caps, including 72 as captain. Not to mention 17,490 runs between them, and 378 wickets — including Geoffrey's seven. Fortunately, there is an almost complete absence of 'All Our Yesterdays' in their approach and, whatever some viewers might think, whenever the odd game from the past is mentioned, it is either to make a point which is technical, tactical or humorous.

Geoffrey completed his first full season in the box, and was soon in the eye of a storm of newspaper criticism, but most of the carpers missed the point. He never has been, and never will be, anything other than his own man, but at least you know where you stand — or sit — with him. He listened, noted and learned and I have no hesitation in saying that, as a commentator, he is easy to work with.

As well as relating the story of the summer of 1991, this book should give the reader an insight into the complex operation which underpins a cricket commentary. Over 50 production and technical staff are necessary at each Test match for the commentators to do our job. I have not set out to justify anything or anybody, simply to explain.

PLAY!

CHAPTER ONE

JACK
IN
THE
BOX

The happy, foot-tapping music of 'Soul Limbo', played by Booker-T and the MGs, was gently faded. The countdown into Tony Lewis's earpiece from production assistant Jane Whitmore ended 'four-three-two-one-zero', and executive producer Keith Mackenzie followed immediately with two words to herald the BBC's long-awaited televised summer of international cricket between England and the West Indies – 'Cue Tony.'

The date was 23 May 1991 and, coincidentally, the 25th birthday of Graeme Hick, who was about to make his debut for England at Edgbaston, after a seven-year period of qualification, in the first of three Texaco one-day internationals. The atmosphere in the packed ground dripped with anticipation, with everyone eager to see if Graham Gooch could haul England out of the depths of poor technique and approach to which they had slumped against the same Australian players who, only a few weeks later, ran the West Indies so close in the Caribbean.

There was a buzz everywhere – certainly among the crowd, Messrs Lewis, Benaud, Illingworth, Boycott and Bannister in the tiny television commentary box on top of the Edgbaston pavilion, and probably in the two dressing-rooms as well – as we all looked forward to the 33 scheduled days of international cricket which would provide many of the answers to questions not only about players from both sides, but also the important one concerning the spirit in which the summer's cricket would be played.

By common consent, the series between the West Indies and Australia in March and April 1991 contained much that was unacceptable, including general sledging and personal abuse with, reportedly, racial overtones, which is why the pre-tour forecast from Viv Richards that it would be 'a friendly tour' was received with a sceptical politeness by the British media.

Gooch had been so close to giving up the captaincy after the disastrous trip to Australia, that speculation was rife about his long-term future if anything resembling another 'blackwash' befell his team. Pre-match chatter centred on the chances of Hick overcoming the chink in his armour against fast, short-pitched bowling, which several judges feared would be mercilessly exploited by whichever four-pronged demolition squad Richards had at his disposal.

Would Allan Lamb survive the summer, now there were increasing doubts about his form and fitness? Could Robin Smith, omitted from the one-day squad, come back after a poor winter? In the bowling department, how could England mask the absence of Angus Fraser? Could Phillip DeFreitas sustain the slight improvement in consistency he made in Australia, and could Richard Illingworth capitalise on his chance in the one-day squad, to nose ahead of Phil Tufnell?

All these and many other issues were debated, but one name dominated the morning chatter. Ian Botham was back in the England dressing-room for the first time in two years, having forced his way into the side with consistent form for Worcestershire with bat and ball, including a spectacular 161 against the tourists. At least he had persuaded the selectors he was still worth an England place, but David Gower had patently not. Even three centuries in six Tests had not wiped clean a slate apparently besmirched by his airborne antics in Australia, although lack of runs for Hampshire was the official party line to explain the absence of the one man who could give the England batting order what it lacked – a class left-hander.

West Indies had their problems – but fewer of them. Desmond Haynes and Gordon Greenidge, opening partners in 89 Tests, had fitness and form problems respectively. If the bedrock of the West Indies batting was to be splintered, could Phil Simmons step in and become an authentic Test cricketer? Was Viv Richards really past it, and how would other senior players like Malcolm Marshall and Jeffrey Dujon stand up to another hard series?

The West Indies pace attack can never be described as 'thin', but the absence of Ian Bishop appeared to leave the front-line quartet of Marshall, Curtly Ambrose, Courtney Walsh and Patrick Patterson short of quality support. For the first time ever in England, their touring party did not include a spinner, and it seemed that the Test & County Cricket Board's curious decision to halt play at 7pm in the Cornhill Tests, even if the minimum daily ration of 90 overs had not been met, could lead to a situation similar to the unsavoury one on the final day of the Trinidad Test in 1990. Then, in the knowledge that bad light would prevent the final 20 overs being bowled, only 17 overs were bowled in the last 115 minutes of play.

By 10am, the commentary box was chaotic. Sound engineers were checking our microphones, and our two studio managers, Dave Bowden and Steve Pierson, were helping the commentators as well as chattering away through portable mikes to the scanner van, in which Keith Mackenzie and his staff were at full stretch, trying to pull all the right strings together as the clock ticked remorselessly towards the on-air time of 10.20am.

Tony Lewis scribbled away, before he was shunted into the in-vision torture-chamber to give his scene-setting brief to the viewing millions. Next time you watch the relaxed and smiling 'AR' take you through the teams, the toss and weather prospects, just remember the babble of cues and instructions which are battering his right ear. The whole exercise reflects great credit on him, Keith Mackenzie and his crew, who are invariably flying a plane, not always totally airworthy, by the seat of their pants.

At 10.05am, our floor managers wanted a commentators' rota so that the Boss in the scanner van could programme Tony when it came to his hand-over to the commentary box, just before the start of play. The compilation of the duty lists of commentators and summarisers is handled separately by Richie and Ray Illingworth. Both deal in half-hour stints, and both take into account any commitments, away from the microphone, of their colleagues. These include a daily newspaper report for the *Birmingham Post* by me from Sunday to Friday, the much more demanding deadlines for Richie and Tony for the *News of the World* and the *Sunday Telegraph* on Saturdays, and the occasional sponsors' lunch for Ray, Geoff Boycott and Tom Graveney.

The daily arrangement among the commentators is that Tony does a maximum of three of the scheduled 12 stints, although any of his allotted three are at the mercy of the weather and intervals when he is on permanent 'in-vision' call. Richie and I share the other nine, five one day and four the next, while the two summarisers share each day evenly. The planning is meticulous and the disciplines are rigid.

An essential member of the team is our scorer, Malcolm Ashton. A Lancastrian with a wonderful, giggling sense of humour, he wet-nurses us with a flow of figures, records and pending landmarks which help keep us ahead of the game. The main commentator is flanked by him on the right and the summariser on his left, with the monitors sited according to the space available in different boxes.

At 10.15am, I moved into my seat, gave a sound level through my microphone, (which is so directional that it allows normal conversation to take place only a few feet away) and hooked up to sound to enable me listen to Tony and his summariser when they went live. My console has volume controls for the producer and summariser, and I can also call up the sound of the programme preceding the cricket on the relevant channel.

I looked out over a packed, expectant Edgbaston, listening to Keith and Tony tidy up the loose ends. I glanced at the monitor and saw the famous BBC globe quickly enmeshed in revolving spaghetti and one meat ball, before the evocative pastische of sepia pictures unrolled to the music which is known to cricket fans all over the world. Frank Worrell and Wes Hall led the way, with Worrell re-appearing to run out Derek Shackleton in the 1963 Lord's Test, before the balletic Michael Holding precedes a subtle switch to colour. Richards, Gooch and Marshall hold centre stage in turn, filmed doing various forms of hand-jive as the music bubbles on.

I watched this fascinating piece of film for the first time and then I heard the countdown from Jane, followed by the two words I was to hear dozens of times more during the summer. 'Cue Tony.'

Gooch won the toss and, under overcast skies, decided to field and see what sort of mess the West Indies could get into against an attack ideally suited to the conditions. When he led England out, I listened nervously as Tony and Ray finished their double act and tried to shut out the noise behind me. Richie's *Sporting Life* rustled as he meticulously dissected the form – a daily labour of love, even though the number of bets he had during the summer could be numbered on one flexible, former leg-spinning hand.

Stage managers Dave and Steve muttered back to base that everything was in order. My stomach churned, as it always does before the first few words force themselves into the mike. *Come on AR! Speak to me!* I could see Botham and Hick in picture and I wanted to speak. Still he went on, calmly giving a re-cap of the teams and toss, and then I heard the magic words from Keith: 'Tony, it's Jack-In-The-Box when you're ready.'

We were off and running.

CHAPTER TWO

THE FIRST CLASHES

ONE-DAY INTERNATIONALS
23, 25, 27 MAY

SELECTION

The England selectors chose 13 players, including the Worcestershire trio of Graeme Hick, Ian Botham and Richard Illingworth, whose big chance it was to nose ahead of Middlesex's Phil Tufnell for a regular place in the full England team. Mark Ramprakash was given deserved senior recognition after a successful 'A' tour of Sri Lanka, and Neil Fairbrother was given another chance to make his left-handed mark for England. Much of the attention of the media, expected to focus on the debut of Hick, was deflected by the return of the Prodigal Son.

Despite playing only eight five-day Tests and eight one-day internationals since he joined Worcestershire from Somerset in 1987, and none in either format for two years, Botham showed that his love of centre-stage had not deserted him when, on the day the squad was announced, six days before the game, he hit a magnificent 161 for his county against the West Indies. Not only that, but his form with the ball in his new medium-pace style proved to the selectors that he was still capable of doing a good job for England as a fourth or fifth bowler. Those people ignorant of his cricketing education were now realising that, far from being a bowler who just ran up and let the ball go, he had a full and deep knowledge of the manipulation of a good hand action – so essential to produce and control movement in the air and off the seam. Not quite a master-craftsman like his mentor, Tom Cartwright, Botham was still light years ahead of most other younger, English qualified bowlers. At the age of 35, it was a tribute to him that he had convinced the selectors that he was worth a place, even if David Gower had not.

In the enforced absence of Angus Fraser, Chris Lewis was chosen to complement a solid-looking one-day seam attack, together with Phillip DeFreitas and the recalled Derek Pringle. Predictably, England omitted Ramprakash and David Lawrence – chosen ahead of Devon Malcolm – on a pitch expected to favour seam rather than pace.

The West Indies chose their strongest available side, with Desmond Haynes not risked because of a recurring back problem and, with Gordon Greenidge suffering a serious knee injury in the second game at Old Trafford, the most experienced opening pair in the history of international cricket was fated never to walk out together again on the tour.

THURSDAY 23 MAY EDGBASTON

Graham Gooch won the toss and decided to field. From the commentary box I watched umpires John Hampshire and Mervyn Kitchen square up the stumps, looked at the monitor and waited. And waited as Botham semaphored to the dressing-room for a long sweater before a ball had been bowled. Everything seemed in slow motion, until I heard the hand-over from 'AR' and heard myself launch the BBC summer of cricket with a great original line: 'And now the first ball of the international summer, DeFreitas to Greenidge.'

With that equivalent of my commentating single to get off the mark out of the way, I settled into my half-hour stint. There is nothing like a couple of statistics to engage the tongue in the right gear, and the viewing public were soon aware that Greenidge was playing in his 127th one-day international, and DeFreitas his 60th.

I needed a wicket to remove any remaining inhibitions, and Phil Simmons obliged by mis-driving a ball from Chris Lewis to his captain at mid-off. With DeFreitas completing a spell of 6-3-4-0, the West Indies were soon toiling on a pitch which was hardly satisfactory for such a showpiece contest. The pace was slow and the indifferent bounce made strokeplay such a risky business that only 13 runs came in the first 10 overs, and that included two fours.

The 18,500 capacity crowd were impatient – not with the failure of Greenidge and Richie Richardson to break the stranglehold, but because they wanted Botham to bowl. He came on for the 13th over, and was captioned on the screen, rightly, with a description he probably found hurtful: 'right arm medium'. The only surprise was that his first ball did not dismiss Richardson, but he put that right with his second ball for his country since 11 August 1989. It swung and seamed away from the Antiguan, and Illingworth took the catch in the covers. Pure theatre, with players and crowd alike marvelling at the return of Golden Arm.

Viv Richards prowled about the crease for 17 overs, while his great friend and former Somerset colleague soured the cream of West Indies batting with three more good wickets. Greenidge got a beauty which lifted and left him on its way to wicket-keeper Jack Russell; Gus Logie was beautifully caught at deep backward square leg by DeFreitas, about 20 yards wide of the boundary ropes over which the little Trinidadian had parked Botham for six off his first ball. As Logie was dropped by Lewis of his second ball, the all-rounder could have taken three wickets in his first 29 deliveries, and the crowd was on the verge of hysteria.

When Logie did finally fall, Botham's figures were 9-2-31-3 and the score was 78 for four after 29 overs. Still Richards was there, having survived an edge off Botham through a vacant second slip area and two mis-hits off Derek Pringle over mid-off when he aimed leg-side. Even Richards could not get away with it for ever, and when Gooch shrewdly brought himself on 25 minutes before lunch, another mis-hit found Neil Fairbrother taking 15 rapid running paces to his left to hold the sort of steeler which gives the fielder at least two re-runs of the cricketing consequences of dropping the catch. It was an intelligent piece of bowling from the England captain, who was not afraid to toss up a slower off-spinner.

Richards' 30 came off 45 balls, and his departure left Carl Hooper and Jeffrey Dujon in charge – but not for long. Botham played his last trump, with the help of another catch for Russell off a perfect outswinger to Hooper, to complete his best figures for England in 99 one-day internationals.

As Richie pointed out, Botham entered the game at 16 for one, and left it in near-ruin as a contest, 21 overs later, at 99 for six. Dujon was well caught by Lewis, low to his right, in the final over before lunch off Illingworth, and even though Curtly Ambrose survived the plumbest looking LBW appeal by Illingworth after offering no stroke and being hit three inches below the knee roll, with his front foot no more than 18 inches forward and a couple of inches outside off stump, England were so much on top, the contest as such seemed almost over.

Geoffrey criticised Gooch for not posting a second slip for his seamers, and forecast the downfall of Malcolm Marshall in exactly the way he was out next ball – caught by Lewis in the gully off DeFreitas.

Courtney Walsh is a joyous tail-ender who offers enormous enjoyment to everyone with a range of strokes which varies from one of the most spectacular leave-alone contortions imaginable, to the sort of flat-batted six over square cover off Lewis which puts the bowler's jaw about knee-height. He and Ambrose added 52 from 60 balls, and the sneaking feeling grew during the mayhem of the last three overs of the innings, which were worth 27, that the West Indies had managed a final total of 173 for eight which would be far from straightforward for England.

Especially when Ambrose followed his opening delivery – a no ball – with the wicket of Gooch. A perfect length delivery pitched 12 inches outside off stump and nipped back to strike a front pad which was no more than a few inches in front of the batting crease.

Hick's first ball in international cricket, for which he had waited seven years, was an age in coming from Ambrose, despite the Worcestershire man passing Gooch on the march, as is his custom, some 25 yards from the pavilion gate. He took a guard of middle and leg, gave the pitch an obligatory tap and was ready. But the West Indies were not. Marshall wandered over to have a chat with Ambrose – though it can hardly have been necessary – and a wasp did its best to fly through the grill of Hick's helmet. The delay was then extended by Logie signalling to the pavilion for a fielding helmet so that he could stand at short leg. All of this could have been done while Hick came to the crease, but Richards and his players clearly had the Worcestershire batsman in their sights, and the trigger would not be pulled until they were ready. I timed it as 77 seconds before Ambrose released the drum-tight tension around the ground with a thunderbolt which was jabbed away.

The first of many play-and-miss strokes followed, with the third ball only kept out with another involuntary jab. Ambrose's third over was ominous. He gloved a static Hick, who only just coped with two break-backs with a bat which was far from straight. Ray Illingworth was quick to spot the fault and forecast trouble later in the summer if it was not remedied.

The light was poor and, at 23 for one in the eighth over, the first of two stoppages which forced the game into the second day took the players off. On their return, the West Indies were unlucky not to win a decision against Michael Atherton, who was shown in the slow motion replay to be run out by Hooper by two feet.

Our producer, Keith Mackenzie, always insists that such an incident is replayed at normal speed to show the viewers what the umpire saw, and this policy offers the perfect defence to those critics who, mistakenly, believe that replays are unfair to umpires. In this case, played at normal speed, the decision was nothing more than marginal, proving that the fast finish of a desperate batsman, together with the outstretched bat and a direct hit, can be too much for the naked eye to computerise into an accurate decision.

Hick's unconvincing innings was worth 14 off 47 balls when he was nicely softened up and dismissed by Marshall. The 48th ball whipped back into his abdomen, and the next one – wide of off stump – was pushed with an open face to Richards standing wide at slip. The torture of Hick had begun.

His wicket was to be one of only three for Marshall in the Texaco series and, like Botham, the fast bowler has never taken five wickets in a one-day international. It is a comment on the nature of the limited-overs format that, whereas between them, two of the leading wicket-takers in the history of cricket have taken five wickets or more 49 times in five-day cricket – as well as ten in a match eight times – their five-wicket hauls in a combined 218 one-day games are non-existent.

After 20 overs, England were 60 for two, but the arrival into the attack of Hooper changed the game. With his fifth ball he bowled Allan Lamb for 18 – the ball turned from three inches outside off stump and kept low, hitting the stumps half-way up – and in his next over he had Fairbrother caught at the wicket. The left-hander got a bottom edge, and did not help umpire Hampshire by standing his ground. As the score was then 87 for four, the wicket was no surprise to Richie, who commented that it was the Australian equivalent of the English 'Nelson' score of 111, which is also considered unlucky. Superstition plays a big part in cricket, irrational though it may be. The rationale Down Under is that 87 is 13 short of 100, and thus is an unlucky number by association. Only an Australian mathematician could have worked that out.

Botham came and went in two overs – all the batting time the indifferent light allowed, and so the unfortunate crowd were denied the *raison d'être* of one-day cricket – a result. At 97 for four from 27 overs, England were well placed – particularly as their batting order unusually contained 11 players who had scored a first-class hundred.

FRIDAY 24 MAY

They were all to be needed on the second day, even though the alarm bells did not ring out for seven overs. The West Indians had heard different bells earlier in the morning, when a false fire alarm forced them out on the pavement at 5.30am, although Walsh and Ambrose seemed lively enough in the first half-hour.

Whatever English or Australian supersitition might decree, a score of 123 proved disastrous for Botham. Atherton called him for a sharp single and, although he made his ground, the replay showed that he tore his right hamstring on the eighth of ten running strides. He went down like a sack of potatoes and a delay of seven minutes followed while he was treated by the England physiotherapist, Lawrie Brown. Fairbrother came out to run for him, complete with helmet as the law demands. He need not have bothered as Botham was LBW next ball, stranded by badly affected footwork, to a ball from Walsh which nipped back. Not plumb, but probably out.

Pringle lasted three balls before he was well caught at slip by Richardson, and when Russell was caught by his counterpart off Patterson, England had lost three wickets in 14 balls and slumped to 134 for seven. Atherton was then 55, and was lucky that, with the depth of batting strength, he never needed to organise the strike.

Richards took two fine slip catches in successive overs off Marshall and Patterson to dismiss DeFreitas and Lewis. England had thus lost five wickets for 29 in eight overs, but the hard-headed Illingworth countered the Richards gamble of bowling out his main four bowlers with only 22 needed from 13 overs when he joined Atherton.

The Worcestershire man actually faced 34 out of 51 balls for the match-winning partnership, and marked his senior international debut by coolly changing his bat four balls before he hit the winning boundary off Hooper. Atherton's unbeaten 69 came off 147 balls and earned him the Man of the Match award.

A happy England squad drove the 80 miles up the M6 for the next game at Old Trafford. Richards had a different sort of trip, during which he must have reflected on how his side could lose a match by one wicket in which his bowlers had tossed 38 no balls and wides at England, only four of which were scored from. More than six extra overs compared with seven illegal deliveries from England was hardly a bargain, especially as seven of his batsmen reached double figures compared with three for England.

SATURDAY 25 MAY OLD TRAFFORD

England called up Dermot Reeve for Botham and Eddie Hemmings as stand-by for Illingworth, who took a knock on his left wrist from a throw from Lamb two days earlier, but finally declared himself fit to play. Gooch and Stewart decided to alter the balance of the side and bring in Ramprakash for Botham – thus committing the captain to a full bowling ration.

The West Indies were unchanged, and the umpires were Harold Bird and David Shepherd. Richards won the toss and, like Gooch at Edgbaston, chose to field first, even though conditions were different. A further change brought Tom Graveney into the box in place of Geoffrey.

Ray Illingworth might not have a degree in agronomy, but he is just about the shrewdest reader of pitches I have known. Like women and horses, cricket pitches are notoriously misleading in appearance, but the former England captain invariably gets it right. At the start of play he said: 'It will have much more consistent bounce than Edgbaston, even though there is no great pace. Batsmen will have much more confidence, and their tactic should be to keep enough wickets in hand to attack the fifth makeshift bowler, be it Simmons, Hooper or Richards.' Prophetic words as the first two were to bowl 13 overs for 74.

Gooch and Atherton delighted another big crowd with a well-paced opening partnership of 156, which blossomed after a careful start in which the England captain took 19 balls to move from nine to ten. For once, Atherton led the way, and Tom was soon purring a compliment about his technique. 'He was the only batsman at Edgbaston to come to terms with the pitch, and he has the best basic technique of all the England batsmen. He keeps his head still, and when he plays back, his back foot stays parallel with the crease and keeps him sideways on.'

When England passed 50 in the 18th over, Tom saw Atherton slip for the third time in the session and, pressing his 'lazy mike' switch, asked for a close-up of the opener's shoes. With nine cameras at his disposal, our executive producer chose a close-up from the wide-angle camera, and I heard him tell Tom: 'Coming up after this ball if nothing happens.'

Tom made the valid point that 'there is juice alongside the pitch where the batsmen run, and it is dangerous in the sort of light rubbers Atherton is wearing. Also you wouldn't want to be hit on the toe, because there is no protection. It's a funny game nowadays. They wear helmets, chest protectors and arm guards, yet wear plimsolls which leave them helpless against yorkers.' That was not just a moan from a former player – as Lamb later found to his cost when Ambrose hit his foot, and he could neither field nor play two days later at Lord's.

Patterson let go a couple of head-high bouncers, which brought forth the following lovely story from Richie: 'Patrick has had a varied career. He has played league cricket, and he also played a season for Tasmania, where he was involved in an intriguing little incident when Tasmania went to play New South Wales 100 miles away from Sydney. The story goes that Patrick was not quite at one with his skipper, Roger Woolley, and the afternoon before the game when Roger went in to have a net, Patrick gave him a series of 32 bouncers on the trot to indicate his displeasure.' A nice pause, and then the dead-pan pay-off line: 'Roger Woolley doesn't play with Tasmania any more' – another pause – 'and neither does Patrick.'

Gooch struggled along at one run per over, but the fluent Atherton delighted his home supporters with a range of strokes which so bemused Richards that he mistakenly paired two of his makeshift bowlers – Hooper and Simmons – for two overs before lunch which cost 18, and five more after the break which went for 27.

The fourth ball of the 36th over, bowled by Hooper to Atherton, was arguably the most damaging of the summer to the tourists. Greenidge was at point, and as he turned to chase a cut for four, he collapsed and, after a delay of six minutes, hobbled his way out of the match – never to be seen again on the tour until he accepted an invitation to join our commentary team for the Oval Test in August. His left knee was badly twisted and an operation quickly followed. If, as seems likely, he does not play sufficient first-class cricket to score the eight centuries he needs to become the 23rd man in history to score 100 hundreds, he will become only the third to 'die' in the 90s together with C. B. Fry and J. W. Hearne.

Hooper finally hit the top of Gooch's leg stump as he aimed to cut, to make England 156 for one in the 38th over, and Tom praised him for 'a good innings, considering he wasn't in good form'. Atherton followed five balls later, caught by substitute Brian Lara for 74, and the rest of the innings was dominated by a scintillating 62 off 50 balls from Lamb.

Hick's second attempt to bed down at number three was a determined one, and he was content to let Lamb blaze away after surviving an appeal for a catch to Dujon off his second ball from Hooper. He tried to run the ball through slip, which prompted Tom to say: 'You really must play with the face of the bat at the start of an innings.' Patently obvious, but rarely said and too often ignored.

Lamb rushed his side from 191 for two after 45 overs to 233 off 50, and two fours off an Ambrose over which cost 13 – 11 off the bat – took him to 50 off 40 deliveries, including nine crashing fours. A somewhat deflated Ambrose bowled Hick off the inside edge for 29 out of 102 added for the third wicket, with Richie noting that 'Curtly has given that wicket the high two and a half, and the inside edge isn't worth much more'.

Lamb's brutal innings ended with a fine overhead catch by Dujon off Patterson, and as Richards stalked off the field, he knew that a target of 271 off 55 overs would have been less demanding but for another rash of 23 no balls and wides.

Dujon partnered Simmons, but although both openers profited from a wayward spell of five overs for 27 from Lewis, DeFreitas held them in check with accurate bowling, which earned him figures of 6-3-8-0, and a splendid running catch at deep third man to 'trap' Dujon off Lewis for 21 out of 34. Such an asking rate – 4·93 at the start of the innings – usually precipitates a run out, and Simmons drew a particularly short straw when he was stranded by

Richardson and a relay to the bowler, Pringle, from Hick to Russell first, after a mis-field by Lewis.

We were warned that the Prime Minister would visit the box and, although I heard him, Minister for Sport Robert Atkins, and their entourage come in, I was behind the mike and did not hear the reason for the general laughter until my half-hour stint was finished. John Major's first appearance in our commentary box was at Lord's the previous year, when Raymond engaged him, as Chancellor of the Exchequer, in matters of general finance, domestic and international. Probably not quite the favourite topic for a self-confessed cricket fanatic, but he can have been even less prepared for Ray's greeting this time. As a handshake was exchanged, Ray said: 'Nice to meet you again. What a game you are in. Every time I see you, you've got a different job.' The reply was to the effect that he hoped there was no change next time.

Gooch brought himself on, and first ball went a long way towards settling the match. An away swinger to Richardson bounced, and the Antiguan's attempted favourite square cut edged a catch to Russell to make the score 69 for three in the 21st over.

Other than an innings from Richards to match the destructive quality of his record unbeaten 189 on the same ground in 1984 – coincidentally that came out of a score of 272 for nine – England appeared to have the game in the bag. They erred four balls before tea when, with Richards and Hooper at the same end, Gooch threw it to their end, and so the fourth-wicket stand was allowed to develop.

Soon after tea, when the target was 191 off 30 overs, Russell thought he had successfully brought off a brilliant stumping of Richards off Gooch, but our 'slo-mo' proved umpire Shepherd made a good decision. Pringle carried on some good work by Illingworth, but Richards was now ready for blast-off. Gooch carefully moved Ramprakash to deep square leg in his final over after a leg-side four and, but for one thing, the move worked perfectly. Richards looked at the fielder over 70 yards away, and deliberately lofted the ball straight at him. Catching practice? Yes, but only for a spectator six rows back. By now, the asking rate was over eight – 124 needed off 15 overs and then 88 off 10.

It was then that substitute Reeve caught a hard square cut from Hooper, whose 48 off 88 balls came in a partnership with his captain of 121 from 152 deliveries. As pressure situations go, it was highly charged for a bowler, especially if your name is Lewis, but he responded manfully with the prized wicket of Richards.

He walked across in a predetermined attempt to work the leg side, and the appeal was such a formality that the West Indies captain hardly bothered to wait for the decision. As he walked off, having scored 78 from 85 balls and so leaving his side with just a sniff, he received a heart-stirring Lancashire ovation which, unusually, was led by the policeman and steward guarding the gate to the pavilion.

With 63 needed off six overs, Gooch stayed faithful to Essex, and left Pringle to keep the England ship off the rocks. He bowled the penultimate over, with 22 needed off 12 balls, and settled the match with what he clearly thought was a hat trick. There was no argument about the dismissals of Logie for 24 off 21 balls and Marshall for 22 off 15. Logie hit a low full toss high to Illingworth at mid-on, and Marshall hit another one straight back to the bowler to prove the value of pitching the ball up. That brought in Greenidge with Hooper as runner. The hat-trick ball pitched middle stump and, holding a touch from leg to off, would surely have hit middle, but umpire Bird believed he heard or saw an edge, and a disbelieving Pringle – the most undemonstrative of bowlers – was pictured in close-up mouthing 'Jesus', and he was not rehearsing his matins.

The 54th over of the innings was thus worth two wickets and three runs, and with the game now won and lost, there was just time for Greenidge to be asked to swallow the bitterest pill of all – run out as non-striker by his runner vainly trying for a bye to the wicket-keeper.

Game, set, match and the series, despite which, Lord's would be another sell-out on Bank Holiday Monday. England's 2-0 lead came from wins by one wicket and nine runs, with the combined no balls and wides count now 61 conceded by the West Indies, and 20 by England.

MONDAY 27 MAY LORD'S

England made two changes, bringing in Reeve for the injured Lamb, and Lawrence for Lewis, thus reverting to a balance of five bowlers. Richards called in Lara to replace Greenidge, and Gooch maintained the pattern of the series by fielding first after winning the toss.

The steep climb of 59 steps from our entrance door at the back of the Warner Stand, and our viewing angle – fine leg and extra cover – are the only drawbacks at Headquarters. Our commentary box area is nearly twice the size of the others, and half a dozen people can be accommodated in comfort sitting down. The desk space is ample, which is of great help to Richie, Tony and myself when the time arrives for us to tap away on our Tandys before we file. In addition, unlike Old Trafford, Trent Bridge, Edgbaston and the Oval, we are not next door to Radio. Not that there is any problem between the two sets of talkers, but when you step outside the box for a break, it helps us and them if we can have a rest from talking shop.

I took the first half-hour, most of which seemed to be taken up with Lawrence's first over to Simmons. He thundered in from the Pavilion end and followed a first-ball wide with two no balls in the next three deliveries. The next ball was wafted away over cover for four, and the transparently enthusiastic fast bowler finally finished his nine-ball over with a roared LBW appeal.

I measured him at 26 running paces – roughly the equivalent of 40 yards, so his nine-ball over stretched to over 700 yards. A normal six-ball over equals around a quarter of a mile which means, as I heard myself develop the equation to the viewer, 'whenever he bowls 20 overs in a day, he covers over five miles, sprinting half that distance.'

In over 40 years' association with the first-class game, I doubt whether I have ever seen so much unbridled enthusiasm spill out from a massive frame that seems all heart. He would not make a world champion at poker, but a captain's only problem is trying to get the ball off him or, when he is bowling, trying to get him to throttle back a little. He gives the impression that he believes if he runs in quickly enough, he can get among the slip cordon to watch the action at the other end. Typically, his cruel injury to his left knee in New Zealand the following winter came at the end of a 'dead' Test, when many bowlers would not have been flat out.

Dujon stood at the non-striker's end throughout the first over, and had still not faced a ball when he finally took guard for the first ball of Lawrence's second over. It is not often a middle batsman gets a first baller after 15 minutes in the middle – especially at the start of an innings, but Dujon, fatally, played back to a ball of full length which nipped back to reduce the stumps from three to two.

'Syd' was relatively restrained. He contented himself with a forefinger 'out' signal, three punches of the air and one high five with Atherton – all taken at the gallop as his momentum took him past the rest of his colleagues. If the crowd needed lifting any further out of their seats, then Russell did the trick seven balls later with a magnificent left-handed catch off the inside edge to dismiss Simmons off DeFreitas. Sometimes a commentator struggles for the right word or phrase for an unexpected piece of action, but my twice-repeated 'brilliant' just about hit the spot.

Lara, playing in only his second one-day international, joined Richardson, who set about taking Lawrence apart so successfully that, after 13 overs, the fast bowler's analysis was 7-1-50-1 compared with the now ever-reliable DeFreitas's of 6-1-13-1. Richardson hit Lawrence for five fours in seven deliveries, including three through the covers, and a majestic hook and pull. It was thrilling batting which the 28,000 crowd loved.

Gooch brought on Reeve at 63 for two after 13 overs, and the Warwickshire man immediately showed his ability to swing and cut the ball about in a good first spell in international cricket of 7-1-17-0. He also showed that he is in little danger of missing an LBW decision through not appealing. Illingworth promoted his chances for the Cornhill five-day series when he had Richardson well caught at deep mid-wicket by DeFreitas, but if Gooch thought that Richardson's 41 off 56 balls was the end of the violence, Richards soon put him right.

From the first three balls he received from Illingworth, Richards slashed him through the vacant slip area for four and then smashed him into the far-from-empty members' enclosure in the pavilion for six.

The Worcestershire bowler kept his composure, and deserved the wicket of Lara, when the left-hander hit a simple return catch after scoring 23 out of 91 for four in the 21st over. Such a run-rate would lead to a big score, if the middle order did its stuff, and Logie did not miss the chance to unleash a cascade of strokes. In his 126th one-day international he was half-way towards his 13th 50 at lunch, by which time his captain was 24 and the score 132 for four off 32 overs.

During the interval, Denis Compton formally opened the new stands bearing his name and that of Bill Edrich, and the reception he got as he limped his way round the ground from the crowd – many of whom never saw him play – was a moving tribute to the legendary nature of his name.

Logie had survived a caught and bowled chance to Pringle in the bowler's first over, but that was the only chance the little man gave as he piled up the runs. Richards was caught at deep fine leg by Illingworth off DeFreitas with remarkable aplomb, although the speed with which his right hand went to cover a fluttering heart told a different story.

Logie's 50 came off 62 balls, and with Hooper also enjoying himself with 26 off 29 balls, the score rocketed to 225 for five after 46 overs, with a total approaching 300 a real possibility – until the return of Lawrence. He was magnificent. With the obligatory opening no ball out of the way, he had Hooper nicely caught by Fairbrother at fine leg, and after Gooch caught and bowled Logie for 82 off 99 balls at 241 for seven in the 50th over, the fast bowler really went to work. He had Marshall caught by DeFreitas at deep third man, and then won the Battle of the Gloucesters by nailing Walsh LBW on the back leg two balls later. Thanks to him, the West Indies loss of four wickets in the final eight overs restricted them to 37 and, at 264 for nine, the target was not out of reach.

Not even when Gooch and Atherton were out to make it 48 for two in the 15th over. The captain was run out in schoolboy fashion – thrown out by a direct hit from Hooper as he veered away from the line of throw and tried to ground his bat 12 inches outside the crease. Had he held his line he might have intercepted the throw and certainly would not have been out by the distance of four feet shown on the replay.

Atherton was caught by Dujon down the leg side off Marshall to ensure that the third examination of Hick and the second of Fairbrother in the series would be a stiff one. With 198 needed off 35 overs, Marshall bowled a phenomenal delivery to start the 21st over. From the Nursery end, it angled in to pitch a couple of inches outside off stump and then lifted and left Hick like a leg-break. Just to gild the lily, as it passed Hick it started to swing back and went so much that Dujon took it level with the end of the leg-side return crease. It was the sort of ball which gives a batsman a cold sweat of thanks for survival every New Year's Eve. Hick blinked and then played an innings somewhere near his normal standard, although as the runs flowed from him and Fairbrother, Geoffrey reminded the viewers 'that it is a different game with no close catchers'.

The Lancashire left-hander clicked into top gear with two fours off Hooper to help the score to 105 for two off 25 overs at tea. They had then added 57 off 60 balls, but even that rate of progress was left well behind after the interval. The long and short of it was that they clattered every bowler except Ambrose all over Lord's, with the West Indies rushed to the biggest defeat of the three games with 53 balls to spare.

The facts are that the two young men hit the last 156 from 22 overs, with Fairbrother hitting Patterson for 2-6-2-4 before he was caught for 113 off 109 balls by Richards off a top edge. His innings won the match, the Man of the Match award, and the hearts of the crowd, who gave him a rare standing ovation as he walked off. Only an innings of such brilliance could deflect media hype from Hick's 86 off 102 balls. The completion of a 3-0 clean-sweep in the series crowned a few days for Gooch which greatly assisted in the rehabilitation of the England team as a unit, following its woeful disintegration four months earlier in Australia.

Like Gooch after the match, Raymond refused to be carried away: 'England also won 3-0 in 1988, but that didn't count for much in the five-day Tests.'

However, the England players and commentators alike left Lord's full of anticipation about two things. The selection of the home side for the first Cornhill Test to be announced in four days' time, and the match itself at Headingley six days later. The first battle had been won ... now for the war.

ENGLAND v WEST INDIES
at Edgbaston on 23, 24 May 1991

WEST INDIES		Runs	6s	4s	Balls
C. G. Greenidge	c Russell b Botham	23	-	3	56
P. V. Simmons	c Gooch b Lewis	4	-	1	25
R. B. Richardson	c Illingworth b Botham	3	-	-	21
* I. V. A. Richards	c Fairbrother b Gooch	30	-	4	45
A. L. Logie	c DeFreitas b Botham	18	1	1	28
C. L. Hooper	c Russell b Botham	10	-	2	11
† P. J. L. Dujon	c Lewis b Illingworth	5	-	-	18
M. D. Marshall	c Lewis b DeFreitas	17	-	1	42
C. E. L. Ambrose	not out	21	-	-	59
C. A. Walsh	not out	29	1	3	26
B. P. Patterson	did not bat				
Extras	(b 1,lb 5,w 6,nb 1)	13			
TOTAL	(55 overs)(for 8 wkts)	173			

ENGLAND		Runs	6s	4s	Balls
* G. A. Gooch	lbw b Ambrose	0	-	-	2
M. A. Atherton	not out	69	-	4	147
G. A. Hick	c Richardson b Marshall	14	-	1	49
A. J. Lamb	b Hooper	18	-	2	26
N. H. Fairbrother	c Dujon b Hooper	4	-	-	6
I. T. Botham	lbw b Walsh	8	-	-	30
D. R. Pringle	c Richardson b Walsh	1	-	-	3
† R. C. Russell	c Dujon b Patterson	1	-	-	8
P. A. J. DeFreitas	c Richardson b Marshall	8	-	-	10
C. C. Lewis	c Richardson b Patterson	0	-	-	4
R. K. Illingworth	not out	9	-	1	39
Extras	(lb 9,w 18,nb 16)	43			
TOTAL	(49.4 overs)(for 9 wkts)	175			

ENGLAND	O	M	R	W
DeFreitas	11	3	22	1
Lewis	11	3	41	1
Pringle	7	0	22	0
Botham	11	2	45	4
Gooch	5	0	17	1
Illingworth	10	1	20	1

WEST INDIES	O	M	R	W
Ambrose	11	2	34	1
Patterson	11	2	38	2
Marshall	11	1	32	2
Walsh	11	0	34	2
Simmons	3	0	10	0
Hooper	2.4	0	18	2

PARTNERSHIPS

	WI			ENG		
Wkt	Score	Runs	Balls	Score	Runs	Balls
1st	8	8	44	1	1	2
2nd	16	8	30	41	40	94
3rd	48	32	50	80	39	60
4th	78	30	47	87	7	8
5th	84	6	10	123	36	56
6th	98	14	15	126	3	9
7th	103	5	18	134	8	13
8th	121	18	57	147	13	19
9th	173	52*	60	152	5	7
10th				175	23*	51

Toss: England
Umpires: J. H. Hampshire & M. J. Kitchen
Man of the Match: M. A. Atherton
RESULT: ENGLAND WON BY 1 WICKET

ENGLAND v WEST INDIES
at Old Trafford on 25 May 1991

ENGLAND		Runs	6s	4s	Balls
* G. A. Gooch	b Hooper	54	-	4	110
M. A. Atherton	c sub (Lara) b Ambrose	74	-	6	123
G. A. Hick	b Ambrose	29	-	2	44
A. J. Lamb	c Dujon b Patterson	62	-	10	50
N. H. Fairbrother	not out	5	-	-	6
M. R. Ramprakash	not out	6	-	-	6
C. C. Lewis					
D. R. Pringle					
†R. C. Russell	did not bat				
P. A. J. DeFreitas					
R. K. Illingworth					
Extras	(b 4,lb 16,w 14,nb 6)	40			
TOTAL	(55 overs)(for 4 wkts)	270			

WEST INDIES		Runs	6s	4s	Balls
P. V. Simmons	run out (Russell/Pringle)	28	-	1	52
†P. J. L. Dujon	c DeFreitas b Lewis	21	-	3	29
R. B. Richardson	c Russell b Gooch	13	-	-	34
C. L. Hooper	c sub (Reeve) b Lewis	48	-	3	88
* I. V. A. Richards	lbw b Lewis	78	2	6	85
A. L. Logie	c Illingworth b Pringle	24	-	2	21
M. D. Marshall	c & b Pringle	22	1	1	15
C. G. Greenidge	run out (Russell)	4	-	-	4
C. E. L. Ambrose	not out	5	-	1	4
C. A. Walsh	not out	1	-	-	1
B. P. Patterson	did not bat				
Extras	(lb 4,w 10,nb 3)	17			
TOTAL	(55 overs)(for 8 wkts)	261			

WEST INDIES	O	M	R	W
Ambrose	11	3	36	2
Patterson	10	1	39	1
Walsh	11	0	56	0
Marshall	10	0	45	0
Simmons	4	0	30	0
Hooper	9	0	44	1

ENGLAND	O	M	R	W
DeFreitas	11	3	50	0
Lewis	11	0	62	3
Pringle	11	2	52	2
Illingworth	11	1	42	0
Gooch	11	1	51	1

PARTNERSHIPS

Wkt	ENG Score	Runs	Balls	WI Score	Runs	Balls
1st	156	156	232	34	34	60
2nd	156	0	5	61	27	49
3rd	258	102	89	69	8	19
4th	260	2	3	190	121	152
5th	270	10*	10	208	18	16
6th				250	42	27
7th				250	0	1
8th				256	6	7
9th				261	5*	2
10th						

Toss: West Indies
Umpires: H. D. Bird & D. R. Shepherd
Man of the Match: A. J. Lamb
RESULT: ENGLAND WON BY 9 RUNS

ENGLAND v WEST INDIES
at Lord's on 27 May 1991

WEST INDIES		Runs	6s	4s	Balls
P. V. Simmons	c Russell b DeFreitas	5	-	1	16
†P. J. L. Dujon	b Lawrence	0	-	-	1
R. B. Richardson	c DeFreitas b Illingworth	41	-	7	56
B. C. Lara	c & b Illingworth	23	-	2	40
* I. V. A. Richards	c Illingworth b DeFreitas	37	1	4	57
A. L. Logie	c & b Gooch	82	-	10	99
C. L. Hooper	c Fairbrother b Lawrence	26	1	2	29
M. D. Marshall	c DeFreitas b Lawrence	13	1	-	16
C. E. L. Ambrose	not out	6	-	- -	12
C. A. Walsh	lbw b Lawrence	0	-	-	2
B. P. Patterson	not out	2	-	-	10
Extras	(b 1,lb 9,w 14,nb 5)	29			
TOTAL	(55 overs)(for 9 wkts)	264			

ENGLAND		Runs	6s	4s	Balls
* G. A. Gooch	run out (Hooper)	11	-	1	29
M. A. Atherton	c Dujon b Marshall	25	-	3	46
G. A. Hick	not out	86	-	8	102
N. H. Fairbrother	c Richards b Patterson	113	2	10	109
M. R. Ramprakash	not out	0	-	-	-
D. A. Reeve					
†R. C. Russell					
P. A. J. DeFreitas	} did not bat				
D. R. Pringle					
R. K. Illingworth					
D. V. Lawrence					
Extras	(b 4,lb 12,w 10,nb 4)	30			
TOTAL	(46.1 overs)(for 3 wkts)	265			

ENGLAND	O	M	R	W
Lawrence	11	1	67	4
DeFreitas	11	1	26	2
Reeve	11	1	43	0
Illingworth	11	1	53	2
Pringle	9	0	56	0
Gooch	2	0	9	1

WEST INDIES	O	M	R	W
Ambrose	8	0	31	0
Patterson	10	0	62	1
Marshall	11	1	49	1
Walsh	11	1	50	0
Hooper	4.1	0	36	0
Simmons	2	0	21	0

PARTNERSHIPS

	WI			ENG		
Wkt	Score	Runs	Balls	Score	Runs	Balls
1st	8	8	15	28	28	55
2nd	8	0	7	48	20	38
3rd	71	63	79	261	213	192
4th	91	20	24	265	4*	1
5th	164	73	101			
6th	227	63	59			
7th	241	14	23			
8th	258	17	15			
9th	258	0	2			
10th	264	6*	13			

Toss: England
Umpires: M. J. Kitchen & D. R. Shepherd
Man of the Match: N. H. Fairbrother
RESULT: ENGLAND WON BY 7 WICKETS

CHAPTER THREE

GOOCH'S TRIUMPH

HEADINGLEY TEST
6–10 JUNE

SELECTION FRIDAY 31 MAY

I have long held the view that the England selectors unnecessarily handicap themselves by picking their side six or seven days before the actual game, and the events of the last Friday in May did little to change my mind. It is curious that, by announcing their team so early, the selectors deny themselves the chance of seeing fringe candidates in action in the championship games over the weekend. The Test & County Cricket Board say there are three valid counter-arguments.

First, players travelling for a new round of three-day games need to know whether or not to take extra kit for the Test match. Second, since the county programme was adjusted in 1991 to allow manager Michael Stewart to have two full days with his team before the start of the Test, an announcement of the team on the Saturday or Sunday, instead of Friday, might make it difficult for every player to report by Monday evening. Third, the lawyers rightly insist that the chosen party must sign a written acceptance of the selection offer, including their agreement to abide by the Board's disciplinary rules.

Knocking those arguments down in order, the Board would have a point if matches started, as they traditionally did for many years, on a Saturday. But now that the starting days have been brought back a day to give Stewart his two clear days, those players concerned have already travelled before the team is announced. Similarly, the necessity to report on Monday evenings before the Thursday start of the Test would remain unaffected whether the side was announced on the previous Friday, Saturday or Sunday. Finally, in previous years when the side was announced on Sunday morning and the players reported the following Tuesday evening, there was still insufficient time for the players to be sent their contracts and return them signed. What happened in most cases was that a verbal acceptance was obtained by telephone, with pen put to paper at the Test match hotel, although I believe that even that rarely happens. I know of one England player who, at the time of writing, has a cap count in double figures, and has yet to sign a contract for a home Test.

It makes little sense for England to forfeit any advantage they might gain by picking and announcing later. A Sunday or even a Monday announcement would give the selectors at least two more days' cricket to watch, and would assist them in clarifying injury problems. When I have put the point to Stewart, he counters that they have the right to announce later if they so choose, and this did happen with the side for the fourth Test match at Edgbaston.

The eagerly awaited announcement of the XII for the Headingley Test was a shambles. The Press Association was told that the names would be available at 10am. The Board spokesman, Peter Smith, then announced several defer-ments – all because, apparently, Gooch wanted to talk to several players privately before they learned their fate publicly. As the side had been picked the previous evening, it is difficult to understand why the captain, manager and Ted Dexter could not share out the dozen names and telephone them early Friday morning, rather than wait until Gooch was on the Bristol ground – where Essex were playing – before he completed his telephonic round of other county grounds.

The frustration of the agencies and national journalists grew, as lunch came and went, still with no announcement, and two things happened which only fuelled the controversy. Warwickshire's Reeve was approached by a local news agency and interviewed during the home game at Edgbaston against Yorkshire on the incorrect basis that he had been chosen. The distress caused the player when he was told the truth later in the day can only be imagined – especially as he was actually batting in late afternoon when the XII was announced over the public address system. No wonder he smashed the York-shire attack for an unbeaten 99.

Lawrence, who had obviously been spoken to by Gooch before the start of the Gloucestershire match against Essex, gave an interview to local television about his omission before it had been officially confirmed, so, even though the selectors were not responsible for the Reeve incident, had the official announcement of the team not been delayed for six hours, neither Reeve nor Lawrence would have been put in such an invidious position.

Most public speculation concerned the probable omission of David Gower, and whether Fairbrother would be preferred to Ramprakash. Although unlikely to play, Illingworth looked certain to keep out Tufnell, and the composition of the seam attack was expected to include the return of Malcolm.

At 4.30pm, the following XII was finally prised out of Lord's: Gooch, Atherton, Hick, Lamb, Smith, Ramprakash, Russell, Lewis, DeFreitas, Pringle, Illingworth, Malcolm. As Gooch and Stewart will only ever consider a five-man bowling attack if a batsman/wicket-keeper is chosen ahead of Russell, it was certain a bowler would be dropped, probably the spinner.

On the final day of Worcestershire's home game against Glamorgan, the Monday the players had to report to Leeds, it was announced that, because Pringle had suffered a back strain, Glamorgan's Steve Watkin had been called up. He gave a pleasant, impromptu interview in the New Road press box, and seemed far from overawed at the thought of making his Test debut.

THURSDAY 6 JUNE

Overcast conditions, with an indifferent weather forecast, put paid to any chance of Illingworth playing but, lo and behold, the announced team included Watkin AND Pringle – for whom the Glamorgan seamer was cover. It seemed that Lewis was unwell and, for the fourth time, ruled himself out of a home Test. The bad press he received subsequently stung him into a denial of a migraine, but undoubtedly his late withdrawal stretched the patience of the selectors to the limit.

I walked into the historic Headingley ground across the rugby field and climbed up the steep steps to the roof of the stand in which we were housed. Boxed is a better word, because the commentary area is really only of box-room size. If there is any truth in the maxim that 'small is beautiful', then it is gorgeous. The front desk space is the smallest on the circuit, and the poor summariser struggles to peer round the double-banked monitors to see the left-hand quarter of the ground as we look out towards the Kirkstall Lane end.

I arrived at 10am, and the usual chaos was fermenting nicely, both in the box and in the scanner van. I grabbed one of only three seats available, other than the three for commentator, summariser and scorer Malcolm Ashton. Tony, Raymond, Geoffrey and our two stage managers, Dave and Steve, were chatting. A sound engineer was on his knees, adjusting wires and muttering into his chest back to base. As yet, there was no Richie, no producers and no assistants – all of whom would appear in the next hour. But I was grateful there was no cat – because already there was insufficient room in which to swing it.

I mugged up a few facts from the admirably packaged Cornhill bundle, and learned that this was the 100th Test between England and the West Indies. The score stood at 41 to 22 wins in favour of the West Indies, with the last home win as long ago as 1969 on the same ground. Our Raymond was captain then and, although that game got the odd mention in the general buzz of conversation, it was from the written hand-out, and not from either of our two Tykes, that I learned that 'West Indies were between fast-bowling eras, post Hall and Griffith and pre Roberts and Holding.' Not a major trump card for me if they kept hammering me with aces, but it would do.

I also spotted that the three wins in 1990 against West Indies in Jamaica, New Zealand at Edgbaston and India at Lord's had improved England's record to four wins in the last 40 Tests.

Another fact of some interest and no little significance was that the last 'played-out' draw at Headingley was in 1968. The draws in 1974, '78, '79 and '80 were all badly rain-affected, and in 1975 the pitch was vandalised. With every other game providing a result, including all nine from 1981–89, the bookmakers seemed to have erred in making the draw favourite at 10–11, with West Indies 11–8 and England 5–1. I was so unimpressed with the England attack that I cheerfully laid 7–1 to one press-box patriot, safe in the knowledge that Malcolm, DeFreitas, Pringle and Watkin could not possibly take 20 wickets, especially as the rain would win anyway. Damon Runyon believed that a gambler was never in greater danger than when he believed he was on to a certainty, so I suppose, wherever his spirit is now, it had a quiet chuckle five days later.

Richie walked in at 10.30am and I watched him with envy as he carefully set out his stall. A briefcase, a word processor and a coat – all were housed as though he was in an aircraft hanger and, after a polite inquiry about my commitments, he compiled our rota, putting me in at number one.

I plugged in to Tony, only ten yards away in our in-vision room, and waited. Despite the three Texaco games, I felt as though this was the start of the summer. I tried to shut out the self-doubts which flooded my mind, but they gnawed away. I tried telling myself that this was my 51st Test match behind a microphone for either radio or television, which must prove something, but I knew I would not settle until 'AR' was told by Keith to throw to Jack-In-The-Box. Malcolm trotted out one of his jokes – this one called for his well developed sense of mimicry, but it sailed yards past my right ear.

At 10.50am we went live. I watched the film of the toss, which had taken place 15 minutes earlier, and heard Richards say to Gooch, after calling correctly, 'I'll let you know.' He then turned to Dave Bowden, who was there to relay the result to Keith, 'No chat today?' Gooch replied: 'No chat if no decision,' and walked off.

The ploy of delaying a decision is not new, but it still baffles people who cannot understand why a captain has not already cleared his mind of options should he win the toss. The only good reason is that it keeps the opposition guessing for a few minutes, but in this case there was little doubt that Richards would open the kennels and give Ambrose and company a run.

Umpires Bird and Shepherd marched to the middle — 'The Old Firm', as I had seen them described in one newspaper, but it was surprising to discover that, whereas this was Bird's 45th Test, it was only Shepherd's 12th.

I heard Raymond's analysis of the pitch. 'It is damp, but it won't be quick. The surface looks flat — it was relaid four years ago with lighter soil. The grass is roughish and the ball should move off the stalky bits. There are no cracks, and Marshall could be the most dangerous bowler. He is the most accurate and he swings it. The outfield has not been cut short and that will take 30 runs a day off the total.'

Ambrose came down the hill towards us, with Patterson 'up the cellar steps', as described by Geoffrey. I am often asked whether we commentate off the monitor or the pitch, and the answer is both. When behind the arm, as we are everywhere except Lord's, then I prefer to watch the live action and switch to the monitor between deliveries so that I know what the viewer is seeing. Another reason why I prefer to watch each ball bowled on the pitch is that, now that we use double-ended coverage, I find it confusing to watch the bowler on the screen and then switch to the pitch. We still receive mail which is divided on the merits of a facility which has been introduced for the benefit of the viewer. Some people get disorientated when they never see a bowler running towards them, but the overwhelming advantage must be the better view that is offered with all LBWs and catches close to the wicket. In most of the domestic knockout games, we do not have double-ended coverage and I find it irksome trying to interpret action which has been masked by the batsman's back.

The clock showed 11.23 as Patterson rushed away from us, and Atherton was bowled as he squared up to push leg-side. That told me it was a good delivery, as was proved by the replay, which showed the ball pitching off stump and hitting it. Bowled from half-way across the return crease, that is good enough for most, even though Raymond was critical because 'both the batsman's toes were pointing down the pitch. He was too square on.' This was true, but had the ball not deviated, he would have played it and, as a former seam bowler, I prefer to give the bowler full credit when he deserves it.

Hick's entry was slower than in the one-day internationals and, although he quickly got off the mark with a boundary to third man, the pattern for the series was soon established. The first bouncer from Ambrose was evaded, but not watched, mid-on was dispensed with, and the fast bowlers began an incessant bombardment at an off-stump line.

Gooch was in such positive form that his dismissal by Marshall came as a shock to the system, but it was a magnificent delivery which made the score 45 for two in the 15th over. The Barbadian had conceded 13 in his first over before, off the final ball, he made one lift and leave Gooch to give Dujon the first of six catches in the game. Gooch's 34 included six fours and came off 49 balls, and with him went more than just one wicket. His growing influence as captain of his country, on and off the field, can be counter-productive when he is out, and so it was on D-Day, 6 June.

Hick must have been praying for deliverance, but although there was no questioning his courage, doubts about his ability to cope with four fast bowlers were hardly assuaged when he was out to Walsh, the ball after a field change was made with Logie moving from short leg to silly mid-off. Tony said: 'That adjustment of the field put maggots of doubt in his mind, hence the edged catch to Dujon.' But Geoffrey was in no mood to be kind: 'That ball was one and a half feet wide, and he should not have played it.' Hick's six runs comprised two scoring strokes from 31 balls and, at 45 for three, Richards was already pleased with his decision to field first, and relished his task of maximising the pressure on Ramprakash, while Lamb was at full stretch at the other end.

Raymond was in his best fortune-telling form: 'His bottom hand strokes are good, like the pull and cut, but he doesn't play forward to the fuller length ball with a straight bat, and Marshall is just the bowler to exploit this.' He did, right on the stroke of lunch to make the score a rocky 64 for four from 26 overs. The ball bounced a little, but Lamb's angled bat cost him his wicket.

If England were in trouble, so was Raymond. We all make slips from time to time, when what we intend to say is phrased, shall we say, somewhat curiously? All the viewer at home hears is the comment, which is assumed to be carefully thought out. If only they realised. Haynes, whose back problems had attracted much speculation before the game, was seen to be feeling the offending area after a good stop in the covers. Like a good summariser should, when a close-up of Haynes appeared, Raymond pointed out that, as the tourists' vice-captain had come into the match with the injury, he would not be allowed a substitute if he had to retire.

Mischievously, Richie said: 'Perhaps he'd be wiser to strain a hamstring,' to which Raymond bounced back with the following switchboard-jamming remark: 'Good thinking, Richie. But I'm not sure they're all that intelligent.'

The point he wanted to make, in joking fashion, was that most cricketers would not think that fast – but try telling that to those people whose sensitivity about race issues is so highly developed, they detect offence where none is intended.

After lunch, it was not long before Raymond was back on safer ground, praising the approach and technique of Ramprakash. I considered that his coolness was all the more impressive, considering the situation and the nerves which must be affecting him. 'Everyone should have them, even after 50 Tests, otherwise you are not thinking right. The secret is to control them, live with them, and not let it affect how you play. He looks a good natural player, and what I like most is his judgement of what to leave outside off stump.'

Geoffrey was not wholly in favour of the way Ramprakash stood at the crease in open fashion, with the front left foot withdrawn towards mid-wicket – doubtlessly influenced by playing in the same Middlesex side as Haynes. 'I disagree with Desmond. It might suit him, but I think there is no substitute for being as perfectly side-on as possible. Desmond gets back into the orthodox position anyway, but copiers might not find it so easy.'

While Ramprakash may have been lucky to survive a big LBW appeal from Ambrose (thanks, perhaps, to 'Dickie' Bird's well-known reluctance to give out anything that is not plumb), Smith was at his pugnacious best, and a wicketless afternoon session was within two deliveries of completion when Marshall produced another beauty to Ramprakash. It held its line and bounced and Hooper took a good catch at second slip, with the youngster's 27 off 103 balls a splendid debut innings for his country. Richie believed that 'all the England players were out to good balls,' and a tea score of 129 for five represented a fighting recovery.

Smith was then 38, and he offered an unaccepted simple slip catch to Hooper soon afterwards off the unlucky Ambrose, just before Marshall left the field, apparently with a strained hamstring. On came substitute Clayton Lambert, who promptly ushered Smith to 50 with an overthrow of four off . . . who else but Ambrose, whose day this clearly was not. Richie summed up the incident with: 'Generous slipped in for the Derby yesterday, and it's happening here as well.'

Anyone who commentates for 38 days' cricket in a summer has a gremlin in his voice-box who is waiting to pounce. Raymond's did an unusual daily double when he spoke about the excellent sightscreens on the ground, compared with when he played over 20 years previously. 'Yes, I remember in the 1960s when Wes and Charlie used to come at you out of the trees.' He said that in vision during a stoppage for bad light and, to his credit, Tony did not even blink.

Smith was so much in charge that when he was run out on his own call for a second run, the West Indies fielders nearly knocked the fielder, Ambrose, off his feet. He was at third man and rifled in a wonderful throw to Dujon to catch

Smith no more than six inches short, even though Richie thought his bat was not grounded. As usual, Keith replayed it at normal speed, and how umpire Bird could read such a photo-finish is beyond comprehension. Richie summed it up thus: 'One of the more brilliant decisions of Bird's career. Players might argue it was too close to call, but that's why the umpire is there.' When I discussed the decision with 'Dickie' much later in the season, he insisted: 'I just saw it Jack. I knew it was out, I just saw it.'

That was the beginning of the end for England, with Russell LBW to Patterson at 154 for seven, a few minutes before the third stoppage for bad light shortened the day by 26 overs. This gave me ample time to write and file my match report for my newspaper, and enabled Richie to do his links for the late-night highlights programme unusually early.

This package is edited as the day progresses, and usually the link comments are recorded in two sessions – at lunch and after the end of the game. Our commentary box then splits neatly into two. Raymond, Geoffrey and Tony disappear, leaving Richie to do his links, Malcolm, who has to stay until they are completed, and me. Studio managers Steve and Dave tidy up our 'house' ready for the next day, and it is at least an hour after the close of play before the hutch is empty.

It had been a long day, with most of it belonging to the West Indies. Only Gooch, Ramprakash and Smith kept their relentless attack at arm's length, and the failure of Atherton, Hick and Lamb was disappointing, even if not overly significant so early in the series. All England could hope for was a total in excess of 200, and similar overcast conditions to obtain the next day.

FRIDAY 7 JUNE

If the first day belonged to the West Indies, the second one went to England – in particular to Pringle and DeFreitas, who scored half of the 24 runs eked out by the last three wickets, and then took five of the six wickets to fall to bowlers, with two run outs putting the West Indies in serious trouble.

Bad light and drizzle extracted another 24 overs from the daily minimum ration of 90, but the spectators had full value for money. I was so confident about the 7–1 I had laid against an England win, that I informed the viewers that 'the morning odds of 6–1 are not generous, because the home attack comprises an out-of-form fast bowler, a debutant, and two all-rounders – one of whom, DeFreitas, has played 21 Tests in five years, and the other, Pringle, 22 in nine, during which time he has been dropped 11 times.'

Oh ye of little faith, as Raymond hinted as soon as DeFreitas was caught by Simmons off Ambrose, making the score 177 for eight. 'If England bowl well, a score of 200 is a good one. There is enough in the pitch to make the West Indies struggle, especially without Greenidge. Their middle order is vulnerable anyway, and much depends on Haynes.' Richie agreed, provided England bowled well. Watkin lasted nine balls before Ambrose bowled him, and then Malcolm played the sort of innings which delights the crowd and commentators but, for some reason, the bowlers and fielders do not find funny.

Logie, normally the safest of fielders, dropped Pringle, and allowed 41 minutes of the best and worst of tail-end batting to evolve. Pringle tried his best to organise the strike but, as Malcolm's 31-ball share of the 58-ball tenth wicket partnership shows, the Derbyshire bowler's occasional inability to recognise which is the first or last ball of an over is an insuperable handicap. His backing-up routine is also eccentric. On the rare occasion when he does take a stride as the ball is released, it is just as likely to be a backward one, so that any run is one yard further than usual.

As Richie summed it up: 'I sometimes think that Devon does it by numbers, which could work – except he often loses count.' He went on to make a valid, but seldom appreciated point: 'Bowlers sometimes forget the common-sense approach against tail-enders. You bowl differently – line and length go as frustration increases, which is why it is sometimes more difficult to bowl to number 11 – your brain ceases to function.'

Pringle was finally well caught by Logie off Ambrose, whose two wickets that morning were his first in the match, and West Indies had eight overs to negotiate before lunch. Simmons tucked into Malcolm and was 23 out of 29 at the break, after surviving an inspection by the umpires of his bat, with a too-recent oiling affecting the ball. The incident launched Richie into a lovely, evocative memory of youth. 'Linseed oil is mostly a thing of the past, because of modern plastic. The wonderful thing as a kid with a new bat, was to use raw linseed oil – and then take the bat to bed with you.' Malcolm's third over cost 15, and Simmons raced to 20 before Haynes scored his first run.

Ominous? Possibly, until the first hour of the afternoon session provided three instances of the uplifting effect youth can bring to a team. The gangling Watkin struck first. His 14th ball for England pitched just outside off stump and bounced enough to force an edge from Haynes to Russell. The catch was not taken cleanly, but as soon as it was completed, it was a toss-up whether the bowler, or his Glamorgan chairman in our box, leaped further in the air and shouted loudest. Those BBC directional mikes paid for themselves in that one shared moment of Welsh triumph.

The 50 was passed in the 18th over, and it was then that Ramprakash put his indelible stamp on his debut Test with two electrifying pieces of fielding which roused even the normally staid Headingley crowd to a fever-pitch of excitement. A magnificent catch and a swooping run out from the covers in 13 balls were brilliantly captured by the high-square cameraman, and Simmons and Hooper were back in the dressing-room, with the innings tottering at 58 for three.

DeFreitas was the beneficiary of a catch which was destined to win the BBC's Catch of the Season competition, and it was a supreme example of anticipation, athleticism and a sure pair of hands. A short, wide ball was hit firmly off the back foot by Simmons, not quite out of the meat, about seven feet wide of Ramprakash, who is five feet nine inches tall, at cover point. In such circumstances, the fielder instinctively stays on his heels when he sees a back-foot stroke played – and that makes the swallow-dive of Ramprakash to his right even more remarkable. Not only did he pick the ball, two-handed out of the air at chest height, he managed to hold on to it as he crashed to the ground. Many such catches convince the spectator that, when the catch was taken, the fielder was in mid-air, although at the key moment, the feet are usually still on the ground. Not in this case – it was a genuine mid-air dive of which any international goalkeeper would have been proud.

If ever Ramprakash takes a better catch, I hope I am there to see it. If that catch was the sort to shake a batting dressing-room, his run-out of Hooper two overs later must have dented the morale of a West Indies side who now knew they were in for a real dog-fight.

Hooper pushed a ball short to Ramprakash, hesitated fatally for a split second before he tried to beat the spinning roulette wheel before the ball dropped into the zero groove. Again it was the superb anticipation of the fielder which brought England another wicket. He had to veer slightly to his left as he raced in, in order to make an angle to pick up and throw at the bowler's stumps. Hooper's frantically moving feet never got out of the treacle, and the splendidly positioned umpire Shepherd confirmed the success of the direct hit.

Richards joined Richardson, whose average against England was under 40 compared with 50-plus against other countries. His supposed fallibility in English conditions was supported by the fact that nine of his 12 Test hundreds were scored at home, and none in England. Geoffrey was more concerned with Richards. 'He has a habit of trying to hit his side out of trouble, but he will have problems if England bowl well.'

The crowd settled to watch one of the crucial partnerships of the match between the Coopers Deloitte number one, Richardson, who averaged 47·18, and his captain who, despite an average of 50·08 was rated 26th because of his relative decline in the previous two years.

Tony was now behind the mike, and clucked like a protective mother hen about the field placings for Watkin. The slip area was packed, but it was the supplementary silly mid-off which reduced the number of leg-side fielders to two that Tony queried: 'It is impossible to bowl to a seven-two field to Viv.' Raymond agreed that it was putting 'impossible pressure' on Watkin. He was to make the point in the Lord's Test that, even if the ball was leaving the bat, a third leg-side defender helped the bowler to bowl a straighter line – otherwise he would err on the safe side outside off stump. This sort of clear, constructive technical criticism is something that, having worked with both sets of commentators and summarisers in radio and television, I have found happens more frequently in television than radio and thus enhances the viewer's understanding of what is happening on the pitch.

When Geoffrey used the telestrator to show the two men posted deep for the hook when Richards was facing, the speed with which Keith and the relevant cameramen picked up the point to pinpoint the two fielders was a prime example of attentive teamwork. The telestrator monitor at Headingley is sited at knee height between the commentator and summariser, which makes it difficult for a right-handed commentator to use. In any case, it should be used more by the summariser to make and develop his analytical points. He asks for it to be available, and then uses a pen to draw on the screen. He has a switch to clear the white circles and arrows, and I think it is one of the more useful innovations of recent years. I am not sure that it is used enough yet, but that is only a matter of practice and confidence.

At 80 for three, Pringle came on to bowl to the usual jeers he and, before him, Keith Fletcher, always receive in Yorkshire. Tony said: 'There is no reason for that any more. I think it's just their way of saying "Hello Derek – nice to see you back".' His size and the appearance of immobility make him an easy target, and although his record in 21 Tests of 512 runs at an average of 15·51 and 48 wickets at 37·64 hardly made his selection an inspiring one, this match was to establish him in both the England side and in the affections of the Headingley crowd.

Richards was 'caught' by Russell off a Malcolm no ball, and an ice-cream vendor was spotted by a camera, much to the amazement of Richie, who has been known to commentate in his Humphrey Bogart raincoat if it is cold. 'They're a tough race, actually buying and eating ice-cream at three degrees. Might even be the first sale of the day – no wonder he's struggling with that £10 note.'

Malcolm's first 11 overs cost 50 and, at 101 for three in the final over before tea, the fourth-wicket pair was clawing back the advantage when another run out was handed to England. Richardson dug out a yorker and took two comfortable runs as Gooch chased from mid-off. With three balls to the interval, Richards was not over-keen to get back on strike, but his fellow Antiguan turned and ran, as he thought, to the danger end.

What the calling was is unclear, but Richardson certainly got half-way before he realised that he was in trouble, as Gooch completed a keen piece of fielding by throwing quickly to Malcolm on the turn. It was really that refusal by the England captain to settle for anything less than a committed effort which forced the error. The throw was relayed by the bowler to Russell, and Richardson dragged himself slowly to the pavilion, carefully avoiding catching up with his partner, who was walking off the pitch for the tea interval.

Geoffrey described the incident as 'a nightmare of a run out – an absolute tragedy.' A repetition of the last word brought an instruction from on high that we must refrain from referring to anything as 'tragic', or 'a tragedy' as it offended those who, with some justification, regard sport as just that, and not to be compared with other serious happenings in life.

Richardson scored 29 out of the 44 added with his captain, who then dominated the rest of the day so completely that he scored 50 out of 62 off the bat in the 13 overs allowed by bad light and drizzle in the final session. He hit Watkin for a four and a six, and also hit Malcolm for six in an over which cost 14. It was a thrilling counter-attack, spoiled for him by the loss of four partners. Logie fenced at a short, wide delivery from DeFreitas, and then Dujon unworthily wafted a simple catch to Ramprakash in the covers off Watkin to start a mini-collapse which cost the West Indies three wickets for nine runs in 18 balls.

Marshall came in with Hooper as runner. Pringle was brought back, and Lamb immediately dropped Richards off an overhead chance at slip. Geoffrey thought he should have tried to knock the ball up: 'I often saw Kenny Barrington do that to high slip catches, and it gives the fielder a much better chance, especially if, like Lamb, he is not tall.'

In the same over, Pringle had Marshall caught by Hick at second slip, and a brilliant low, left-handed catch by the same fielder five balls later off DeFreitas convinced Richards to accept the light when it was offered. Raymond believed this was a mistake: 'It must have been to Viv's advantage to stay on. He is going well, and has more chance of scoring runs than tomorrow, when he has to play himself in and the bowlers will be fresh again.' At 166 for eight off 49 overs, with Richards on 73, the game was perfectly balanced for the expected large Saturday crowd.

The second day illustrated the faulty approach of the West Indies, under conditions which, DeFreitas apart, the England bowlers did not exploit to the full. Only three of their eight dismissals were not self-induced, with the run outs of Richardson and Hooper only marginally more destructive than the forcing strokes played by Simmons, Logie and Dujon. The brilliance of Ramprakash in the covers plucked two wickets out of nothing but, with Richards still there, it seemed that unless the home team could fire on a greater number of cylinders, England would struggle to stay in the match. The form – or lack of it – of Malcolm was particularly worrying.

SATURDAY 8 JUNE

On Saturdays, Tony is spared an in-vision introduction, because the hand-over comes from Grandstand. As a result, this is the one day when he takes the first shift, and he and Raymond were in good form. Pringle began with a couple of sighters which brought this grumpy comment from Ray: 'I don't know. The England players have been in the nets for an hour, yet you would think they hadn't bowled for a week. Particularly in these conditions, it's a complete waste to give them a couple of sighters.'

He need not have worried, because off the third ball of the over Richards edged a catch to Lamb at first slip to give the Essex all-rounder his 50th wicket for England. With some justification, Raymond repeated his comments of the previous evening. 'That really proves the point I made about the light last night. He never once played a stroke like that yesterday. He must have wanted at least another 20 or 30 runs, and I'm sure he would have got them last night.'

The last-wicket partnership between Walsh and Patterson produced nine runs and more misses than hits. Of its 26-ball duration, 18 were missed, three deliberately, before Walsh was well caught by Gooch off DeFreitas. The steepler was, in Richie's words, 'a particularly difficult catch, because as you circle it you know there are 15,000 people and watching television millions who know exactly how it should be caught.' Nicely put.

The psychological balance of the game was now with the home side, having turned a likely deficit, when the tourists were 102 for three and 156 for five, into a lead of 25 runs. More importantly, they got away with Malcolm and the inexperienced Watkin failing to exploit as helpful a set of conditions as they could really hope for at international level. Their combined 28-over share of the 54·1 bowled in the innings cost 124 for two wickets, while DeFreitas and Pringle aggregated six for 48 off 26·1 overs.

England expected, and got, a torrid pre-lunch session. Their ship was battered by an Ambrose hurricane which, this time, was touched with the luck which had been missing on the first day. Geoffrey warned: 'For me, the game will be won and lost today. So often the West Indies bowlers come back and blow sides away, and England need sensible, controlled batting, but it won't be easy.'

While Gooch took guard, in that schoolboy fashion, with a couple of fingers on the top of the handle, Richie told the viewing public that it was 'the coldest Test day in England since 1965 at Edgbaston, when the England and New Zealand players were given hot soup on the field'.

The first ball of what was to be one of the greatest innings ever played for England could have been Gooch's last. He drove Patterson in the air just past Marshall at mid-off, with Geoffrey pinpointing a recurring fault with the help of the slow-motion replays. 'This is his biggest fault. His front foot is stuck in the block-hole. He was working on it in the nets yesterday, but after transferring the weight to the back foot, the left foot goes nowhere and only finishes on the batting crease.' The replay he asked Keith for, from the high-square camera, illustrated his astutely observed point perfectly, with the impetus of the stroke taking Gooch a yard further than the batting crease after he had made contact.

Not only has Gooch's batting record improved dramatically since he became captain, so has his approach to running between the wickets, and his eye for the short single soon helped his side to 20, with Raymond noting that the West Indian quicker bowlers were clearly not getting the same movement as the England seamers. No sooner had he made the point than Ambrose gave the perfect reply with the first of six successive wickets he was to take that day. Atherton edged a lifting delivery, which also left him, to Dujon and, although Raymond initially believed that he did not have to play at it, he altered his view when he saw the replays from front-on and reverse.

Hick came in at 22 for one and, 14 runs and six overs later, Raymond did what all commentators do from time to time. The law of averages, as well as Sod's Law, decrees that if you make enough forecasts, some are bound to be wrong. And so it came to pass. 'England now have a lead of 62, and I would expect them to make a reasonable total. If they concentrate and bat well, they'll be in the box seat.'

If that box seat was in the dressing-room, he was proved right in the next minutes, when Hick and Lamb were both out. Hick received a four-ball short-pitched working over from Ambrose, followed by a classical yorker, which found its way on to the stumps from the bottom edge of a far from straight bat. Geoffrey had replaced Raymond, and the dismissal brought his second use of the word 'tragic', which was also to be the last time it hit the airwaves that summer. Lamb was caught first ball by Hooper at second slip but, although a lunch score of 47 for three was disappointing, the spectators and commentators preferred to pay tribute to the magnificent hostility of Ambrose.

Gooch was superb, and so was his young partner, Ramprakash. Raymond said: 'There are fewer bad balls in Test cricket – full marks to Ramprakash for coming to terms with the greater need for patience.' With the ball still darting around, albeit less frequently for the faster West Indies bowlers, any batsman needed luck to survive. Gooch played and missed at one from Walsh which came back, and flicked something on its way through to Dujon which prompted a huge, concerted appeal for a catch.

The reverse-angle camera from behind Gooch showed that the ball and bat were never in contact, which brought from Richie: 'Remember, the umpire only has the blur of the ball to separate from the movement of bat and pad – he has no replays. If the laughingly-termed "neutral" umpires were now operating, officials of the quality of Bird and Shepherd would not be standing in this game.' I listened with interest as the Ice Man smartly extricated himself from possible trouble with a neat verbal side-step which avoided offence, but still conveyed his point to the watching millions. 'We would have, instead, two umpires from another country like ... Australia for instance.' Classy.

Gooch reached 50 out of 83 off 112 balls, and Ramprakash confirmed the deep impression he made in the first innings, with another solid display of technique and temperament. The middle session was wicketless and worth 67, with the overall lead now a healthy 139. As I took my tea and biscuits, I began to regret my pre-match odds of 7–1, but Ambrose was in my corner.

Immediately after the interval, he had Ramprakash caught by Dujon for a repeat 27 in, coincidentally, the same time of 141 minutes as in the first innings. At the same score of 116, Ambrose put himself on a hat trick for the second time in the day, winning the LBW appeal against Smith, about which the height was the only query.

Once more, the difficulties facing umpires were underlined by a disagreement in the commentary box when Geoffrey thought the ball hit Smith on the knee roll, while Richie thought it was above. Ambrose was a magnificent sight, loping in with a lively controlled run, now in full rhythm, and he threatened a wicket with every ball. Russell was next to go, caught by Dujon. The wicket provided the perfect example of how even slow-motion replays are sometimes unable to help, unless there is a thick edge.

Russell had to be given out, with Ambrose now showing so little sign of fatigue that his sixth set of high fives were completed with much more force than the others. There was so nearly a seventh reason to celebrate, but umpire Shepherd decided that Pringle got his front leg outside the off stump when the ball ripped back to hit the front pad. Again, to illustrate the fractions on which match-turning decisions rest, and not to criticise the umpire, the 'slo-mo' replay revealed that his foot was outside the line, but the knee was not. On the move, as it was at the crucial moment, it was impossible to get it right, other than by guesswork.

The offer of the light to Gooch was refused, much to the pleasure of Raymond, who was not slow to draw a comparison between the attitude of both captains on successive evenings. Admittedly, a slight drizzle had started, and Gooch clearly wanted it to affect the pitch and the ball, but eventually play was halted, with England's 143 for six giving them a lead of 168. Gooch was then 82, having faced 189 of the 330 balls bowled, leaving the first Sunday crowd to watch Test cricket in England since 1983 a mouth-watering spectating prospect to anticipate.

The puzzle of the day was the decision by Richards to use Ambrose so sparingly after lunch, when England were on the floor. Instead, the captain and Hooper bowled eight of the 32 overs bowled between lunch and tea, with Gooch and Ramprakash enjoying the only uninterrupted wicketless session of the match. The unusual tactical error was underlined when the magnificent Ambrose finished the day with all six England wickets to fall, with Gooch standing firm as he fashioned what was to become one of the great Test innings of all time.

SUNDAY 9 JUNE

Before the start of play, Raymond conducted an interesting exercise to illustrate, for viewers, the difficulties of bowling down the slope from the Kirkstall Lane end. He was filmed rolling a ball down the pitch towards the stumps at that end, and it disappeared to show that, although bowlers came down the slope for 20 yards, they then had to run uphill for the last few yards.

Regarding the pitch, he said that 'the moisture content was the same as Saturday – 4·7 compared with 7 at the start of the match. The coarse grass will still guarantee movement off the seam and, although a target of 200 will be difficult, that will leave Gooch on a shoe-string. Another 50 runs will give England a good chance, especially as then they will have a bit more elbowroom with Malcolm, who hasn't yet bowled anywhere near his best.'

As for Gooch, Malcolm Ashton dug out the surprising fact for me to pass on, that he had already passed his best score for England on the ground of 68, and this innings was only his fourth half-century at Headingley. Safe in the comforting knowledge that his Essex colleague would have to be prised out, Gooch concentrated on turning a fine innings into a great one.

In 40 more overs, he scored 72 out of 96 from the bat from 143 balls. Pringle played his most valuable innings for England, and their seventh-wicket partnership of 98 was not only the biggest of the match from 40 pairings, it established the first real advantage in four days.

Only 15 overs were possible before lunch, because of rain, but in that time Gooch reached the 14th and best hundred for his country. It was a monumental piece of concentration and application. This was his fifth hundred against the West Indies, following 123 at Lord's in 1980, 116 and 153 at Bridgetown and Kingston in 1981, and 146 at Trent Bridge in 1988, and it earned this praise from the normally low-key Raymond: 'It's been a brilliant innings. He's getting a standing ovation round the ground, and that is very rare here. I think there is now a difference in the pitch – only the occasional ball now seams and bounces – it was three or four an over earlier in the match. Gooch and Pringle are showing what can be achieved if two batsmen get in.'

The bowling tactics after lunch were curious. Ambrose bowled only seven overs out of 40 in the day, and none after lunch. Marshall received so many looks and 'friendly' chats after running too close to the leg stump that Richie went off into one of his flights of well thought-out fancy. 'At school we used to say two pints equals one quart. Four quarts equals one gallon – how many conversations equals one warning?'

Marshall it was, operating off a short run, who finally broke the epic stand, getting one to move away from Pringle to give Dujon his fourth catch of the innings. Pringle fought successfully for 145 minutes during which he faced 94 of the 202 balls in the partnership, and he walked off to an ovation so warm that those first-day welcoming jeers seem unlikely ever to be repeated on the ground.

At 233 for seven, Raymond was asked how long England should bat for, if they were not bowled out. 'In many ways it would be best if they were bowled out for about 260, and then bowled late today. This is a game they can win, and remember the pitches at Lord's and the Oval are likely to help the West Indies.'

He got his wish, with Walsh and Marshall dismissing DeFreitas and Watkin in three balls, to make the score 238 for nine. Malcolm was more amenable to instruction from his captain than he had been from Pringle in the first innings. After facing only six balls in the next five overs, he had still faced only 11 from 37 when he was bowled by Marshall to leave his captain on 154, the final total 252 and the target for the West Indies a demanding 278.

I was commentating when Malcolm was bowled and, after watching Gooch leave the field to a wonderful ovation, I let the facts underline the merit of a staggering innings which was to take him to number one in the Coopers Deloitte ratings. 'What an effort this has been. It is his sixth score of over 150, but in the context of the match, the pitch and the attack, I doubt whether he has played a finer innings for England.' Even if it were possible, I would not alter one of those spoken words. Gooch became the first England player to carry his bat since one Geoffrey Boycott at Perth in 1979, with his runs exactly two thirds of those from the bat – 154 out of 231.

In between innings, Richie suggested that perhaps Gooch might 'try something unorthodox and not even open with Devon Malcolm this evening.' Raymond did not disagree. 'I suggested it in the first innings, because you've got to keep putting the ball into the right place.'

Any thoughts Gooch might have had of following this advice – probably none at all – disappeared when DeFreitas made the perfect start by bowling Simmons first ball off the inside edge. Unlucky? No, because the ball bounced too high just outside the off stump for the forcing stroke Simmons tried, and the ball was deflected on to leg stump.

With the light fading fast, Richie spotted Gooch having a talk with Malcolm. 'He is probably telling him that we don't want to go off now, so keep it up.' As Raymond put it, after an immediate bouncer: 'He must have been speaking to Devon's deaf ear.' After another stoppage for rain, Pringle replaced Malcolm.

Only 48 overs were bowled in the weather-affected day, making a total of 247 in the first four days out of the scheduled minimum of 360, yet we were still in line for a cliff-hanger.

At the end of the first-ever Sunday of Test cricket on the ground, England's advantage could be traced to the actions of the two captains. Gooch was magnificent, but must have been relieved that Richards chose to give Ambrose only seven of the 40 overs needed to prise out the last four England wickets. It was difficult to realise that England were well ahead on points, despite another triple batting failure at numbers two, three and four. The wintry conditions seemed to have snuffed out much of the West Indies' traditional ebullience and, for the first time in the match, England were now favourites.

MONDAY 10 JUNE

Tony had recorded Gooch's thoughts the previous evening, which were typically cautious: 'The match could still go either way. We've got something to bowl at – if we bowl well you never know what could happen. It should be a good game.'

Geoffrey was more positive, showing admirable prescience when commenting that 'DeFreitas is such a good line-and-length bowler that he's bound to cause the West Indies big problems – especially now he's got the outswinger going as well as the nip-back ball. That makes like for batsmen so much more difficult.'

The breakthrough England needed went begging when Haynes cut a ball from the Lancashire bowler straight to Ramprakash in the covers, but the awkward chest height of the chance caused it to be dropped, and with Richardson hitting Malcolm for two fours and a three, followed by 11 more in the next DeFreitas over, it was clear that the West Indies had decided to attack the target.

Raymond wanted Pringle to use the outswing cross-wind from the Kirkstall Lane end, and Gooch obliged him after the first eight overs from Malcolm and DeFreitas cost 39. Haynes set himself to anchor the innings, and with Richardson, Richards, Hooper and Logie all capable of winning the match, his wicket was the crucial one.

It fell to the Essex all-rounder in particularly satisfying fashion. At 61 for one, with Haynes on 19 from 51 deliveries, he offered no stroke to a ball which came back and caught him in front of his stumps. The fact his front foot finished three feet in front of the batting crease saved him in the eyes of umpire Bird, although the replay showed that the ball hit him on the knee-roll when his moving left leg was neither very far forward nor outside off stump.

No matter – two balls later another break-back was edged via bat and pad to Smith at short leg, and England were on their way. Geoffrey complimented Pringle on the wicket and his foresight in practising on an old pitch before the start of play, to get used to bowling down the hill. That is the sort of attention to detail the former opening bat loves, which is why sometimes his intolerance with a less-than-thorough approach gives people the wrong impression of a man who simply wants England to do well.

I thought that Pringle's batting and bowling performances had fully justified his selection, but Raymond pointed out that he may not have been selected had Lewis been fit. For once our captions department got it wrong when, putting Pringle's bowling career record for England on the screen, the viewer read that, while the Essex man had never taken five wickets in an innings – which he had at Edgbaston in 1984 and at Headingley in 1988 – he had somehow managed to take ten wickets in one Test, which he had never done. I switched down my 'lazy mike' to tell Keith, and heard the temperature in the kitchen rise several degrees. Computers may be infallible, but their operators are not.

Watkin was brought on at 70 for two and Richardson immediately hit him for four and three to pose Gooch with a big problem. Already Malcolm was a question-mark and, in a four-man attack, the England captain did not want another. Richardson's 50 came up after 98 balls, but Watkin, as in the first innings, revealed his priceless asset of taking wickets, when he had Hooper smartly caught at slip by Lamb to make the score 77 for three and thus place an enormous responsibility on Richardson, Richards and Logie.

Geoffrey voiced a big doubt about Vivian's ability to negotiate the start of his innings against medium pace. 'At the start of his innings, it's almost as though he has got too much time to play against medium-pacers. You feel he has a choice of at least two strokes, he sees it so quickly, which is why I reckon he's much happier against the quicks.'

How would Richards tackle the task of winning the match? Would he graft it out, or would the recently adopted Welshman go for the jugular of the young man from Maesteg? The question was answered off the eighth ball faced by the West Indies captain who, in roulette terms, decided to back number six instead of betting red or black.

It is not over-dramatising his dismissal to say that with him went the match. It was Glamorgan Present v Past, and a good-length ball around middle and off did the trick. Richards aimed to hit it in the air wide of mid-on, but a steepling top edge went over the head of Gooch at mid-off. It was a difficult catch to take, even in fielding practice, but in the context of the Test match, it was horrid. Gooch turned and ran 12 paces directly away from the batting stumps and, as the ball plummeted over his left shoulder, he took it two-handed about 18 inches away from his chest.

Geoffrey was succinct. 'That shot of Richards will demoralise the West Indies dressing-room. An instantly forgettable stroke.' Gooch's influence on the result of the match was already massive, but he had one more ace to play.

With Richardson still there, and Logie the hero of so many rescue and escape acts in his previous 48 Tests – only two hundreds but 15 half-centuries – England did not dare count even one chicken until they took another wicket. Against all the odds, the same bowler-fielder combination did it again nine balls later. This time Gooch was at third slip, where he pulled off a catch which was certainly more spectacular than the one to dismiss Richards, although possibly not so difficult. The edge, low to his left, was one of those which either sticks or it does not, whereas the first one gives the fielder ample time to consider his fate if he drops it.

Raymond summed up the way the match was going for England's captain with a nice northern turn of phrase: 'I think if Graham Gooch fell off the pavilion, he'd fall into a feather bed.' His wonderful slip catch gave Watkin three wickets for 15 in 15 deliveries. Richie agreed about the merit of Gooch's two catches: 'Although the one to get rid of Logie was a marvellous reflex effort, I'd go for the Richards one – beautifully judged.'

But Ray rightly drew attention to the part played by Pringle. 'There is no doubt in my mind that his steadiness has helped the other bowlers. He has blocked the Kirkstall Lane end, and created doubts in the minds of all the West Indies batsmen, and that has helped Gooch to switch the other bowlers and keep attacking fields.'

With a lunch score of 99 for five, only Richardson on 58 not out stood between England and a certain win, and the Antiguan continued after the break with a mixture of stern defence and flashing stroke-play. Dujon took ten off DeFreitas's first over, including two sumptuous back-foot cover boundaries, but providing England's two best bowlers held their nerve, the result was inevitable.

The sixth-wicket partnership had added 48 off 96 balls when the next one was, effectively, the last nail in the coffin. Richardson could only parry a useful delivery to Lamb at first slip, who took his fourth and most important catch of the game with understandable relief and joy.

Marshall was LBW next over from Pringle, with the bowler not getting the usual bunch of high fives, but a much more painful set of low ones when, in the rush to congratulate him, either Russell or Gooch spiked the big toe which always protrudes from his 'cut-out' left boot. At that stage, the Essex all-rounder had taken two for 28 off 20 overs, and if there was a working man's Man of the Match award, it would have been his.

Once the West Indies lower-middle batsmen start a helter-skelter descent, there is no stopping them, and the loss of Dujon and Marshall to DeFreitas and Pringle completed a slump from 136 for five to 139 for eight in 14 deliveries. Walsh came in to the sound and sight of the National Anthem and fluttering Union Jacks, with only the threatening rain offering an undeserved escape route.

He and Ambrose were both dropped, before the last two wickets went in five balls to complete a crushing win by 115 runs, compared with the last home win against the West Indies on the same ground, when England won by 30 runs. Atherton's catch to give Malcolm his only wicket in the match was hardly orthodox. Walsh steepled one into the covers, which Atherton, in the gully, decided was his. The further he went, the more likely a collision with Ramprakash, whose catch it was. Atherton ignored his colleague, but Ramprakash fortunately did not, and the result was a full-length diving catch which, had he not clung on, would have brought a stewards' inquiry, for 'crossing and taking my ground'.

Geoffrey hailed the win as 'a fully deserved one, because England played the better cricket.' Richie attributed the victory to 'top-class fielding, and even though there were three blemishes today, the big difference from Australia is how they fielded. Victory came just after 3pm – the last win was 1969, and that's a long time between drinks.'

Man-of-the-Match adjudicator Fred Trueman played with the crowd by mentioning Smith, Richards and Ambrose but, even without his three catches and a run out, Gooch's unbeaten 154 made this particular award one of the biggest formalities ever. In the after-match interview, Gooch was quick to mention the contributions of Ramprakash with the bat, Watkin with the ball, and Hick for his slip catches. Pringle toasted his new friends in the crowd with champagne, and they responded with 'God Save Our Pring'.

Gooch's first Test hundred at Headingley made him the fourth England batsman after Ken Barrington, Ian Botham and Geoffrey Boycott to score a century on each of the six English Test grounds, and he also became only the fifth home player to carry his bat through a completed Test innings. He is in exalted company with Bobby Abel, Plum Warner, Len Hutton (twice) and Boycott.

Another fact to be assimilated by both sides before Lord's, was that Richards had now lost two successive Tests as captain for the first time, Australia having won in Antigua in May. Richie wound up the telecast with a blend of caution and shrewdness. 'West Indies are never more dangerous than when they have been stung. At Lord's and in the rest of the series, they'll be very hard and difficult to beat.'

ENGLAND v WEST INDIES
at Headingley on 6, 7, 8, 9, 10 June 1991

ENGLAND

		Runs	Balls	Mins		Runs	Balls	Mins
* G. A. Gooch	c Dujon b Marshall	34	49	61	not out	154	332	449
M. A. Atherton	b Patterson	2	16	23	c Dujon b Ambrose	6	33	38
G. A. Hick	c Dujon b Walsh	6	31	50	b Ambrose	6	20	24
A. J. Lamb	c Hooper b Marshall	11	37	55	c Hooper b Ambrose	0	1	1
M. R. Ramprakash	c Hooper b Marshall	27	103	141	c Dujon b Ambrose	27	109	141
R. A. Smith	run out (Ambrose/Dujon)	54	88	133	lbw b Ambrose	0	1	1
†R. C. Russell	lbw b Patterson	5	29	44	c Dujon b Ambrose	4	12	14
D. R. Pringle	c Logie b Patterson	16	73	110	c Dujon b Marshall	27	94	145
P. A. J. DeFreitas	c Simmons b Ambrose	15	33	43	lbw b Walsh	3	27	41
S. L. Watkin	b Ambrose	2	9	14	c Hooper b Marshall	0	5	6
D. E. Malcolm	not out	5	31	41	b Marshall	4	11	28
Extras	(lb 5,w 2,nb 14)	21			(b 4,lb 9,w 1,nb 7)	21		
TOTAL	(79.2 overs; 366 mins)	198			(106 overs; 449 mins)	252		

WEST INDIES

		Runs	Balls	Mins		Runs	Balls	Mins
D. L. Haynes	c Russell b Watkin	7	38	54	c Smith b Pringle	19	51	80
P. V. Simmons	c Ramprakash b DeFreitas	38	62	72	b DeFreitas	0	1	1
R. B. Richardson	run out‡	29	62	98	c Lamb b DeFreitas	68	141	192
C. L. Hooper	run out (Ramprakash)	0	5	9	c Lamb b Watkin	5	25	33
* I. V. A. Richards	c Lamb b Pringle	73	98	130	c Gooch b Watkin	3	8	10
A. L. Logie	c Lamb b DeFreitas	6	15	24	c Gooch b Watkin	3	7	7
†P. J. L. Dujon	c Ramprakash b Watkin	6	13	14	lbw b DeFreitas	33	62	72
M. D. Marshall	c Hick b Pringle	0	5	9	lbw b Pringle	1	7	5
C. E. L. Ambrose	c Hick b DeFreitas	0	3	4	c Pringle b DeFreitas	14	26	34
C. A. Walsh	c Gooch b DeFreitas	3	16	26	c Atherton b Malcolm	9	23	32
B. P. Patterson	not out	5	14	18	not out	0	-	2
Extras	(lb 1,nb 5)	6			(lb 1,nb 6)	7		
TOTAL	(54.1 overs; 236 mins)	173			(56.4 overs, 239 mins)	162		

WEST INDIES	O	M	R	W	O	M	R	W	FALL OF WICKETS				
										ENG	WI	ENG	WI
Ambrose	26	8	49	2	28	6	52	6	1st	13	36	22	0
Patterson	26.2	8	67	3	15	1	52	0	2nd	45	54	38	61
Walsh	14	7	31	1	30	5	61	1	3rd	45	58	38	77
Marshall	13	4	46	3	25	4	58	3	4th	64	102	116	85
Hooper					4	1	11	0	5th	129	139	116	88
Richards					4	1	5	0	6th	149	156	124	136
ENGLAND	O	M	R	W	O	M	R	W	7th	154	159	222	137
Malcolm	14	0	69	0	6.4	0	26	1	8th	177	164	236	139
DeFreitas	17.1	5	34	4	21	4	59	4	9th	181	167	238	162
Watkin	14	2	55	2	7	0	38	3	10th	198	173	252	162
Pringle	9	3	14	2	22	6	38	2					

Toss: West Indies
Umpires: H. D. Bird & D. R. Shepherd
Man of the Match: G. A. Gooch
RESULT: ENGLAND WON BY 115 RUNS
‡ = Gooch/Malcolm/Russell

CHAPTER FOUR

CONTROVERSY AND STALEMATE

SELECTION FRIDAY 14 JUNE

The England selectors understandably rubber-stamped the winning XI of the first Test match, although the inclusion of Lawrence for Lewis in the XIII showed their acknowledgement of the problems concerning half the pace attack in that game. The combined second-innings analysis of DeFreitas and Pringle at Headingley was 43-10-97-6, whereas the erratic Malcolm and the inexperienced deputy, Watkin, combined to produce 13·4-0-64-4.

Again, the XIII was announced on the Friday before the start of the Lord's Test – only four days after the end of the first Test – with the Benson & Hedges semi-finals and the Derbyshire game against the West Indies offering the only cricket to the selectors. Had Malcolm played in that solitary three-day game, the selectors would still have been able to watch only seven of their XIII, but he missed the match.

Had the selection and announcement of the team been delayed until Sunday, the selectors could have watched the first two days of the five Britannic Assurance County Championship games which started on Friday 14 June. Often it is not easy for Gooch to fit in meetings with Stewart and Dexter, because of his Essex playing commitments, but his county had three days off. They were due to have a Refuge Assurance League game against Hampshire on Sunday, so it would have made sense to have met that morning in Chelmsford. Such a delayed announcement might have posed an administrative problem to the Board, who need to supply the list of names to the printers of the official souvenir programme as early as possible, but the priority should always be the duties of the selectors, and how best they can carry them out.

With Illingworth again unlikely to play in the second Test, the form of Watkin and Malcolm was crucial to England's chance of avoiding defeat on what was likely to be one of the two best batting pitches of the series. Figures are not always conclusive but, at Test level, they are ignored at peril, especially when they show that the DeFreitas–Pringle pairing at Headingley produced match figures of 69·1-18-145-12 in nine spells, whereas Watkin and Malcolm managed 41·4-2-188-6 in eight spells. Gooch, Stewart and Dexter had to evaluate the performance of both bowlers. They had to decide if loyalty to a young man who took five good wickets on his debut, together with allowance for first-match nerves, should earn him another chance under conditions which were certain to be much less favourable for seam bowling than at Headingley. The fact he was a stand-in bowler meant they did not have to stick rigidly to the policy of giving a new cap at least two successive games. If he did play, they would gamble that Malcolm would be in better form because, in a four-man attack, even with the back-up of Gooch himself and Hick, a side can just about afford one bowler to be out of sorts, but not two.

The six days between the announcement of the team on Friday and the start of the match the following Thursday were marked by two astonishing public personal attacks on Stewart and Boycott. Derbyshire chairman Chris Middleton launched himself at the England manager for travelling to Derby on the Saturday to try to sort out Malcolm's run-up which, since Australia, was now unrecognisable in length and rhythm. Boycott, whose abrasive microphone delivery had already sparked much public argument, found himself, on the morning of the match, the subject of an attack by *Daily Mail* writer Ian Wooldridge which was surprisingly personal and unusually unbalanced from such a well-respected writer.

Having decided to pick Malcolm in the squad, Stewart contacted Derbyshire to tell them he would like a one-to-one session with the fast bowler in order to try to re-establish a run-up which the two had worked out during the winter tour of Australia. Kim Barnett, the club captain and Bob Lark, chief executive, were in agreement, and so Stewart had a session with Malcolm in the indoor nets on Saturday.

The following day, during the Refuge League game against Somerset, in which the bowler was to bowl his only eight overs in competitive cricket between the first and second Tests, chairman Middleton voiced his views in the press box on what he saw as unwarranted interference by Stewart. His objection to the publication of the indoor-net session on a rainy day, included comments which, later in the season, earned him a fine of £750 from the Test & County Cricket Board's disciplinary sub-committee of which, piquantly, he was a member.

Gerald Mortimer of the *Derby Evening Telegraph* quoted Middleton next day as saying:

> The England manager appeared like Mount Joe from on high, to put everything right on a pouring wet day. After all, Devon will be at Lord's tomorrow when there will be two full days in which to iron out any faults. If there was anything wrong, Derbyshire could have sorted it out. Phil Russell should be getting the credit for turning Devon from a raw fast bowler into one of Test ability. What we now find is that he returns from Tests and tours in a state of complete exhaustion. He is still recovering from the tour of Australia, yet we are criticised for leaving him out of the recent match against the West Indies. Six or seven years' hard work have gone into his cricket, but if we're not careful, England will burn him out.

As the weekend before the Lord's Test was 16 weeks since the fast bowler's return from Australia, during which time he had bowled 73 overs in nine one-day games, and 138 in first-class cricket, including the Headingley Test, he had hardly been overworked. He did return from the winter tour with a shoulder strain, but attributed that to throwing in from distant boundaries, rather than an excess of bowling. However, Derbyshire could point out that on that tour, he bowled 74 more overs than any other England bowler in the Tests, and 145 more overs in first-class cricket than any other touring pace bowler.

Whatever the merits of Middleton's comments, it cannot have eased the cricketer's nerves, and the public disagreement between a county chairman and the England manager did little for the good name of cricket.

THURSDAY 20 JUNE

Unusually, there was tension in our commentary box before the start of the game. A tight-lipped Geoffrey was clearly upset about the attack on him that morning in the *Daily Mail*. The first few paragraphs of the article, entitled 'A querulous, carping voice of cricket that leaves a sour taste', contain opinions from Wooldridge, which he is entitled to hold and write, but not if they are presented as facts without any substantiating examples. He complained that

Boycott was 'incapable of voicing criticism with either sympathy or sensitivity', and all this with 'a limited vocabulary and no wit'. He was 'the meanest-spirited commentator in the history of televised sport'. This was because Boycott had discovered that 'the sheerly provocative bludgeon' will win through, and, as well as being easy to do, is 'very profitable'.

Geoffrey is better equipped than most to look after himself in an argument, but his expression that morning told us that Wooldridge had hurt him, which perhaps was the object of an exercise that, it seems, began following a lunchtime difference of opinion with another racegoer at the Royal Ascot meeting two days earlier about the merits of Geoffrey's style and content.

As for the subsequent remarks that Boycott was 'mildly criticised' by 'a very senior BBC executive' for unbalanced comment at Headingley, I can only say that I found the content of what he said entirely unexceptionable, whether talking about batsmen or bowlers. I cannot recall one criticism that was malicious or destructive, even though during the first third of his broadcasting summer, he may have laboured a point in a repetitive manner.

Summarisers are experts first and broadcasters second. Of course he has his critics, so do we all, but the content of what he says is as near flawless as any summariser with whom I have worked.

Perhaps jokingly, perhaps not, the comment of Wooldridge's which Geoffrey said caused the most offence was the claim that they had been friends for 27 years. Like the Middleton–Stewart affair, the Wooldridge–Boycott matter did little for the good name of anyone, and the two former England cricketers sensibly decided to stay silent, take a fresh guard and get on with their jobs.

Tony, rightly, did not ignore the Malcolm controversy and quickly brought Raymond into the discussion as soon as the game started. He gave the teams – Illingworth and Lawrence were omitted for England, and the injured Patterson was replaced by Ian Allen for the West Indies, who batted after Richards won the toss.

Raymond said that it could be a good toss to lose, with a little moisture explaining why, again, Richards dangled the England dressing-room for ten minutes before announcing his decision. He also pointed out that the pitch was a new one, because of damage done in the recent Middlesex county match against Kent by Ramprakash fielding in the covers. As a result, groundsman Mick Hunt had to prepare a different strip, nearer the Mound Stand.

Malcolm bowled from the Pavilion end, and was soon in trouble with a leg-side attack which was heavily punished by Haynes and Simmons. Raymond's suggested solution was to show him a video of his bowling in last year's one-day international at the Oval against New Zealand: 'He bowled well, his rhythm was good and he got through the crease so well, it would be bound to help him to see it again. Today, his left side is collapsing too early, and from this Pavilion end, he's bound to go leg-side. The former Middlesex and England fast bowler Alan Moss used to bowl six inches outside off stump, and you've got to play at that line because of the slope.'

There are people who believe that the importance of the lateral slope at Lord's is over-emphasised, but a study of the relevant figures shows otherwise. From the Grandstand to the Mound Stand is a distance of 450 feet with a left to right slope, looking out from the pavilion, of eight feet. That gives an average gradient fall of one in 56 which, with the width of each cut pitch being ten feet, as laid down in Law Seven, means that, on average, each pitch has a drop of slightly over two inches. The widely accepted results of this concern bowling from the Pavilion end and batting at the Nursery end, rather than the other way around – presumably because there is also a much more noticeable slope away from the Pavilion end.

This means, as Raymond said: 'Fast bowlers need to adjust their normal line about six inches towards the off side, and batsmen need to re-assess what they can leave alone and what they must play.' With the batsman having to counter the slope from off to leg as he faces the Pavilion, any ball which pitches around off stump and holds its line against the slope is the equivalent of a leg-break. Conversely, bowling from the other end, a delivery which moves back off the seam has a similarly exaggerated effect. Traditionally, off-spinners have always bowled with the slope from the Pavilion end, and slow left-arm spinners from the Nursery end.

The effect of the slope is therefore far from being a myth, and batsmen and bowlers, unused to playing at Lord's, do need to make technical adjustments. Small wonder that, after his poor first Test match, Malcolm was drawn, as though magnetised, towards leg stump, despite Gooch having given him three slips and a gully. After two boundaries to leg, Gooch went from third slip to square leg, much to Raymond's disapproval. 'That is just a field for poor bowling,' to which Tony added: 'It must be a terrific temptation for Gooch to go back to slip.'

He did, despite the warning from our Yorkshireman that 'Haynes will probably get one down leg-side now'. In fact, he was only half right, because a four to mid-wicket was followed by a majestic pull for another boundary, and the West Indies innings was well and truly launched.

DeFreitas was a model of economy, with his first five overs costing three runs, while 28 came from the other end. Raymond spotted that 'Malcolm is also bowling into the breeze and it's a stiff one. I would have bowled him the other end with it and it would also have helped his action. He bowls from the outer half of the return crease anyway, and although DeFreitas does as well, his hand action is still okay. Devon's is not, which is why he is firing everything legside.' That was a perceptive analysis of a fast bowler which, coming from a slow bowler, made it even more impressive to me.

When Gooch rested Malcolm, his six overs for 33 included five leg-side fours of the six hit off him, and when Watkin was hit for four by Simmons off his first ball, the selection of the same attack that won the first Test was already shown to be a mistake. The nearest Malcolm came to success was when a desperately difficult return catch from Haynes went begging, although perhaps Geoffrey's comment that he preferred to 'call that a save of runs, not a missed chance,' was nearer the mark.

Richie compared the problems of Malcolm with similar ones overcome by Craig McDermott a few months previously. 'He was falling away in the delivery stride and, in order to counter so much leg-side bowling, he found he had to aim 15 inches outside off stump. It worked, and gradually his natural action returned.'

By this time, Gooch had turned to Pringle, but with his first three deliveries going for 11 runs, Gooch was close to despair after 70 minutes play. DeFreitas had then bowled eight overs for as many runs, while 54 came from nine at the other end. Fortunately, the Essex all-rounder soon settled into a better rhythm from the Nursery end, and started to swing the ball away from the right-handers.

Gooch set his field accordingly, giving his Essex bowler a seven-two split, which Raymond thought was too taxing. 'I reckon that sometimes a man by the square leg umpire helps the bowler to bowl a straighter line at middle and off, rather than as Pringle is doing at the moment, starting the outswinger too wide.' The theory is a sound one and does not contradict his earlier thought that a square leg to Devon was a field for poor bowling. The difference was that Malcolm had to forfeit a slip whereas, when Gooch finally moved a man for Derek, it was from the off-side in front of the wicket. He later pointed out that because the field set for him forced him to bowl outside the off stump, this meant that batsmen could leave alone perhaps three or four an over.

The more I listen to Raymond, the more impressed I am with his analysis of the minutiae of captaincy and technique. Unlike Geoffrey, he prefers the low-key approach which is why, although they are both Yorkshiremen, they provide an ideal contrast as summarisers.

With Haynes and Simmons going along at more than three runs per over, I voiced my growing doubts about England's selection, and forgot to avoid the use of 'we' in referring to England. 'We got 20 wickets at Leeds in 110 overs, but England will do well to get ten in that number in this innings.'

When the score was 87, just before lunch, Richie prophesied an Australian-inspired superstitious wicket, and he was proved right as soon as Haynes completed a fine half-century, including nine fours, off only 75 balls. The viewers missed the wicket because, as usual, live transmission is halted at 12.55pm to accommodate regional newscasts before the 1pm national news. The growing criticism levelled at programme controllers is presumably balanced by the complaints they would receive if they shifted the main mid-day bulletin, because the lunch break in Tests begins at anything from exactly 1pm through to approximately 1.05pm, if a fast bowler begins an over just before the hour.

It is much easier to sympathise with criticism from viewers concerning other departures from live cricket – in particular when a batsman is in sight of a landmark, or when perhaps a side is in danger of following-on. This is even more galling when the move is to racing, with ten minutes or so to go before the off. Again, it is a matter of balancing the protests from racing enthusiasts against those of cricket watchers.

Where the viewer does have a legitimate grouse is the timing of the highlights programme late at night. The only consistent feature of the programme is that it is tagged on towards the end of the nightly schedule, either side of midnight. If it is worth doing, it needs a reasonably regular programme spot, and should be earlier in the evening.

The wicket missed by the viewing public came a couple of minutes before 1pm, when Gooch brought on Hick from the Pavilion end. With his third ball in Test cricket, a gentle off-spinner did not turn, and Simmons edged a catch wide of Lamb at slip, who took a fine, low, diving catch. Having played with considerable restraint and responsibility after his two dismissals from attacking strokes at Leeds, the opener looked understandably distraught as he walked off, with 33 off 88 balls as his share of the opening partnership of 90.

Hick put together such an effective, teasing spell of off-spin at the beginning of the afternoon session (his figures were now 5-4-3-1), that the early fears of wrong selection became stronger, even after Haynes was undone by what I think was one of the best deliveries of the series for 60 off 106 balls to make it 102 for two.

A perfect outswinger from Pringle first squared him up to play towards mid-on, and from that position he did well to get an edge to Russell. Geoffrey drooled over the dismissal, and commented thus over the replay: 'That was a gorgeous delivery. The ball goes towards leg stump and then cuts away, late in the air and then off the pitch. A fine innings has ended because Haynes was out-thought by clever swing bowling by Pringle. He is a good craftsman – knows his limitations and needs watching, even on a pitch where batsmen think they should be whacking him around.'

The cameramen love a full Lord's, with an abundance of famous faces a sitting target – literally – for their attention during any gaps in play. Various visual tours of boxes during the afternoon revealed a splendid mixed trio in one box of Imran Khan, Mick Jagger and Spike Milligan, with other branches of entertainment and politics represented by Sir Richard Attenborough, Leslie Crowther, John Major and Peter O'Toole – all carefully listed alphabetically.

They watched England's problems increase, with Richie surprised that, after 45 overs, Malcolm had not yet bowled down-wind from the Nursery end, and Tony spotted that 'Watkin has still to relax. He seems tense around the shoulders.' Richardson hit his first ball for four, square on the off side, with Watkin's chairman pointing out that 'that was the sort of ball you can get away with in county cricket, with batsmen more likely to pad up to it. Alan Jones says if you could pinpoint an improvement Watkin has to make, it's in his concentration.'

Geoffrey expanded the point: 'I don't think a lot of people realise how important concentration is to bowlers as well as batsmen. Top bowlers don't just bowl a length – they pinpoint a spot on the pitch they want to exploit a batsman's weakness. They have to concentrate every ball at this level.' As he spoke, another poorly-directed delivery was hit for four to square leg, causing Geoffrey to add: 'There is the perfect illustration of the difference with class batsmen. They don't need a rank bad ball to hit, just a fraction off line is enough.'

Gooch pulled what few tight strings he had, switching DeFreitas, but Watkin could not find the fuller length Geoffrey insisted he should be bowling. A better ball was edged through the vacant third slip area, which proved the point made. 'It was a good ball, but it was played off the back foot – the batsman would have been in much more trouble forward.'

Yet again Boycott was displaying the thoughtful criticism which negates much of what Wooldridge wrote that day. And the remarks were not forthcoming because of the article, because similar comments were plentiful in the first Test as well as in the one-day internationals.

With Gooch unable to create any pressure, the third 50 came off 111 balls, compared with 93 and 112 for the first two, before Malcolm finally appeared down-wind for the first time, just before tea, when the score was 169 for two.

As the players went off, Richie summed up the ragged bowling performance thus: 'It is an easy-paced pitch – nothing for short, yet all the punishment has come off the short stuff.' It was a bull point, with the bowling figures revealing that, from the first 50 overs bowled by the four seamers, DeFreitas and Pringle's combined 29 cost 59, while 21 from Malcolm and Watkin were heavily punished for 90. The lesson of the performances from the first Test had either been ignored, or were considered unlikely to be repeated.

Richardson's half-century came off 100 balls, including ten of the 25 fours hit in the first 182 runs – a statistic which tells the story of a first day which was to end with the West Indies in complete command at 317 for three. The third session was expensive – 141 coming from 30 overs, although that looked unlikely when Richardson threw his wicket away, trying to hit Hick over the top. DeFreitas took a well-judged catch at deep mid-off and, just as he did at

Headingley, the batsman studiously avoided the gaze of his captain as he passed him on the way out, with 57 out of 198 for three a relatively disappointing score, taking into account the sort of total the tourists were seeking.

Hick's off-spinners delighted Richie: 'What impresses about him are the subtle changes of pace – just slightly slower or quicker – and it looks to me as though he knows exactly what he's about.' Raymond was also impressed: 'He's got a nice action, he bowls from close in to the stumps – he's got a lot going for him. He's only bowled about a dozen first-class overs this season – if ever he bowled a thousand in a season like we used to, he would become a good bowler.'

Richards, as Hooper had done earlier, got away with a mis-hit in the air over the covers, which Geoffrey thought 'a sloppy shot – he hates being tied down'. With the fourth-wicket pair ready to attack Hick, Gooch reverted to seam and his most reliable bowler, DeFreitas, although Geoffrey wondered if 'DeFreitas can find his rhythm from the Pavilion end, which is not his favourite.'

Sure enough, the next ball was a long hop, which Hooper hit for four, and that signalled an acceleration to the fastest tempo of the day, with 53 runs coming from the last 12 overs. Hooper's 50 had come earlier off 112 balls, with his captain reaching the same mark off only 63, with two fours and a six in one over off the now-suffering DeFreitas.

The thin England attack was torn to shreds, with the century stand coming off 121 balls, and the second 50 hit off 49. It was stirring stuff, although the spectators and viewers could reflect overnight, as Gooch surely did, that his bowlers had let themselves down badly by conceding 184 of the 317 runs scored in the day in boundaries, with most of those hammered off the back foot. Gooch vainly tried no fewer than 17 bowling changes in a day which the West Indies batted well, but were given far too many easy runs.

FRIDAY 21 JUNE

Play started 75 minutes late because of rain, but the extra hour ensured that the capacity crowd of 28,000 were denied only 14 overs of the daily minimum ration of 90. England's day was of the switchback variety, with the last seven West Indies wickets falling for 97 in 27 overs, and then England losing their first five wickets for 110 in 45 overs.

The pre-lunch session of nine overs began with the surprising decision by Gooch to take the second new ball after ten minutes, despite the damp outfield. At least it was a surprise to Messrs Illingworth and Benaud, with Richie's reaction to Raymond's tentative explanation that 'moisture is less likely to get into a new ball', a positive one of 'I can't work that out – Gooch must have great confidence in shellac.' From Ray: 'He's got less in Devon, it seems that DeFreitas and Pringle will get it.'

If Gooch had been wired to sound, his smile, five balls later, would have been even wider when Richards went back to a full length ball from DeFreitas and was nailed plumb LBW. For the second successive Test, his well of brilliance on one day had dried up the next, and the stroke and minimal footwork were so uncertain that Raymond said: 'Sometimes Viv seems to play by numbers.' Richie agreed, using the replay to illustrate the length of the ball to which he had played forward on the previous day and not back and across his crease.

The wicket offered much-needed relief for Gooch, whose decision to give the new ball to his only two trustworthy bowlers probably came after hours of reflecting on the lopsided work-load of his four pace men the previous day. DeFreitas and Pringle's 41 overs cost 111, while 50 from the rest cost 201. The fourth-wicket pair had rattled up 124 from 169 balls, of which Richards faced 89 for an innings of 63 which was studded with brilliance.

Logie, playing in his 50th Test, was all but out first ball to another break-back from DeFreitas before, at the other end, Hooper was fortunate in the next over to survive a complete misjudgement against one from Pringle which held from leg to off. Umpire Ken Palmer's refusal of the appeal brought an unusually strong comment from Raymond that 'as it pitched on and straightened, and the height was all right, I'm not sure which stump it would have missed.'

Richie, who wraps up his little darts in a more understated manner, explored the other possible avenue of escape – that Hooper had played a stroke, which might have saved him. 'If he did play a stroke, it was a pretty ordinary one – he was at least nine inches away from the line of ball.' An offered stroke only keeps the batsman out of trouble if his pad is outside the line of off stump and the ball comes back, but, as this delivery went the other way after pitching around middle, a study of the replay – which umpire Palmer did not have at his disposal – offers no valid reason why I should disagree with the view of Raymond.

Logie's innings lasted for only ten deliveries, but in that time he got the sort of working-over from DeFreitas with which Hick was to become all too familiar. One delivery threatened to cut the little man in half, and another hit him amidships, before he was bowled off the inside edge. As Raymond said: 'That one didn't bounce like the other two – that's why he got the deflection and lost his off stump. Good, hostile bowling on exactly the right line from the Pavilion end.'

Those two wickets in nine balls gave England a real chance of preventing West Indies from scoring around 500, unless Hooper could turn his elegant innings into a major one. He reached his hundred just before lunch, and that it was only his third such score in 48 Test innings says much for the continued faith in his ability held by Richards, especially as he had reached 50 on only five other occasions. He became the 14th West Indian to score a Test hundred at Lord's, with George Headley the first when he scored 106 and 107 in 1939. Geoffrey said: 'The West Indies Board and Viv are to be congratulated for continually picking him, and they probably think it is time he repaid them with a big innings. After all, he is such a technically correct player and is always beautifully balanced.'

It was not to be, with the deserving Pringle helped by a neat slip catch by Lamb to dismiss Hooper on 111 from 202 balls, to make the score 366 for six. I greeted Marshall with a comment which landed me in *Private Eye*. I made the mistake of launching myself into a reference to the fast bowler's batting at Headingley without calculating the speed the information took to reach me from Malcolm Ashton. By the time he passed the sheet to me, I had already said that 'Marshall only got a handful of runs in the first Test', and then had to add, 'nought and one'. A fingerful perhaps, but no more, as at least one keen-eared viewer noted.

DeFreitas was now generating sufficient bounce from the Pavilion end for Dujon to send for an arm-guard, which probably did little for the peace of mind of the three England batsmen who were most in need of runs – Hick, Lamb and Atherton.

With the new England new-ball pair bowling so well, the West Indies seventh-wicket pair could scratch only 16 runs before Pringle took his third wicket of the innings with another outswinger taking the edge of Dujon's bat and finding its way to Lamb at slip, following a double-handed parry from Hick. Raymond thought that the extra bounce and movement off the pitch today was 'perhaps off the cracks, as the pitch is dry and has not had as much preparation as usual. The enforced move from the original strip at least means a central pitch, with both square boundaries an equidistant 72 yards from the middle.'

The weather was now hot and sunny and among the cutaways offered to Richie was a shot of several men – none of whom was in the first flush of youth or possessed of a 32-inch waistline. As the camera's wandering eye finally settled on one weighty, bare-chested sun-worshipper, Richie said: 'We always say we'll even up the Page Three pictures for you – there's one of them.'

The last three wickets could muster only 37, with Pringle completing his third five-wicket bag for England by deceiving Marshall with a slower off-spinner and then having Walsh caught by Atherton off a slog into the covers.

In between, Ambrose pushed a simple catch back to Malcolm to make his figures so far in the rubber read 39·4-3-171-2 to underline the danger, in a five-match series, of giving an out-of-sorts player one chance too many to find his form. A Test match should be for displaying good form – not finding it.

Marshall, not without justification, thought he was hard-done-by when umpire Palmer gave him out LBW, and Geoffrey sympathised with the batsman: 'It was a lovely slower off-spinner. It actually turned back up the slope, and I thought it might have missed leg stump.' After another look at the 'slo-mo', he was much more positive: 'It was definitely missing leg stump.'

There are two schools of thought about such a comment. The first believes that little is achieved by showing up the umpire and that he should never be directly criticised. The opposite view is that, when the pictorial evidence points to a definite conclusion, it is less than honest not to say so. In any case, cricketers recognise that umpires make mistakes like anybody else, but also feel that they should be pointed out, as are their own errors. What replays do show, like those in soccer, is that the officials are usually right and, even when they are not, an occasional fault is understandable. Richie is a firm believer that, even when replays of LBW decisions appear to show a mistake has been made, allowance *must* be made for the angle of the camera, compared with that of the umpire, and also the height – even when the camera is situated exactly behind the bowler's arm.

Knowing all the English umpires well, I know that they are always keen to hear if they might have got something wrong, and they appreciate the invariable corollary to any critical comment that their decision has to be made without recourse to seeing a replay. Cricket has always been full of the rough and smooth sides of justice but, just because modern television is able to point out most of the errors, there is no justification for the increasing tendency among the modern players to 'show out' after being given out. After all, they do not see any replay until later, so there should be no difference in the giving and taking of decisions in the modern game, compared with the past. The umpire must be right, even when he is wrong, and the sooner players accept that, the sooner cricket will improve some of its deplorably fallen standards.

Between innings, Richie enthused about the performance of Pringle. 'His figures of 35·1-6-100-5 assume considerable significance in the absence of Angus Fraser. Gooch has had to find someone to do Fraser's job, and Pringle has done it for him.'

Tony and Raymond went through the wickets in vision, with the point repeated about Pringle's contrasting luck when he appeared to be denied a better LBW appeal against Hooper than the one he won against Marshall. Asked about the pitch, Raymond was at his prophetic best: 'I think England will have problems. There are cracks there, it is dry, and the extra pace of the West Indies bowlers is bound to cause trouble.'

His crystal ball was to prove nice and clear, as was mine after the first four overs: 'So far there has been no real problem for the England openers, but we saw enough from their bowlers to know that when the West Indies pace attack finds its range, it's going to be a tough battle.'

The next ball from Ambrose caught Atherton in no-man's land in mind and body, and a late leave-alone stroke dragged the ball back and down into middle stump. The Lancashire opener's eighth and final ball of his third innings of the series took his aggregate to 13 runs from 57 balls in 77 minutes at the crease. The first of three cracks in England's top order was already beginning to widen, with the man astride another, Hick, now taking guard.

The first two balls from Ambrose to Hick were outside off stump, and the third was completely unplayable. It pitched around off stump, lifted chin-high and moved back up the slope towards first slip like an 85 mph leg-break. With the ball nearer to the Hick profile than his bat, as it whistled by, that was the end of his troubles for the moment – but Dujon's were only starting. With his weight on the right foot to take the ball, it suddenly swung the other way after passing the crease, and he finally took it, still rising, reverse-handed to his left as he ducked. Raymond gulped before he admiringly said: 'I don't know that you need spinners when Ambrose can do things like that.'

When Geoffrey replaced him, he soon noticed that 'they've done their homework on Hick after the Texaco games. They have got the normal short leg, but they've added a leg gully because he tends to stay on leg stump when playing the short ball.'

In Ambrose's next over, he really went after his man in a manner that could have only one ending. The first ball was a bouncer, which Dujon took high to his left, but Hick turned his head away and did not watch the ball off the pitch. Either side of two forward stabs, he was hit on the thigh pad and then came the final thrust. His tenth and last ball lifted from not too far short of a length and gloved the static Hick on its way to Richardson at third slip. That was six for two, with Ambrose's figures now 4-4-0-2, and Geoffrey could only marvel at the quality of bowling. 'The ball was short and straight, and Hick froze a bit. He couldn't get his hands out of the way. But all credit to Ambrose for super, aggressive, top-class fast bowling.'

The second-wicket partnership lasted 17 deliveries, as did the one for the third wicket, with Gooch able only to gaze in horror at the mayhem taking place at the other end. This time, it was self-inflicted, with Lamb ballooning a one-handed cover drive off Marshall to Haynes, who easily took the overhead catch. The stroke was beyond the comprehension of most people, especially Geoffrey, who made his most damning remark of the summer – and remember this was *after* the *Daily Mail* feature was published. While Richie thought it was 'a loose and needless stroke,' Boycott condemned it as 'dreadful. You'd expect something different from a club cricketer.'

Gooch trudged off for tea, having made half of the 16 runs scored while the top order was blown away, and he had then faced 38 of the 59 balls bowled. It was proving a grim end to a twelve-month period which ranks among the most successful of any batsman in history. In the year since he went in to bat in the second Test against New Zealand to this day he had 1672 Test runs behind him, including six of his 14 Test hundreds. He averaged 88 in that time, compared with 36·75 in the preceding 15 years, and his record ranks with that of Richards, whose 1710 runs for the West Indies in 1976 is a world record for a calendar year.

Small wonder that he was now top of the Coopers Deloitte world ratings, and his points total of 903 was only the seventh ever in excess of 900 out of a possible maximum 1000. From his lofty position, he could consider the contrasting dreadful figures of his numbers two, three and four. At tea on that Black Friday, Atherton, Hick and Lamb stood at a combined 37 for nine off 159 balls faced in a crease occupancy of eight minutes short of four hours in three innings each. A cruel, but apt, paraphrase of Churchill is that 'never have so few been owed so little by so many'. It must be doubtful if any top three England batsmen have ever achieved so little in their first three innings of a Test series.

As the players came back on to the field, Raymond thought that 'if England lose another quick wicket, they will be bowled out and have to follow-on. I don't understand Gooch's thinking behind Ramprakash batting ahead of Smith. It worked at Headingley, but usually the younger player bats behind the more experienced one.'

Looking at Ambrose, winding himself up for another ferocious burst, Tony sketched a pretty picture of the beanpole fast bowler. 'Just imagine Curtly – a genial character in his own little village of Sweets in Antigua, lolloping around the roads quite harmlessly, but look at him now: a Test-match bowler of the highest quality.'

He went on to paint a different picture – this time of the England dressing-room during the interval. 'It must have been disturbing there at teatime to see number seven with his pads on after ten overs, practising evasive action in front of the mirror.' Raymond provided the perfect double-act punch-line: 'Especially if you're number eight and you've just come out of the bath.'

It all reminded me of a Warwickshire dressing-room in the 1950s when the Derbyshire pace attack whipped out the first six for very few. Skipper Tom Dollery came in from a telephone call, took one look at the scoreboard and turned to two of his side with:

'You go in next.'

'I can't – I've been in.'

'Well you go in.'

'I've been in as well.'

Ambrose started the final session as he had finished the middle one, bowling with fearsome hostility off 13 rhythmic running paces. Unlucky for some – particularly batsmen. Keith supplied, on the screen, the career details of the fast bowler, including a world rating of fourth, with which Raymond disagreed. Referring to Ambrose's solitary ten-wicket haul against England in Barbados 14 months earlier, he made the point that 'when you're playing with three other class quicks, it's not easy to take ten in a match'.

Tony and I had other problems, because we knew we would be staying for live cricket throughout the extra hour, although the original schedule called for a split with the Pilkington Glass Ladies' Championship in Bournemouth. We had to keep the tennis fans informed about play there when it finally began after rain, without actually telling them when they could watch live tennis.

Ramprakash impressed for the third successive time and the 50 came in the 23rd over. Meanwhile, I was having a good Test, having already used 'we' about England and referred to Marshall's solitary run at Headingley as 'a handful'. With things reputed to happen in threes, it was no great surprise when, in response to a suggestion from Alan Griffiths through my earpiece that I recap on the day, I blithely told the public that 'we started play 75 minutes late today because of drivel.' Many a true word . . .

Richards permutated his three main bowlers for as long as he could, but finally turned to Allen, a bowler who is fast-medium with a whippy arm action, but more of a 'skidder' than someone who hits the pitch. Clearly nervous, he completed two innocuous overs before, with the third ball of his next over, he produced a decent delivery from the Nursery end to force a slip catch from Ramprakash. Raymond thought: 'It was a good ball which went down the hill, but it was Ramprakash's right hand coming through which made the ball carry to Richards.'

While Smith came in to join his captain, Raymond pointed out the big difference between Gooch's method of avoiding the short stuff, compared with that of Hick. 'He should watch Gooch, and see that he moves to the off side to get inside the line. Hick tends to stay leg stump and stay flat-footed so he can't move either way.'

Early in his innings, Smith – like Lamb before him – played a one-handed stroke which was obviously becoming the fashion. Raymond made the interesting point that the heavy bats and thick handles used by many batsmen make it harder to keep under control.

Gooch had been dropped when 13 by Hooper off Ambrose, but Walsh repaired the damage with what I described as 'a great over which softened up Gooch with the pressure of different deliveries. He had to face such varied problems that he was finally pushed into fatal indecision.' A wonderful delivery, bowled from wide of the crease at the Pavilion end, pitched 12 inches outside off stump and clipped the top of that stump, as Geoffrey put it, 'like a lightning off-break.'

Gooch walked off with 37 runs chiselled from 115 balls received and, at 87 for five, England were on the brink of disintegration when Russell joined Smith. The pair were the two heroes of a rearguard action in Barbados in 1990 which went close to saving that match and, with it, the series. Russell batted for five hours for 55 then and, with 136 still needed to save the follow-on, similar heroics were needed.

Geoffrey believed Jack Russell to be 'a limited player, but he's got two or three scoring strokes and he's a better player when he plays naturally and uses them. Too often in Australia he seemed to come in with purely a defensive approach.' Not this time though. By the close of play he was 16, Smith 23, and the score coaxed along to 110 – exactly half of the follow-on target, with half the wickets gone. Russell's one close call came during that magnificent spell from Walsh, which included one ball which pitched six inches outside leg stump and brushed his chest on its way to Dujon, who took it diving to his left. Richie saw the replay and said: 'What an extraordinary delivery. Russell is shaking his head and nodding. That's how it gets you when you get a ball like that.'

As our commentary box emptied at the end of the day, I looked out over the empty ground, and wondered about the thoughts of the selectors after another poor performance from roughly half the side. The near-unstoppable nature of Ambrose's bowling made it difficult to point the finger at Atherton and Hick, but the inability of Malcolm and Watkin to repeat the basic tenets of bowling had already eliminated any hopes of an England win. The inability of the Glamorgan bowler to come to terms with the mental demands made by running up in front of a 28,000 crowd was there for all to see, but Gooch knew the risk when he settled for a four-man attack half of which was suspect.

SATURDAY 22 JUNE

Smith and Russell continued their recovery partnership, although not without their problems after the wicket-keeper escaped a lobbed stroke off Ambrose's first ball of the day to short square leg, with Logie two yards too straight. Raymond summed up the Russell technique thus: 'His strength is to use the pace of the ball in playing square either side of the wicket – he doesn't hit too many through mid-off and mid-on.' On Smith, he was just as perceptive. 'In

Australia he was getting forward too far too quickly. Now he's trying to stand still longer, and that is essential against the swinging ball.'

Speaking from bitter experience, Tony countered by saying that the problem 'is to stand still when the nerves are on the move'. And when his summariser noticed that Russell's first back-foot movement was towards leg stump, Tony put the case for the defence with: 'Mostly he's behind every ball, but the body isn't obeying the mind at the moment.'

The fourth over of the day from Ambrose was the most hostile, including two bouncers and another better-length delivery which Smith could only push shin-height to Logie at short leg. The catch went down, and the crucial first hour was gradually weathered.

Richie had obviously had a mixed morning of study of the *Sporting Life*, and his first target was the front-foot no-ball law, which was to keep finding out Marshall in the innings. 'A humourist said that there are only two things certain in life – death and taxes. There is a third. It is that cricket administrators never think through a major change in law – like the front-foot no-ball rule brought in in the early 1960s, which comp 'cates the umpire's readjustment to length and line of LBWs.'

He then switched to his unmatched ability to milk the last drop out of a picture with a minimum of words. Keith offered him a cutaway picture of a multi-coloured parrot floating, kite fashion, across the middle. Our Ice Man made three references to it in the next few minutes. The first was innocent enough: 'Don't know which team has that as its mascot.' The second came like a flash, as Walsh suddenly lost his run-up next ball. 'It's done for Courtney – probably a secret parrot-fancier.' If that was enough to set Malcolm on an increasing spiral of giggles, imagine him one minute later when Russell went to umpire Barry Meyer to have something removed from his eye: 'You see, those parrots are so dangerous. You never know what they're going to do.'

The sixth-wicket pair started to flourish and Richards, like Gooch on the first day, turned to spin a few minutes before lunch and with equal success. Geoffrey awarded the first six rounds of the day to England for defeating the pace attack and getting spin on, and this after the top order had been destroyed the day before. I reminded him of Hick's success against Simmons and, sure enough, Hooper struck with his tenth delivery. Smith had just got to 50 off 134 balls – his fourth against the West Indies, when 'Nelson' struck for the second time in the game.

The 111th ball received by Russell was bottom-edged to Dujon to end a fighting partnership of 96 from 218 balls, and their two and a half hours together re-lit a flame of hope in the England dressing-room. Pringle could have gone for a duck, but Logie was on his heels when a chance was offered him off Allen, with the fielder already standing unusually deep – some ten feet from the bat.

The West Indies bowlers beat the outside edge at least a dozen times in the morning, but a session worth 76 from 27 overs had given the home team a life-line.

Saturday afternoons are messy affairs in the commentary box, because we are at the mercy of the comings and goings of Grandstand. Until we go on BBC 2 at about 4.40pm, the viewers are on short rations of live cricket and their understandable frustration is shared by us if either wickets or runs, or both, are coming thick and fast. We still have to commentate for the highlights programme and, of course, viewers always see replays of wickets before they return to us live.

The first live stint after lunch was difficult to talk about, with Smith and Pringle settling in against good fast bowling from Marshall and Ambrose, whose over-rate was little better than a ball a minute. At times like these, the commentator needs to keep his eyes and ears open for items to develop in discussion for the benefit of the viewers, and Richie's chance came when Geoffrey referred to the famous Lord's ridge, which the authorities have always insisted was never as pronounced as players said, and had more or less disappeared in the last few years.

Mockingly, Richie queried its existence. Geoffrey made an interesting and typically well thought-out reply: 'I saw groundsman Mick Hunt before the game – he says there is still a slight crown batting at the Nursery end – and if the ball hits it on the seam, it gets extra bounce.' Richie asked if the groundsman had any ready explanation why they had not got rid of it. 'Yes, 25 years ago, when I first batted here, it was much more pronounced – it was almost frightening to stand in the crease and look at this mound. Mick says that each year they've tried to reduce it in a gradual process rather than trying to remove it in one go. That is why it is only slight now – but it is still there.'

Which is why, with the ridge and the cross-slope to deal with, cricketers find playing at Lord's is different from any other ground in the country. Marshall was having his most frustrating time in the series. His post-prandial spell from the Nursery end was one of his best, but nothing would go right and he ran into his worst no-ball problem of the summer. He bowled 16 in the innings, and his humour was hardly improved when Smith, on 73 and playing with increasing authority, edged him between Richards and Hooper, with both slip fielders looking at each other for comfort.

The score was then 207 for six, and with that missed chance went most of West Indies' slim hopes of enforcing the follow-on. Raymond termed it a particularly bad effort for neither man to go for the chance because 'Smith was forward, so they had an extra yard to see it off the bat'. The bowler had a close LBW appeal turned down and then watched a run-out escape involving an

Ambrose fumble at fine leg. Picture Marshall's face when the next ball went for four, making ten off an over in which a wicket could have fallen off three deliveries.

Another capacity crowd excitedly indulged in their own public count-down to the follow-on avoidance figure of 220, and roared Pringle home off the final run of a three he hit off Ambrose. The fast bowler was still keeping both batsmen at full stretch and he suddenly let Smith have four bouncers in five deliveries, with the fifth one so short it all but qualified as well. Umpire Meyer spoke to the bowler, who promptly put on that misleading genial smile – rather like Al Capone must have done when he was given his only meaning-ful conviction for income-tax evasion.

Marshall kept looking skywards, but there was no help forthcoming next over either, when Pringle edged him for another four. It was easily the most frustrating period of the innings for the West Indies, with the seventh-wicket pair now scoring at the fastest rate of the innings. Smith completed a marvel-lous hundred – his fifth for England and the first against the West Indies. The crowd gave him a standing ovation, recognising that he was the linchpin of a rescue act which had then taken England from the darkness of 60 for four and 84 for five, into the relatively blinding light of 259 for six.

His cutting and pulling rank among the most powerful in world cricket, and his courage in withstanding the firepower of Ambrose and Walsh, brought this tribute from Richie: 'That is quite a comeback after what happened in Australia ... it is a great innings.' He had then faced 199 balls and batted for five minutes short of three hours, and he became the 13th Englishman to score a century at Lord's against the West Indies – a list, incidentally, which included Geoffrey and Raymond, both of whom did it in 1969.

The second new ball had been taken 40 minutes before tea, but it was Allen who broke through when Pringle, now in a free mood, ambitiously tried to pull a short delivery and gave Simmons an easy catch at mid-on. His 35 off 86 balls came out of a spirited stand of 89 from only 25 overs, and contributed much towards what was to be a near-complete England recovery. Undoubt-edly, the West Indies were handicapped by the absence of Patterson, with the preference on tour of Allen over Ezra Moseley becoming increasingly difficult to understand.

Smith was stuck on his own personal 'Nelson' throughout tea, but he was now above superstition, and shared two more partnerships with DeFreitas (29 out of 47 for the eighth wicket), and Watkin (six out of 37 for the ninth) to restrict the first innings deficit to 65. Geoffrey was unstinting in his praise: 'He was made to work damn hard for his runs, and it was half an hour before lunch before he started to blossom, and eventually get on top of the fast bowlers. A stupendous performance. To get a hundred is a psychological breakthrough.

He's had four fifties against them, but to know he's capable of hundreds against the best bowling in the world will stand him in good stead for the rest of the series.'

Smith is a man of great contrasts. In the middle, he oozes confidence from a thick-set, muscular frame which generates enormous power in his strokes. He is unflinching against the most intimidatory of bowling, and never complains about the sort of overdose of bouncers he received in Antigua, when he sustained both a broken finger and a badly bruised cheek. Yet, off the field, he is diffident to the point of shyness and our Mr Fixit, Dave Bowden, had a difficult job persuading him to agree to record an interview with Tony for use on Sunday. He agreed only after a promise that, if the interview went wrong, it would not be used. As it happened, despite being so nervous before the cameras turned that the odd tremor of his upper lip was spotted, he was soon put at ease by Tony, and gave a good, natural interview in which he did himself justice.

After DeFreitas gave Marshall a well overdue reward with an edge to Dujon to make it 316 for eight, Watkin came in to watch Smith receive an unintentional beamer from Ambrose, followed by a bouncer that was definitely meant. Richie, almost thinking out loud behind the mike, said: 'Now, do you think to yourself, should I give it the forward prod?' This the number ten bravely did as he faced 32 of the 74 deliveries in a ninth-wicket stand of 37.

Raymond commented that he believed Smith was standing still longer than at any time in his career, whereas previously he had been getting on the front foot so early that he had been exposing his leg stump and had no idea where his off stump was.

At 5pm, Richards brought back Walsh for Ambrose at the Pavilion end, and his first ball was square cut, like a shot from a gun, to the Grandstand boundary. Raymond and Richie could only wax lyrical. The Yorkshire view was that it was 'the shot of the Test match – he absolutely murdered it past Haynes'. Quite a compliment considering 750 runs had been scored in the first three days. Richie added: 'There were two men behind square on the boundary . . . I tell you it went like a rocket and neither had a chance. Worth paying your money just to see that.'

Richie then made a rare mistake, although it was not his fault. When Godfrey Evans brought the up-to-date odds of the match into the box, as he always does before the start of play, Ladbrokes were quoting 1–3 West Indies, 5–2 the draw and 50–1 against England. Richie must have been half-listening to me when I told him: 'A quote of 50–1 must have at least a nought missing – they are really 500–1.'

I thought no more about it . . . until I heard it quoted to the world on Saturday evening. 'The satchel-swingers [lovely Australianism] had West

Indies 1–3 this morning, with England 500–1 – like they were at Leeds ten years ago in Botham's Test match.' What could I say? Nothing – the damage was done.

Ambrose finally turned his figures into something like a realistic reflection of his performance when he bowled Watkin and Malcolm in four deliveries, to leave Smith 148 not out. It was an innings which proved many things, including the fact that he was undoubtedly batting at least one place too low. Yet again he had been left with the tail, and only because, unlike in Australia, they resisted for 86 overs was he able to play a major innings.

He hit 20 crackling fours, faced 271 balls and battled away for close on seven hours – a monumental effort which the crowd was not slow to appreciate as he led the players off. His innings altered the whole shape of the match, with the West Indies now unable to take the sort of risks in their second innings that they could have done with a bigger lead than their final one of 65.

MONDAY 24 JUNE

In the end it did not matter, with rain allowing only 37 more balls in the final two days. No play was possible on the Sunday but, even though the game was then condemned to be a draw, the brief amount of cricket on this morning emphasised the swing of psychological balance achieved by Smith's innings on Saturday, which made the Man of the Match award a formality.

DeFreitas brought one back to have Simmons LBW in his third over, which prompted Raymond to wish that Pringle would bowl at Richardson before he was settled in. It seemed a classic case of foot-in-mouth when, next ball, Malcolm had the Antiguan smartly caught at slip by Hick to make the score nine for two. How could Raymond get out of that? We should have known better . . . it was easy.

'That's why I wanted Pringle to bowl – he'd have got it in the right area more often.'

Tony did not let that pass. 'It didn't do a lot, Ray.'

'The way he plays, it doesn't have to. He doesn't play properly forward, only half and half with the weight on the back foot and not going into the stroke.'

You can beat a Yorkshireman, but sometimes it is particularly hard work.

After five more balls, the rains came, and we were left to reflect on the England performance, possible changes for the Trent Bridge Test, and the reasons for the huge improvement since the end of the Australian tour. Richie dealt with that one: 'In Australia the injuries to Gooch and Fraser were crucial.

Also the fielding was bad there, but it is good here. Above all, the return of Gooch has had most to do with the improvement.'

Geoffrey believed that Lawrence and Illingworth would come in for the next Test. 'We got it wrong here – Illingworth should have played in front of Watkin. I wouldn't make any batting changes, and of course England have a good, athletic catching side. Fielding gives the spectators such a lift.' Richie took up this point, reminding the viewers that when Border took over from Hughes in 1984 against the West Indies, they dropped 51 chances in the Tests and one-day internationals, which inevitably destroyed their hopes.

Tony broadened the in-vision chat by inviting Richie to talk about Hick. 'Ask him to count the number of bad balls he's received in three innings and the one-day games. They can probably be counted on one hand. That is the difference between Hick in county cricket and Hick in Test cricket.'

So ended a game in which Haynes reached 50 for the 50th time, and the ground record of Tests between the two sides stayed level – four wins each and six draws. The draw meant that England's woeful post-war record at Lord's against Australia and West Indies was not improved. In 1957, England beat the West Indies by an innings and 36 runs, and that remains the only win against either country in 45 years.

Despite his ill luck, Marshall went past Imran Khan's 362 Test wickets into fourth place on the all-time Test list behind Hadlee, Botham and Kapil Dev.

With the first round of the NatWest Trophy taking place on Wednesday, the England selectors had no significant cricket to watch, assuming that they would announce the team for the third Test four days later. It would have thus made sense to delay their meeting, especially as Gooch and Essex were at Lord's on Saturday and Chelmsford on Sunday, which would cause a minimum of inconvenience to the selectors.

ENGLAND v WEST INDIES
at Lord's on 20, 21, 22, 23 (‡), 24 June 1991

WEST INDIES		Runs	Balls	Mins		Runs	Balls	Mins
P. V. Simmons	c Lamb b Hick	33	88	116	lbw b DeFreitas	2	11	19
D. L. Haynes	c Russell b Pringle	60	106	142	not out	4	18	-
R. B. Richardson	c DeFreitas b Hick	57	124	141	c Hick b Malcolm	1	3	3
C. L. Hooper	c Lamb b Pringle	111	202	281	not out	1	5	-
* I. V. A. Richards	lbw b DeFreitas	63	89	113				
A. L. Logie	b DeFreitas	5	10	10				
† P. J. L. Dujon	c Lamb b Pringle	20	43	64				
M. D. Marshall	lbw b Pringle	25	40	58				
C. E. L. Ambrose	c & b Malcolm	5	17	24				
C. A. Walsh	c Atherton b Pringle	10	14	23				
I. B. A. Allen	not out	1	11	15				
Extras	(b 3,lb 7,nb 19)	29			(lb 2,nb 2)	4		
TOTAL	(120.1 overs; 501 mins)	419			(5.5 overs; 30 mins)	12 (for 2 wkts)		

ENGLAND		Runs	Balls	Mins
* G. A. Gooch	b Walsh	37	115	148
M. A. Atherton	b Ambrose	5	8	16
G. A. Hick	c Richardson b Ambrose	0	10	12
A. J. Lamb	c Haynes b Marshall	1	3	13
M. R. Ramprakash	c Richards b Allen	24	48	65
R. A. Smith	not out	148	271	412
† R. C. Russell	c Dujon b Hooper	46	111	151
D. R. Pringle	c Simmons b Allen	35	86	108
P. A. J. DeFreitas	c Dujon b Marshall	29	48	50
S. L. Watkin	b Ambrose	6	32	53
D. E. Malcolm	b Ambrose	0	4	3
Extras	(lb 1,nb 22)	23		
TOTAL	(118 overs; 521 mins)	354		

ENGLAND	O	M	R	W	O	M	R	W
DeFreitas	31	6	93	2	3	2	1	1
Malcolm	19	3	76	1	2.5	0	9	1
Watkin	15	2	60	0				
Pringle	35.1	6	100	5				
Hick	18	4	77	2				
Gooch	2	0	3	0				

WEST INDIES	O	M	R	W
Ambrose	34	10	87	4
Marshall	30	4	78	2
Walsh	26	4	90	1
Allen	23	2	88	2
Hooper	5	2	10	1

FALL OF WICKETS			
	WI	ENG	WI
1st	90	5	9
2nd	102	6	10
3rd	198	16	
4th	322	60	
5th	332	84	
6th	366	180	
7th	382	269	
8th	402	316	
9th	410	353	
10th	419	354	

Toss: West Indies
Umpires: B. J. Meyer & K. E. Palmer
Man of the Match: R. A. Smith
RESULT: MATCH DRAWN
(‡) = no play

CHAPTER FIVE

THE TURN
OF THE TIDE

TRENT BRIDGE TEST
4–9 JULY

SELECTION FRIDAY 28 JUNE

When the XII was announced, Malcolm and Watkin were replaced by Lawrence and Reeve, with Hugh Morris later put on stand-by because of growing fears about the back and abdominal fitness of Atherton. This meant Gooch would have a new attack to support DeFreitas and Pringle, although it also meant that the three batsmen in trouble, Atherton, Hick and Lamb, were in the same situation as Malcolm and Watkin at Lord's – in receipt of selectorial support which was straining loyalty to the limit.

At least England could go to Nottingham still enjoying a 1-0 lead, despite four players having contributed little towards either Test, and the fifth, Watkin, earning one chance too many, despite his wickets at Headingley. The inclusion of Reeve ostensibly gave Gooch the chance of fielding a five-man attack, if he included the Warwickshire man instead of Hick or Lamb, but the track record of the captain and Stewart put that particular balance of selection at around the 500–1 which the misinformed Benaud quoted against an England win at Lord's.

Reeve's ability to organise the middle-lower order, together with his record against fast bowling and an average in county cricket of over 50 in 1990 and the current season, would not entice the casting of the die. He does not look a fashionable cricketer, but there have been better looking players who have received chances in five-day cricket.

WEDNESDAY 3 JULY

The day before the game, the pitch looked well-grassed and green – or rather it did to the BBC Radio's new cricket correspondent, former Leicestershire seamer Jonathan Agnew. Facing a deadline, he was unlucky enough to have to conduct an interview with Gooch in front of the assembled national press, and when Gooch, dead-pan, refuted Agnew's description of the pitch 'as a good one for bowling', Agnew came off his long run.

'Well, I wouldn't mind bowling on it.'

Gooch hit him straight over the top. 'And I wouldn't mind facing you on it.'

The hacks laughed, but their turn came when Gooch, impatient with what he thought was a stupid line of questioning about England's chances, and the level of their morale, wearily kept repeating: 'Like I told you before the last Test, and the one before that, if we play well, we can compete. If we don't, we won't. You keep on asking the same questions and I'll keep giving the same answers.'

There was a general moan afterwards at his unco-operative attitude, but I can only admire the man for refusing to play their game of 'quotes'. If he has nothing to say, then he says nothing. It does little for tabloid circulation, but that is unlikely to cause Gooch any loss of sleep.

In the evening the England players, keyed up for the next day's events, were possibly unaware that the last home Test win at Trent Bridge was in 1983 against New Zealand, since when they had drawn with Australia, West Indies and New Zealand, and lost to New Zealand and Australia. Coincidentally, both Gooch and Haynes needed 58 to join the distinguished list of batsmen to score 2000 runs in Wisden Trophy matches between the two countries. Advance bookings were close to £500,000, and the feeling I had that this series was to be one of the best in this country for many years, as Lewis Carroll put it, just grew and grew.

THURSDAY 4 JULY

Independence Day it might have been in the US, but we five commentators and our scorer, Malcolm, soon discovered that, because the area of the tiniest commentary box in the universe was reduced still further by the presence of a bulky power generator in one corner, we were entirely dependent on a shuttle service of commentators to and from the adjoining in-vision room if we were to fulfil our microphone duties.

It was physically impossible to place more than four chairs in the hutch, and the three in the front desk had to be squeezed together much closer than is satisfactory. I have commentated under all sorts of conditions in Australia, West Indies, South Africa, India and Pakistan, but never under such restrictive conditions as Trent Bridge. At least the commentators are not distracted by the comings and goings of other people, but I find it a considerable disadvantage not to be able to listen to my co-commentators when I am off duty, so that I can avoid unnecessary duplication or contradiction.

The difference between Richie and the rest of us is that we grumble, but he acts. A quiet appraisal of the situation, with particular regard to how and where he and Tony would fulfil their newspaper commitments on Saturday, and Steve was dispatched to buy a small, folding desk, to erect in the larger, but well-cluttered, in-vision room. Brilliant. It actually seemed to create, rather than diminish, space, and the portable office-top was to come in useful for the rest of the summer, particularly in the small working areas at Edgbaston and the Oval.

Tony and Raymond led off, with Tony revealing that Lawrence and Illingworth were in the England XI, which also included Atherton, surprisingly declared fit after a pessimistic bulletin the previous day. Morris thus continued his fringe contact with the Test scene, and Reeve could only hope that he might get his first cap in the next Test on his home ground in three weeks' time.

Gooch won his first toss of the series, and proved his point with Agnew by batting first on a surface which Raymond said would be 'a good pitch to play quick bowling on. It should have nice bounce and not be too quick, so you won't be playing in front of your throat. Again, England have got plenty of depth in batting ... on paper anyway. The first ten have all got first-class hundreds – only Lawrence can't bat.'

If the sound was turned up on the television in the home dressing-room, the Gloucestershire fast bowler could point to his match-winning unbeaten 36 out of an unbroken eighth-wicket stand of 59 with Russell three days earlier against Northamptonshire.

The forecast comfortable pace was quickly evidenced by one stroke from Gooch. Ambrose dug one in – the opener went forward, then back and paddled it away through square leg for two runs. Little went past the bat, and what was to become one of only two decent opening partnerships of the series for England took on a comforting shape, with the 50 coming in the 17th over.

Marshall was soon in trouble with umpire John Hampshire for running too close to the stumps or, as Tony graphically interpreted the replay, 'a good trampling run – straight down the middle of the flowerbed'.

Raymond was incensed: 'I had a look at Lord's, and there were patches much too close to leg stump. Bowlers should be stopped, not just spoken to. If this goes on, Richard Illingworth could well have some dangerous rough to bowl into here.' Prophetic words, with the Worcestershire spinner bowling most of his 35 overs in the match from over the wicket. In order to clarify the relevant Law 42(13), Keith used a graphic drawing, superimposed on the pitch, of an oblong into which the bowlers must not step. The area at each end extends four feet from the front batting crease, and a width of one foot either side of middle stump. The width of a set of stumps is nine inches, and the graphic drawing illustrated the seven-and-a-half-inch sacred area outside off and leg stumps.

Marshall frequently transgressed in the series, as did Terry Alderman in the 1989 series in England. There is no doubt that these two bowlers take umpires on, and push them as far as they dare. When they are forced to bowl from further away from the stumps, the resultant wider angle of delivery reduces their effectiveness, and it is not long before they creep back. Some people regard it as an acceptable game of chess between bowler and umpire. I prefer to call it cheating, the remedy for which is in the hands of the umpires. Nobody wants to see a bowler ordered out of the attack – nor do I think that would happen more than once. Cricket coaches have long realised that the closer a bowler is to the stumps when he releases the ball, the more effective options he has because, by transgressing, the bowler achieves two things: the facing batsman is disadvantaged, and the resultant rough on, or too close to, leg stump, makes life impossible for left-handers later in the match, and much more difficult for right-handers than should be the case.

Like Raymond, Geoffrey and Richie (who had already pointed out the number of talkings to received before a warning that summer), I believe that the modern umpire is much too lenient with bowlers. Geoffrey was now in residence and he agreed: 'Malcolm always likes to get close for the LBWs, because movement from there is so much more dangerous. The umpires know him, yet all they do is to keep chivvying him.'

He was interesting on the pace of the pitch. 'For once, Ambrose is going to have to show the same patience as batsmen always have to against him. He must not get frustrated because the ball is not moving around or bouncing.' I asked him to compare the difference in pace between this strip and the one in the exciting game on the same ground in 1980, when West Indies sneaked in by two wickets after David Gower dropped a crucial catch off Botham.

'I remember watching a maiden from the other end from Roberts to Gooch. Then Michael Holding ran in to me from the Pavilion end, and it went straight over my head, and Dujon's, and pitched twice before it hit the Cornhill sign for four byes. It didn't do a lot for our confidence.' Geoffrey's recall is usually flawless, but this time he got it wrong. Not regarding the delivery — that sort stays with you for life — but the wicket-keeper in that series was Deryck Murray. He also made the valid point that 'the other batsmen who have not yet contributed in this series, won't get a better opportunity than this . . . a nice sunny day and a nice-paced pitch.'

A double change of shift brought Richie and Raymond into our chairs — not without severe contortions — and they both criticised Atherton, after he was seen to slip on the edge of the pitch. Keith screened a close-up of the offending rubber-soled footwear, which brought from Raymond: 'There is always moisture on the first day of a Test. I can't say I'd be happy batting in rubbers on the first day.' Richie went further: 'And what about his muscle strain? It really is tempting fate to wear rubbers, even ribbed rubber, whatever your choice — half spikes or whatever — you must ensure you always have a firm grip.'

In Australia's Sheffield Shield competition, it became compulsory for batsmen to wear spikes in 1986, and the reason is interesting. The South Australia groundsman, Les Burdett, told me on England's tour that year: 'Our groundsmen persuaded the Board to do this, because we reckon that rubbers and crepes have a bad effect on the nature of pitches. They scuff and compact, whereas we have found out that spikes help break up and aerate the turf. Also they help the surface to wear more naturally, and that is a help to spin bowling.' I remember talking to Micky Stewart about it, but his reply was that his batsmen had tried spikes in the nets and couldn't get used to batting in them. Times certainly have changed.

Gooch continued to take more of the strike. Not by intent, but it sometimes happens that way for no good reason. When the score was 80 in the 21st over, he had faced 78 balls and Atherton 59, as the figures on the screen showed. That they came up so quickly after I had broadcast the information made available to me by Malcolm, was yet another good example of the teamwork which is essential in broadcasting. If either the producer or the computermen had not been listening to me, the viewers would not have had such rapid visual confirmation of the information.

The continued absence of Patterson meant that the West Indies were firing, effectively, on three cylinders, and the inexperienced Allen conceded 25 from his first five overs. When four fast bowlers are reduced to three and a fast-medium operator, there is a pronounced knock-on effect on the entire bowling unit, with Richards unable to rotate his four in pairs to maintain unrelenting pressure. Geoffrey commented that it was a long time since he had seen the West Indies so quickly on the defensive. 'No third slip, no short leg —

it almost looks like a county match. The bowling is straightforward, the batsmen are in control and everything is going smashing for England.'

Gooch completed his 52nd Test score of 50 or more, 14 of which he turned into hundreds, and then came his 2000th run against the West Indies. This time, I warned Keith, via my 'lazy mike', and the ball had only just reached the boundary when viewers saw a breakdown of his Test record against the West Indies, with his 2003 runs coming in his 46th innings. Or, rather, the viewers did not see those figures 'live', because it was now 12.55pm, and they were watching regional news. At lunch the score was 106, with Gooch's 63 scored off 104 balls, and Atherton's 31 off 77. Little should be taken for granted concerning the West Indies, but both sides must have considered, during the break, that England now had the base for a big total. Even the England captain – never outwardly over-optimistic – must have thought that the match situation, considered in the context of England's 1-0 lead in the series, had shortened the odds against his side doing anything other than sharing the final spoils, at the very least.

It took exactly nine minutes for Ambrose and Marshall to expose such ideas as wishful thinking. Ambrose won an LBW decision against Atherton from umpire Kitchen with which Raymond agreed: 'He didn't get outside, and he certainly played a shot, although his front foot went nowhere.' Keith then played in the 'slo-mo' from high-square, which showed that there was no doubt concerning height, and also confirmed Raymond's point that Atherton did not get properly forward.

Hick walked in to join his captain, but a partnership that, before the start of the series, was expected to be a productive and assertive one, lasted seven deliveries before Gooch was undone by a superb piece of thoughtful, technical bowling from Marshall. The over comprised a set-up followed by a clinical sting which climaxed a wonderful battle of wits between two world-class cricketers.

It started with three away swingers, one of which brought an appeal for LBW, before a boundary was followed by a perfect inswinger. Not only did it move sharply back, it did it in the air so late that Gooch offered no stroke, and, suddenly, 106 for none had turned into 113 for two. Richie's verdict was: 'That was beautifully bowled by Marshall – it cut back enough to hit ... a lovely piece of deception.' All this was recorded of course, because of 'Neighbours', with live cricket rarely resumed promptly after lunch during Test matches, except occasionally on Saturdays.

Tony welcomed the viewers back with the bad news and, after the two wickets were replayed, Geoffrey commented on the different approaches of the out-of-form third-wicket pair of Hick and Lamb. 'Hick has got to learn to settle himself, then we'll see how he plays. Lamb is different – he's seen it all and give him anything wide or short and he'll clatter it ... he doesn't care if it goes off the middle or the edge.'

Marshall's Test record was screened, with Tony noting that 'he has played only 79 Tests for his 365 wickets, while Kapil's 376 have come in 110 games. He's certainly packed them in ... Trent Bridge has certainly packed them in too,' was neatly added as a cutaway showed three girls in bikinis.

Umpire Hampshire was wearing darkened glasses to counter the glare from the pitch, but it was the naked eye of his partner, Kitchen, which exacerbated the problems of Lamb and England. Ambrose was now hurtling in, and he brought one back to catch Lamb in front and make the score 138 for three. Geoffrey thought that there was not much doubt about it: 'Lamb gets caught on the back foot to the in-between length. That ball would not have gone over the stumps.'

I was not so sure. My study of the replay showed that, although the ball hit Lamb on the knee-roll of the pad, the decision was only a marginal one concerning whether the ball would have hit leg stump. In the next two minutes, which was roughly 118 seconds longer than Kitchen had in which to make up his mind, I came to the conclusion that, as the ball pitched about 12 feet in front of Lamb before it hit him in front of middle stump, it had already cut back some ten inches, and there was another four feet to go on the angle, before ball and stump would have come together.

Neither plumb nor palpably not out but, as Lamb's expression showed as he walked off, the sort of decision that goes against a batsman when he desperately needs a bit of luck. Richards brought back a third slip and short leg for Ramprakash, and Ambrose went after Hick. When he was 16, he received three bouncers in four balls, the third of which hit him on the back of the helmet. Raymond pointed out that 'it pitched well in Ambrose's half of the wicket, yet he still didn't watch the ball. By the time it hit him, the back of his head faced down the pitch, and that can't be right.'

The storm was weathered, to underline the contrast between the iron-clad determination and courage of Hick and a technique that was much more tentative. At tea, the England ship was not exactly back on course, with a score of 175 for three, but it had been righted by the two tyros – Hick was 35 and Ramprakash 12.

At the start of the final session, in which 40 of the 90 overs were to be bowled, Raymond said: 'This should be a 450 wicket and a great chance for Hick to score his first Test hundred.' Marshall suffered a double blow, straining a leg muscle and receiving yet another warning from Hampshire, but Hick was still in trouble despite having now batted for over two hours. Ambrose hit him on the helmet again – this time the ball went for four leg-byes – to further underline Raymond's point about him turning away from the ball.

The unsettled batsman then wafted twice at Walsh outside off stump, bringing from Richie: 'The difference between Hick and Lamb is that Lamb gives it a cross-bat stroke, while Hick is still trying to play it with a straight bat.'

A problem that batsmen have, even against a three-pronged West Indies pace attack, is that they can rarely dominate, even after a lengthy time at the crease, and both young men were out within 20 minutes of each other to put the innings back in the balance at 192 for five. Ramprakash missed a perfect yorker from Ambrose, with Richie admiring 'a wonderful bit of bowling. It was the classic yorker. You'll see no better example than that.' Raymond suggested that Ramprakash may have had difficulty in picking up the ball because Ambrose can get above the sightscreen.

Hick was then caught down the leg side by Dujon, to give Ambrose wonderful figures, considering the conditions, of 22-5-51-4. Geoffrey shared Raymond's reservations about Hick's technique: 'His problem is when the ball is banged in short and straight at his ribs. He is flat-footed and freezes.' Ambrose was finally rested after bowling 24 of the first 72 overs of the day, but Allen was immediately handed two wickets on a plate in seven balls, and England were nearly over the cliff.

Russell and Pringle, whose resistance with Smith at Lord's was instrumental in England's recovery, were both out to catches at square leg which might have been smart, but came off loose strokes. Logie caught Russell, and substitute Lambert (Marshall was now in the dressing-room) gratefully hung on to a flick by Pringle.

Gooch must have despaired at the collapse, which continued when DeFreitas was bowled through the gate driving at Walsh. Since tea five wickets had fallen for just 53 runs, with the last three wickets coming in 23 balls. From the relative prosperity of 186 for three, the innings was in tatters at 228 for eight, with the added problem that Smith was again left to look after the tail, as well as himself. The tactic of batting him after Ramprakash cannot have been in the best interests of the side, as was recognised later in the series.

The refusal to alter the order might not have proved so costly if both openers had not gone so quickly after lunch, but at such a time, the positive approach of Smith was badly needed to help Hick through. It is impossible to know if this Test match would still have been lost if Smith had batted higher but, as his unbeaten 64 showed, it certainly did not help England to have one of their two best batsmen come in so late. Illingworth somehow survived the last hour, when the score was 269 for eight, and he had then faced 43 out of 80 balls in the partnership.

FRIDAY 5 JULY

Raymond shared the opening stint with me and, with the help of a close-up picture, emphasised the importance of the rough patches close to leg stump. 'There's quite a big patch there, and Richard [Illingworth] should cause problems. The surface is a touch crusty — it dried yesterday quickly after the wet spell of weather, and the bowlers should get more help today.'

Marshall was back on the field and, although the match odds still favoured the draw at 4–5, with West Indies a generous 9–4 and England 11–4, they seemed to owe more to an indifferent weather forecast than the winning chances of the two sides. I said that the game was nicely poised. 'A couple of wickets and the West Indies would be in charge, and another 50 or 60 runs would make England happy.'

When Ambrose's third ball of the day deceived me as well as Illingworth, the game seemed firmly in the control of Richards. A short delivery appeared to strike Illingworth, batting with his back to us, on the elbow, and I told the viewers: 'There's no question of that ... oh yes there is. Out.' Had I watched the action on the monitor, I would have seen the ball take the glove, but in our behind-the-arm position at Trent Bridge, I prefer to watch the actual play.

On the dismissal of his namesake, Raymond said: 'He turned away from it, and just didn't look. It has been a tremendous piece of bowling by Ambrose. The pitch was good, particularly in the first three hours yesterday. At lunchtime the West Indies were dead and buried, and he got them back in the match by bowling superbly.'

Smith now had only Lawrence left, and set about Marshall with such a powerfully struck four that Richie said: 'All I can tell you is I wish I could have played a stroke like that. It's one of the most superb things you'll ever see in cricket. The back-foot drive through the covers, and so perfectly played.'

The tenth-wicket partnership was now beginning to niggle the fielding side, especially when Walsh dropped a sitter off an ambitious Lawrence attempt to pull a short delivery from Ambrose. If the West Indies cup did not then runneth over, it did next over when Richards put Smith down at slip off Marshall. Richie chuckled: 'It's no good saying you won't read about it, because you will.'

Occasionally cricket metes out a particularly rough sort of justice, as Lawrence discovered when he got to the other end, and promptly and undeservedly got the bouncer from Ambrose. The number eleven certainly livened things up for the capacity 13,500 crowd, especially when he lost count of the balls remaining in an over, and ran nearly two full runs, while Smith stood firm at the other end.

It needed something to end a stand of 30 from 68 balls, with the score now 300. I reckoned that 'Walsh should replace Marshall for two reasons. Marshall will be needed in the second innings and it makes little sense to give him such a long bowl after his injury yesterday and surely Walsh's county rivalry with Lawrence is more likely to produce the wicket Richards now wants badly.' There could be only one outcome to that prophecy, and I got it next ball, when Allen caught Lawrence off Marshall. Smith's 64 came off 150 balls and he hit five fours in a stay of 190 minutes that could have been doubled with better support.

Lawrence bowled the second over of the innings and it contained everything except a wicket. Haynes square cut the first ball for four, and then got a beamer in an over which included three no balls, and made it seven minutes before DeFreitas bowled again at the other end

Geoffrey immediately thought that 'mid-off and mid-on are too wide for DeFreitas. It makes it too easy and safe for a batsman to drive straight. Make him drive the wider deliveries, by moving those two straighter.' Straight out of the deep well of personal experience.

Haynes and Simmons made their most positive start of the series, but the wildly enthusiastic Lawrence broke through in his fourth over, when Smith took a sharp, right-handed catch at short leg when Haynes, to quote Geoffrey, 'played with a straight left leg and never got properly forward'.

Already the morning session was a good one for England and the crowd, but it was to be touched with history two balls later, although the public could only watch it happen later on a recorded replay. Gooch brought Illingworth on to bowl who, after taking great care with his field-setting, bowled his first ball in Test cricket. As another slow left-arm spinner from Worcestershire, Dick Howorth, had done against South Africa in 1947, he took a wicket with it, with Simmons watching in horror as the ball ran down the face of a defensive bat on to the stumps.

Tony captured the moment by saying: 'Phil Simmons will be the name on his sideboard for the rest of his life.' The delighted home team went in for lunch with the score now 32 for two off 52 balls. Illingworth became the 11th man in the history of world cricket to achieve the feat, and only the third since the Second World War. He became the sixth Englishman on the list, and the fourth to do it in England. Simmons joins Dennis Dyer of South Africa and Australia's Colin MacDonald (out to Intikhab Alam in Karachi in 1960) as the three batsmen involved in the previous 45 years.

With 'Neighbours' still reigning supreme, Hooper's dismissal 25 minutes after lunch was the third successive wicket to be missed, and when live action was resumed, the viewers saw that the delivery from DeFreitas was one of the best of the series. Raymond paid this tribute to the ball and the bowler: 'It was a great delivery – it went away off the pitch like a leg-break. It bit on the crusty top and it has given DeFreitas figures of 7·3-5-7-1 ... absolutely superb bowling, as he's provided in every international game this year.'

With the crowd now roaring encouragement to the home bowlers, Richards was only saved from a first ball LBW dismissal by a faint inside edge, and England's score of 300 began to look better. Until, that is, the West Indies fourth-wicket pair launched a violent counter-attack. Richardson square cut DeFreitas twice for four, and then Richards turned his attention to Illingworth, albeit with no great conviction according to Geoffrey: 'When I've played against Viv, I've noticed he doesn't play the spinners that well early on. If he's pressured by men around him, he's so afraid of getting a nick that he tries to take the attack to the bowler. One shot in that over wasn't a cricket shot – it was a half slog, but he got away with it.'

The next over from Illingworth contained a delivery that gave Richards just enough width, and Hampshire signalled four, which was also the signal for Gooch to take his spinner off with slightly disappointing figures of 7-0-29-1. Lawrence came back, but still with mid-on and mid-off too wide according to Raymond, who shared Geoffrey's view that 'Viv finds it harder to drive through extra cover, so make him try it by bringing those two fielders much straighter.'

With Richardson also punishing some wayward bowling, the 100 came up in the 26th over – a rapid rate of progress that was accelerating furiously, with the second fifty coming off 56 balls, compared with 108 for the first one.

In the middle of the afternoon, Keith offered Tony a crowd cutaway, showing one spectator guarding against the hot sun with an Arab-type handkerchief draped over neck and shoulders. Tony commented 'Lawrence of Nottinghamshire', paused until Lawrence filled the screen, and then rounded it off with 'and Lawrence of Gloucestershire'. Nice one. Even nicer when the fast bowler squeezed a yorker off the inside edge of Richardson's flashing bat onto the stumps and, at 118 for four, the West Indies were rattled. The best and worst of Lawrence was reflected in figures of 7-1-44-2, but what you see is what you get with the big man. He got the crowd right behind him, with each delivery to Richards and new batsman Logie accompanied by drawn out oohs and aahs. Enjoyable to watch, and enjoyable to listen to and commentate upon.

Illingworth returned, this time over the wicket, with Raymond saying: 'He must bowl on or just outside leg stump. Providing he pitches it right, he'll cause problems.' Logie responded to the ploy with a sweep and an on-drive for four, and then Richards seemed lucky to escape being given out LBW by Kitchen to one from Lawrence that came back a lot. Geoffrey thought 'the ball probably hit the pad outside the line'. Another replay showed that was not the case, but Richie came to everyone's rescue with a typically shrewd remark:

'Lawrence bowls from wide out, and Richards was forward — all enough to create enough doubt in Kitchen's mind.' It was a high-quality piece of mind-reading, which carefully avoided passing an opinion on something that was more out than not.

In a vain attempt to get in another over, Lawrence came off a short run, only for Logie to hit him for six over fine leg off what, to add insult to injury, was the last ball before tea. During the interval, the crowd buzz reflected the quality of the middle session of the day — 110 runs coming from 27 overs and two good wickets to boost their hopes. Raymond was disappointed that Lawrence had not yet bowled from the Pavilion end where, he believed, the cross-breeze would help him move it away. Illingworth could not settle, and switched to round the wicket after four overs from the other side had contained 12 deliveries which were left alone and six which were swept. The others were much too wide, and it was disappointing that the slow bowler had yet to show he could command respect at this level, with either mode of attack.

Richards hit the spinner twice through the covers for four and, when Logie followed suit next over off a wide long-hop, it was the eighth four off Illingworth in an analysis of 14-1-58-1. Worse was to come, with 13 coming off his next over, and Richards completed his 69th score of 50 for his country off 106 balls.

Gooch tried Pringle and Hick in an attempt to regain control but, as at Lord's, the decision to field a four-man attack was exposed once a member of it was below form. Then it was Watkin, now it was Illingworth. A slow left-arm spinner can usually be relied upon to fill the stock bowling role, which is why Gooch was now in deep trouble. The spinner's first over from the Pavilion end, bowled from over the wicket into the rough, comprised one ball which was played and five which were not, including one which pitched three feet outside leg stump. A second moderate over followed, although Logie played one false sweep stroke, and another delivery passed between his legs as he left it alone. The main criticism must be levelled at the bowler's poor direction. The tactic is a defensive one, but viable if bowled well.

Richards then hit Lawrence for a savage six over long-off and, with 80 to his credit out of 239 for four, looked set to crown a run-riot in the final session with his 25th Test hundred, only to fall to a delivery which effected the most confusing dismissal of the summer. He advanced two strides down the pitch to Illingworth, still bowling from over the wicket, missed contact and, as I saw the triumphant gestures of Russell and the bowler, I told the viewers: 'It's bowled him.'

Richards regained his crease and stood there, clearly unsure whether he was out and, if so, how? A bail was on the ground, but the fact it had come forward baffled him. He was clearly unhappy because he did not know where the ball went after he missed it. Both umpires gave him out, which further fuelled the argument that was already raging in the commentary box and the adjoining room, where Tony and Richie tried to analyse the sequence of events.

We were in agreement that:

1. The bail came forward.

2. Kitchen then gave him out.

3. Hampshire also raised his finger, thus indicating that he thought Richards was bowled.

But was he? And how could the bail have come forward? The more replays we studied from the bowler's end, the more confused we became. Richie and I were sure we could see the ball beating Richards and going straight onto the leg stump, but Tony was just as confident that the ball missed the stumps on its way to Russell. A replay from our reverse camera behind the wicket-keeper seemed to support Tony, while Keith is to be congratulated on getting any replays at all, as the ball before, Geoffrey asked him for a 'slo-mo' to illustrate the danger of not getting the bat out of the way in a leave-alone stroke. It is always a risk to replay an incident in an over from a spinner, but the golden rule was adhered to, which meant live action always takes precedence, and so Geoffrey's request was refused.

On the umpteenth replay, Geoffrey joined the corner of Richie and me: 'You can see the ball hitting the leg stump.' Tony refuted this, and the more often we saw it, the more we disagreed. The cricket went on, with Logie and Dujon taking the score to 262 for five at the close, but downstairs in the kitchen, the incident was studied in great detail. It was only when we were given access to a wide-angle picture from Sky Television that the mystery was solved.

The ball went from the left foot of Richards to the right foot of Russell, from where it rebounded back onto the stumps, with the batsman still well out of his ground – thus proving the correctness of Kitchen's first decision. At the end of play, Russell insisted that the ball grazed the stump before hitting his foot, and the bail may have been about to fall backwards when it was forced the other way by the rebound.

Richards was thus out stumped, even though the umpires later agreed that Hampshire's original decision of bowled should stand. What the incident did prove once and for all, is that if 30 replays from front, back and square can still leave five commentators in total disagreement, what chance have the umpires got under freakish circumstances like that? As for Richards, whose fifth-wicket partnership with Logie of 121 came to such a confused end, his only consolation is that, one way or the other, he was undoubtedly out.

However, with the series now nearly halfway over, England's bowling deficiencies were a serious worry. The search for decent support for DeFreitas and Pringle would, on the evidence of the second day's play, still continue. The performance of Illingworth was particularly disappointing, although his chance of settling into five-day cricket was hardly helped by the apparent need for him to bowl over the wicket.

The West Indies batsmen, sensing the rewards if they could hit him out of the attack, did just that and, again, the risk of fielding a four-man attack was fully exposed, with a run-rate of 3·54 earning the tourists valuable extra time in which to bowl England out again.

SATURDAY 6 JULY

The start of the middle day of the pivotal game of the five-match series was delayed until 1.10pm, following an early morning thunderstorm, but with lunch taken early, the capacity crowd was still able to watch 71 overs of exciting cricket, in which 189 runs were scored for the loss of eight wickets.

Gooch's decision to persevere with Illingworth lasted for one over, thanks to Logie hitting one four over the top, and another through the covers off a wide delivery. An analysis of the slow bowler's performance from over the wicket the day before proved all-too-revealing. Of $11\frac{1}{2}$ overs bowled aimed at the rough, 16 deliveries were played defensively, 15 were swept and 38 kicked off, with 11 of those pitching at least three feet too wide.

There is a corridor from nine inches outside leg stump across to middle and leg – a width of 12 inches – into which a Test-class spinner should be able to pitch more frequently than Illingworth managed, and his inability to keep the batsmen quiet, together with the heavy punishment handed out to Lawrence, left Gooch with little chance of restricting the West Indies run-rate to around three runs per over. Again it was DeFreitas and Pringle who were the only bowlers to whom Gooch could turn with confidence. They combined to take five wickets for 138 from 56 overs, while Illingworth and Lawrence aggregated their five wickets for 226 off 57 overs. For the second successive Test, Gooch found himself with a marked shortage of paddles as his ship floated out of control.

DeFreitas replaced Illingworth, and his first ball brought him a lucky wicket, but one which, on balance, he deserved as compensation for the many good deliveries he had bowled in the series which earned him nothing. A real loosener – a wide, short ball – was smashed by Logie into the covers where Ramprakash took a fine catch, low to his right. Logie's first good innings of the series was worth 78 sparkling runs from 132 balls, and he hit a six and eight fours in his share of 154 runs added in partnership with Richards and Dujon.

At 272 for six, England were close to parity, and much depended on the size of any lead the West Indies might secure. The second new ball was rightly taken, but Dujon and Marshall played their natural attacking game so successfully that 53 runs came off the next 14 overs. Dujon was beautifully caught by Hick off Pringle, whose first seven overs of the day cost nine runs. He had started to swing the ball away, but Raymond was critical of DeFreitas for bowling too short:

'He can't swing it from that length, and when it moves off the seam, it does too much and beats everything. Mike Hendrick was a similar bowler who tended to be about half a yard too short. If only he would pitch it up, he'd have a better chance of getting Ambrose to nick one.'

Illingworth came back for his fifth spell, and his first-ball full toss should have dismissed Marshall, who swung it high towards Ramprakash at deep backward square leg. Unfortunately, the fielder was in no-man's land, some ten yards in from the boundary, and the ball went for four and not six, thus emphasising his faulty positioning.

Ambrose finally lost patience and was bowled, trying to hit Illingworth over the top to make the score 358 for eight – a lead that was already substantial, if not yet a match-winning one.

Walsh could have been given out LBW to a full toss from Illingworth which struck him on the foot, with no stroke attempted, but umpire Hampshire ruled for the batsman. Walsh immediately hit two fours and Geoffrey said: 'That is poor bowling. You want the batsman to try to hit you over the top, but long-hops are not what are wanted.' It is curious that Illingworth bowled much better, and with more flight, in the one-day games than in this match and, even allowing for first-match nerves, his performance was a sore disappointment to those critics who had pressed for his inclusion in the previous Test.

Walsh is such a law unto himself with a bat in his hand that, after a mid-wicket chat with Marshall, Richie said: 'Now what were the instructions from Malcolm to Courtney ... and if there were any, will Courtney pay any attention to them?'

Marshall reached 50, with the score then 371 – his tenth half-century for the West Indies, and just before tea, Walsh avoided being stumped thanks to the momentum of his follow-through. He aimed to hit Illingworth over the pavilion, missed the ball by miles, but the effort swung him round to face the stumps and he grounded his bat as the bails were removed. The replayed photo-finish showed a dead-heat, and Kitchen rightly disallowed the appeal.

During the interval, with the lead now 81, Richards was the happier captain, and although his last two wickets went for 16 in 27 balls, he knew he was now firmly in charge. Pringle brought one back a long way to win an LBW decision against Walsh that must have had the batsman reflecting that he had

had better shouts refused. The ball pitched three inches outside off stump, darted back sharply and, although his foot was on off stump, his leg was covering middle.

Richie was offered a cutaway, showing the use of sun-cream by a man who was far from being your nine-stone weakling. 'Nice to see people protecting themselves. That could be an expense because that's quite an expanse. In Australia we have a campaign called "slip, slap, slop". You slip on a shirt, slap on a hat and slop on some sun-cream.' It was the sort of abstract musing which was guaranteed to break up our Malcolm, and it took another over before he caught up, and his charts were up to date.

Marshall was the last man out, swinging a steepler to Illingworth at mid-wicket, with the fielder running 17 paces to his left to complete a well-judged catch. As it was in the air, Richie commented: 'I think it's going to be Richard Illingworth's catch – I'm not sure he wants it.' Clearly, the other fielders were not exactly queuing up for it. Marshall's 68 came off 133 balls in an innings which lasted just over three hours, and it was thanks to him that the last four wickets produced 125 crucial runs.

The final session would go a long way towards settling the match and, between innings, there was much speculation whether England could emerge unscathed and enjoy their only rest day of the series. I was on air and said; 'England have two hours to negotiate tonight which, with that lead of 97, effectively means they have to bat all the fourth day and probably the first session of the fifth. That means five sessions ... which is asking a lot. The balance of the match is now firmly with the West Indies.'

It took 12 balls to prove the point. Bowling the second over of the innings, from the Pavilion end, Marshall bowled Atherton off the inside edge, with the opener again unsure whether to play the ball or not. As Richie said sympathetically: 'This can happen when you've had a long, hot day in the field. Your concentration wavers for a split second ... and that's that.'

As Hick came in to face another onslaught, Raymond was already in favour of England altering their batting order. 'There is a strong case to bring Smith in at number four.' We soon knew. Hick's third ball was his last, with Ambrose blowing another hole with a break-back which took the inside edge of a bat that was well away from his body as he played back. That recurring fault of the back foot not getting in line proved fatal again and, at eight for two, Lamb passed his fellow-sufferer.

Richie recognised the familiarity of the scene: 'This is the sort of situation in which the West Indies excel. They get a lead and then, late in the day with the opposition concentrating only on survival, they pile on the pressure.'

This time, even Gooch could not keep his finger in the dyke, and Ambrose's exultant war dance was even more uninhibited after he bowled a firm-footed Gooch between bat and pad. It was a spectacular dismissal and an equally spectacular celebratory routine. There were three high tens, four one-handed high fives, interspersed with several double-arm punches of the air. His figures read 7-4-11-2, and our two Yorkshiremen were torn between admiration and pessimism about the rest of the day. Geoffrey said: 'I'd always have a short leg in for Lamb – he plays stiff-legged with only a short stride.' Raymond compared the more solid and safer technique of Ramprakash – still batting in front of Smith – with that of Hick.

After the youngster avoided two short, off-side deliveries from Ambrose, Raymond's analysis was an incisive and constructive one which would have interested the subject as much as the audience. 'Ramprakash gets his head facing down the pitch, so both eyes are facing the ball. Hick's problem is he gets too sideways on and when he is facing the off side to a bouncer, he is blind to it.'

Then came the highest of compliments to the Middlesex batsman: 'He reminds me of someone who used to play here – Reg Simpson, who was one of the best avoiders of short bowling I have ever seen. He just used to sway a fraction either way and he was out of trouble. Like Viv yesterday, and he never wears a helmet.'

The fourth-wicket pair survived to the close but, with the score of 54 for three still leaving a deficit of 43, and the rest day to refresh Ambrose and company, England's 1-0 lead in the series looked certain to be wiped out. As the players left the field, Richardson walked up to Lamb and put a sympathetic arm around his shoulders. A nice gesture.

MONDAY 8 JULY

Before the start of play, Raymond drew attention to the shift of direction in the wind – no longer easterly, but from the south-west. A quick word to Alan on the 'lazy mike' and the fluttering flags filled the screen while their shift of direction was explained. 'If Marshall bowls from the Pavilion end, it will now be a big help to his inswinger.'

As usual, his observation hit the spot – in this case Lamb's left pad as he offered no stroke to a Marshall inswinger. Umpire Kitchen thought about it, and then gave Lamb out, with the replay showing that, although his front foot was outside the line of off stump, his leg was not. Raymond thought that it would have hit around middle, and noted that 'the ball is now moving more than at any time in the match.' I was less certain than my colleague about the middle stump comment, but any batsman who offers his pad instead of bat is taking a big risk.

Bad light and drizzle shortened the session by 20 minutes, but not before Richie and Geoffrey disagreed about another Marshall appeal for LBW – this time against Ramprakash. Richie thought that, against a big inswinger, 'he played a shot which, because he got outside the line, probably saved him, as it might well have hit the stumps.' Geoffrey would have none of it. 'No he didn't. The bat was nowhere near the pad when the ball hit his leg. He was lucky to get away with it. It was the perfect inswinger like the one to Lamb.'

Smith was in similar trouble to a good delivery from Walsh, but at 96 for four at the break, the door to escape was still open. The loss of 24 overs meant tea would not be taken until 4.10pm, and the cheer that greeted the single which took the score to 98 was noted by Tony: 'England are now one run ahead. They're in credit . . . it's like saving your pocket-money, only unfortunately there's no interest. You have to earn every run.'

The bank threatened to foreclose in a desperate next hour in which England slumped from 100 for four to 115 for eight, with Walsh finally getting the bit of luck he did not enjoy in the first two Tests. He had Smith nicely caught at slip by Richards for 15, which so affected 'AR' that he used the forbidden word 'tragic' as he dolefully informed his public that 'England were now effectively three for five.'

Ramprakash was next to go, victim to an outstanding catch from a brute of a delivery from Ambrose. It bounced and cut away, and the deflection was certainly more to the two hands of Richards at first slip than the outstretched right glove of Dujon, whose poaching foray was successfully concluded to avoid what would have been a pretty searching court of inquiry from bowler and captain.

Tony watched Simmons in the gully, remarking on such a junior player constantly clapping his hands and exhorting his seniors to greater effort. 'I must be getting old, but I must say if a young player did that in a side I played in, the captain would tell him to belt up.'

Russell was next to go – bowled by one from Walsh which moved from leg to off and hit half-way up the stumps. Good enough, I thought, but our Yorkshiremen are hard task-masters. Raymond argued that it had pitched outside leg stump, 'so if he'd got behind it he would have got away with it'.

While DeFreitas came in to join Pringle, I referred to a chat I had had that morning with Ted Dexter, who thought that Ambrose was a little in front of Joel Garner. Geoffrey and Raymond thought they were about equal, with Raymond saying: 'It is difficult to assess different bowlers unless they play in the same game. I think Garner was capable of possibly bowling a bit quicker, but I can tell you one thing: I would not want to face one at one end and one at the other. Also remember that Joel bowled with a better three fast bowlers than Curtly, so he didn't get the same opportunities to act as spearhead.'

With Raymond noting that, after the rain, the pitch was at its liveliest in the game so far, DeFreitas needed a charmed life to begin his best innings for England. He played and missed at Ambrose and then almost pushed a short ball to Logie at short leg, before he lobbed Walsh over gully. When Pringle was caught in the gully for three, the eighth-wicket partnership had added a meagre nine runs off 63 balls, and Walsh then had figures of 17-6-20-3.

Ambrose bounced the ninth-wicket pair and was spoken to by Kitchen, but there was a tiny wag of the tail in Walsh's last over before tea, with fours to DeFreitas and Illingworth taking England to 141 for eight – a lead of 44.

After the break, Richardson made a wonderful diving attempt to catch DeFreitas at wide long-on off Walsh. His first dive preceded a second one which Raymond gave '9·8 for effort and style'. Walsh soon had Illingworth taken by Simmons off a steered, rather than hard-hit, square cut and, at 153 for nine, England were down and seemingly out.

Initially, DeFreitas refused singles to keep the strike, but, so well did Lawrence cope with the bowling, including several bouncers, that the Lancashire all-rounder reverted to playing normally after a few wild heaves. The next team-talk revealed a switch of tactics. Lawrence instructed – DeFreitas listened and nodded, and promptly took a single off the first ball of the next over. The light was poor, but Lawrence hooked Walsh for four and then hit his county colleague through the covers with what Geoffrey described as 'a peach of a shot ... the best he's played yet'.

Lawrence then hit Allen for four to prompt from Richie: 'Not only is there excitement round the ground, but there is sheer enjoyment.' A cutaway picture showed Ramprakash and Reeve on the England balcony with huge smiles as Lawrence pulled another four to mid-wicket and, although there were three lights on the scoreboard indicator, nobody wanted the players to go off.

The umpires kept a close watch on their own light meters, clearly trying to reconcile the deteriorating light with the fact that the ball was disappearing to all corners. Finally, the last-wicket pair accepted the offer, and a sporting Ambrose applauded them as they left the field. Haynes also congratulated them and Richie said: 'There is a new spirit in this team and it is all down to Gooch. Since Australia he is back and whipping his side into line. This last-wicket stand has shown an enormous amount of determination and courage.'

The players came back with 80 minutes left, and the partnership finally ended when Hooper caught Lawrence off Allen, to leave the West Indies needing 115 to win. DeFreitas was left on 55 not out off 85 balls, and Lawrence trudged off with his 34 including five fours off only 39 balls. The stand of 58 did more than irritate the West Indies, it actually gave the home side an admittedly faint chance of snatching a win, always providing they could take early wickets.

Tony asked Geoffrey if the tourists would go for the win that night. 'I think they should play normally for 30 or 40 runs and then have a go – just in case it bounces down with rain tomorrow. Low totals can cause problems, so it is essential the West Indies go out and don't throw the bat straight away, lose a couple of wickets and get the nervous nellies. The odds are they won't get them tonight, but they must keep it in mind.'

With two lights showing on the board, it needed only one mishap to send the batsmen heading for the dressing-room, and it happened off the third ball of the second over of the innings. Simmons launched a wild drive at one from Lawrence and Russell took the catch – pandemonium! The crowd were convinced the man from Gloucestershire was about to take the West Indies apart with the ball, as he had done with the bat.

Haynes and Richardson had different ideas but, after each man had hit a four, the rain came with the score 20 for one in the sixth over, to leave the result of the game far from settled.

Earlier in the day, Tony interviewed the England physiotherapist Laurie Brown on the merits of the methods now used to train England cricketers. Tony voiced a popular view that 'the more they train, the more they seem to get injured'. Laurie replied: 'There is some truth in it. Like racehorses, the nearer you get to thoroughbred condition, the greater the risk. We want a happy medium between carthorses and thoroughbreds. We tested the England players before the season and at the end . . . treadmill sprinting, strength, blood, et cetera, so we had facts and figures for them. They were less fit at the end than at the beginning, because they either play or travel. I get annoyed when people like you say we do too much.'

'Yes, but fit to bat and fit to bowl surely is what you want. I naively believe you must be fit for something. Presumably you analyse the types of injuries as well; i.e. Fraser and Small.'

'Yes, sometimes it's different when muscles are tired. They can bowl anything from 10 to 25 overs a day, and it is when muscles are tired they are susceptible. Before a game in the morning, we concentrate on stretching, it is *not* a matter of getting them fit for that day. We try to prevent them getting injured that day. The difference between soccer and cricket is that it is far easier to train footballers all week just for 90 minutes. In cricket I have to be sure that an 80:20 risk is worth taking to get a man through a five-day game. I never try to persuade a player to play. He must want to play.'

All of which still does not explain why far more England bowlers miss Tests nowadays through injury than used to be the case. Perhaps it is because so few have a sound basic action.

Graham Gooch dispatches the ball to the boundary during his
masterful second innings at Headingley. His 154* turned the
match England's way.   (*Patrick Eagar*)

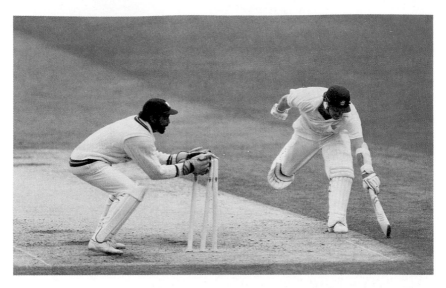

Ambrose's throw to Jeffrey Dujon had to be inch-perfect to beat Robin Smith in the first Test, and was. *(Allsport/Adrian Murrell)*

The sting. Gooch is LBW in the first innings at Trent Bridge. He offers no stroke to a perfect inswinger after three outswingers earlier in the over. *(Graham Morris)*

(Above) Curtly Ambrose gave Graeme Hick a torrid introduction to Test cricket. This time Dujon takes the inside edge at Trent Bridge in the second innings. *(Allsport/Adrian Murrell)* But his slip fielding was a triumph, as Dujon found to his cost (below) at Trent Bridge. Derek Pringle was the bowler. *(Patrick Eagar)*

Richard Illingworth is delighted as he becomes only the 11th
man to take a wicket with his first ball in Test cricket. Phil
Simmons is his victim, bowled at Trent Bridge off the face of
the bat. *(Patrick Eagar)*

The controversial dismissal of Viv Richards at Trent Bridge.
Was he bowled or was he stumped? The records say he was
bowled, but television has shown that he was, in fact, stumped.
(Graham Morris)

Richie Richardson was in fine form at Edgbaston, reaching his first-ever Test century in England. Here he drives Richard Illingworth for four.   (*Patrick Eagar*)

Work and play. If it is Tandy time for Tony, it must be Saturday. Richie is poised to recoup the purchase price of the *Sporting Life*.

Viv Richards is chaired off the ground at Edgbaston having steered his side to victory in the fourth Test, and thus ensuring that he would retire never having lost a Test series as captain. (*Allsport/Adrian Murrell*)

David Lawrence wins the battle of the Gloucesters, nailing
Courtney Walsh LBW at the Oval.   *(Patrick Eagar)*

Robin Smith pulls Courtney
Walsh to the boundary at the
Oval, where his first-innings
century helped England to
victory.   *(Allsport/Chris Cole)*

If England were going to win in spectacular fashion at the Oval, it was perhaps inevitable that Ian Botham would come in to score the winning runs (above). And so it was. Botham was delighted (below) at finally beating the West Indies for the first time in his 98-Test career. *(Patrick Eagar)*

TUESDAY 9 JULY

Atherton did not take the field because of strained stomach muscles, and Reeve was his enthusiastic substitute – termed by Richie 'the sliding sub', because of his penchant for throwing himself about the field. Before play started in fine weather, Richie and Ray discussed the art of preparation of pitches, with our Aussie full of admiration for the former fast bowler Andy Roberts, who prepared 'a lovely cricket wicket for the recent Test against Australia in Antigua. It had pace and bounce, and the difference in his method is that he waters and rolls in sections. That way, he says the same amount of water gets into each section, instead of a general flooding which leaves water lying around and can result in uneven waterings. It certainly worked. He does it in a couple of hours in sections of about three yards each. Take Lord's or anywhere with a slope, and you can have uneven watering.'

The two distinguished former Test captains then switched to a fascinating discussion on fast bowling. Raymond thought you 'need at least two out of pace, direction and length to make it at top level.'

Richie agreed: 'Take Tyson for instance – the quickest I ever faced all the time I played. He was not too bothered about length, but was straight and fast once he'd shortened his run. As for Fred, he was simply a master of swing and control, while Brian Statham always made you hurry your shot and bowled with pinpoint accuracy.'

The modern player tends to be dismissive of players of the 1950s and '60s, but they should listen and note appraisals like that. The average spectator finds it difficult to grade bowlers in speed, so perhaps my own list will help, always remembering that I have taken the top speed of bowlers like Michael Holding and Andy Roberts who used to vary their pace. The following list is of bowlers at full throttle: Frank Tyson, Jeff Thomson, Michael Holding and Cuan McCarthy are the leading four genuinely fast bowlers I have seen. The next group were perhaps two or three miles an hour slower, with the bowlers concerned all capable of exceptional hostility – an intangible, but priceless quality: Fred Trueman, Dennis Lillee, Wes Hall, Ray Lindwall, Curtly Ambrose, Malcolm Marshall, Andy Roberts, Brian Statham, John Snow and Charlie Griffith.

Any such judgement is subjective, but my point is that I have only seen four fast bowlers let the ball go at a speed I cannot believe anyone else has ever exceeded. Sheer speed is given to few. My two lists exclude, among others, Sir Richard Hadlee and Imran Khan, but they would head another category.

If pressed for my all-time number one fast bowler, it would have to be Fred Trueman. A magnificent action and fitness record makes a mockery of the fact that his 67 Tests were out of a possible maximum 121, and he made only four full tours out of a possible ten. Contrast that with Richie's record of 63 Tests out of a possible maximum of under 70. Fred might talk more than most, but he *did* more than most. As for England's two fastest current bowlers, Malcolm and Lawrence, they occasionally border on the genuinely fast category, but most of the time they do not generate sheer speed and, as yet, show little signs of compensating with other qualities.

Gooch permed his three pace bowlers but, apart from an edged four over slips by Richardson off DeFreitas, and a good LBW appeal by Pringle against Haynes, the second-wicket pair made light of the 95 runs they needed to square the series. Pringle moved one two inches from leg to off – which is more incisive than six inches the other way – but all to no avail. DeFreitas bowled a fuller length than earlier in the match, but Lawrence thundered his way to another analysis in which the runs-per-over rate edged towards five.

Haynes completed his 2000 Test runs against England, and his and Richardson's unbeaten half-centuries were their 35th and 18th respectively for West Indies, in addition to their total of 16 and 12 hundreds each. They both hit six fours, with the winning run coming on the stroke of 1pm.

Haynes, in his 100th Test, passed 2000 runs against England to follow Sobers, Richards, Greenidge, Kanhai and Lloyd past this total. A cutaway to the tourists' balcony showed Richards moving around his team, exchanging a volley of hand-slapping high fives. Their delight was understandable – they had come back from an England first-day lunch score of 106 for none to victory in 306 overs bowled in the next four days.

Richie said: 'That was an excellent performance. They played the cricket of champions after coming here 1-0 down. The match was won and lost between lunch and the end of the first day's play.' While Geoffrey, looking ahead to the fourth Test, said: 'Edgbaston does help seam bowlers ... it's not a great place for pace or spin. The places of Lawrence and Illingworth will be under discussion because of the type of attack needed.'

Match figures of England's main four bowlers confirmed that. DeFreitas and Pringle's were 74-20-187-5, while Lawrence and Illingworth produced 72·2-10-287-6. Such remarkably contrasting figures seemed to point, incontrovertibly, to change. If only we knew.

ENGLAND v WEST INDIES
at Trent Bridge on 4, 5, 6, 8, 9 July 1991

ENGLAND		Runs	Balls	Mins		Runs	Balls	Mins
* G. A. Gooch	lbw b Marshall	68	110	129	b Ambrose	13	42	53
M. A. Atherton	lbw b Ambrose	32	80	122	b Marshall	4	6	7
G. A. Hick	c Dujon b Ambrose	43	113	154	c Dujon b Ambrose	0	3	10
A. J. Lamb	lbw b Ambrose	13	21	38	lbw b Marshall	29	82	118
M. R. Ramprakash	b Ambrose	13	64	87	c Dujon b Ambrose	21	118	171
R. A. Smith	not out	64	150	190	c Richards b Walsh	15	37	60
† R. C. Russell	c Logie b Allen	3	22	32	b Walsh	3	19	28
D. R. Pringle	c sub (Lambert) b Allen	0	6	10	c Simmons b Walsh	3	33	45
P. A. J. DeFreitas	b Walsh	8	12	12	not out	55	85	129
R. K. Illingworth	c Hooper b Ambrose	13	46	62	c Simmons b Walsh	13	16	28
D. V. Lawrence	c Allen b Marshall	4	23	46	c Hooper b Allen	34	39	55
Extras	(lb 17,w 1,nb 21)	39			(lb 14,w 3,nb 4)	21		
TOTAL	(103.5 overs; 451 mins)	300			(79 overs; 357 mins)	211		

WEST INDIES		Runs	Balls	Mins		Runs	Balls	Mins
P. V. Simmons	b Illingworth	12	25	40	c Russell b Lawrence	1	3	5
D. L. Haynes	c Smith b Lawrence	18	26	37	not out	57	97	148
R. B. Richardson	b Lawrence	43	76	96	not out	52	100	141
C. L. Hooper	c Russell b DeFreitas	11	22	25				
* I. V. A. Richards	b Illingworth	80	155	209				
A. L. Logie	c Ramprakash b DeFreitas	78	132	190				
† P. J. L. Dujon	c Hick b Pringle	19	79	112				
M. D. Marshall	c Illingworth b DeFreitas	67	133	187				
C. E. L. Ambrose	b Illingworth	17	44	61				
C. A. Walsh	lbw b Pringle	12	35	55				
I. B. A. Allen	not out	4	4	5				
Extras	(b 2,lb 13,w 1,nb 20)	36			(nb 5)	5		
TOTAL	(118.1 overs; 517 mins)	397			(32.2 overs; 148 mins)	115 (for 1 wkt)		

WEST INDIES	O	M	R	W	O	M	R	W
Ambrose	34	7	74	5	27	7	61	3
Marshall	21.5	6	54	2	21	6	49	2
Walsh	24	4	75	1	24	7	64	4
Allen	17	0	69	2	7	2	23	1
Hooper	6	4	10	0				
Richards	1	0	1	0				

ENGLAND	O	M	R	W	O	M	R	W
DeFreitas	31.1	9	67	3	11	3	29	0
Lawrence	24	2	116	2	12.2	0	61	1
Illingworth	33	8	110	3	2	0	5	0
Pringle	25	6	71	2	7	2	20	0
Hick	5	0	18	0				

FALL OF WICKETS				
	ENG	WI	ENG	WI
1st	108	32	4	1
2nd	113	32	8	
3rd	138	45	25	
4th	186	118	67	
5th	192	239	100	
6th	212	272	106	
7th	217	324	106	
8th	228	358	115	
9th	270	392	153	
10th	300	397	211	

Toss: England
Umpires: J. H. Hampshire & M. J. Kitchen
Man of the Match: C. E. L. Ambrose
RESULT: WEST INDIES WON BY 9 WICKETS

CHAPTER SIX

A SHAMBLES

EDGBASTON TEST
25–28 JULY

SELECTION SUNDAY 21 JULY

It is incomprehensible that the England selectors managed to get so many things wrong for the Edgbaston Test, bearing in mind that they had ten clear days after the end of the third Test in which to take soundings before they sat down in Southend to choose their next squad. Curiously enough, after announcing the first three squads of the summer on the Friday preceding each Test, they delayed the announcement of this one until the Sunday – which made their previously rushed arrangements even more illogical.

This time, they left Nottingham in the knowledge that they could divide their attention among eight NatWest second-round ties on Thursday 11 July, the Benson & Hedges Cup final on Saturday 13, a full programme of Refuge Assurance League games the next day, seven Britannic Assurance County Championship matches starting Tuesday 16 July, and the first day of eight more on Friday 19 – or the first two days if they met on Saturday evening after the close of play at Southend where Essex were playing Somerset.

At the beginning of the week, we were told that the squad would not be announced until Sunday 21 July, so there was no valid reason for not using the day before as a final check on form or fitness of fringe candidates – of whom there was no shortage.

Yet the fateful meeting took place on Friday evening, and contrived to choose the wrong alternative in every instance. I can speak with some authority about this, because my presence for the *Birmingham Post* at Portsmouth during Hampshire's three-day game against Worcestershire gave me a close insight into the background of at least three of the glaring mistakes. That game started on Tuesday 16, two days after Worcestershire won their carried-over Benson & Hedges final against Lancashire, and was attended by Michael Stewart on the first day.

He could have been looking at several players in the match, but undoubtedly he came to check on the fitness of Robin Smith and Ian Botham. Smith was not playing, because of a reaction to a finger injury he had sustained over two weeks previously at Southampton in a three-day game against the West Indies, five days before the Trent Bridge Test – but more of that later.

When I knew the England manager was present, I arranged to have a few minutes with him to pass on what I thought was important information about the Edgbaston pitch, given to me a few days earlier by the Warwickshire captain, Andy Lloyd. He told me that the Test pitch would be much drier than usual, and the presence of cracks so far in advance of the game indicated the bounce would be inconsistent. Although it might turn, his long experience of the pitches on his home ground convinced him that England should choose their strongest hand of seam bowlers. Pace would be ineffective, and therefore there was no point in naming either Lawrence or Malcolm in the squad. I asked him, if one of Warwickshire's in-form trio of seamers, Small, Munton and Reeve, was chosen, which one would he favour?

'If I thought they would pick Dermot to bat at six and be the fifth bowler, I would have him – but they won't. Gladstone is now bowling much better again, but because I think it's going to be the sort of pitch on which it is almost a case of the slower you put it onto the pitch, the more difficult it is for the batsmen, I would pick Tim Munton.'

I thought such a positive view was well worth passing on to Stewart, especially as Warwickshire were top of the table, thanks to the efforts of those three seamers supporting fast bowler Allan Donald so successfully. I had known Stewart for over 30 years – one of our first jousts being in an historic three-day game at the Oval in 1960. In a game uninterrupted by rain, he was the first batsman to lose his wicket in the match – at 12.45pm on the second day, when he was caught behind the wicket off me. On the first day Warwickshire's openers, Norman Horner and 'Billy' Ibadulla, shared an unbroken opening partnership of 377 – still a record in English cricket, and still the second highest unbroken first-wicket stand in the history of cricket.

By the time we walked round the pleasant ground, Botham had already bowled the only two overs he managed before 5.10pm – and this after Phil Neale had put Hampshire in to bat. The 12 deliveries cost 17 runs, after which the all-rounder retired to slip, wearing sunglasses. Having come to check whether Botham was now fully recovered from the hamstring injury he sustained eight weeks previously at Edgbaston, and knowing that Botham knew he was on the ground, the England manager was understandably perplexed at what he saw – or, rather, what he did not see. It was almost as though Botham was telling Stewart he should take him on trust, because he was not going to bowl the 15 overs or so he must have known Stewart wanted as proof of his fitness for a five-day Test.

I passed on Andy Lloyd's views to Stewart who, so it seemed to me, took them on board during our ten-minute chat. In the belief that I had done my bit for my country, I concentrated on the match in hand, which was drawn, after Hick played well for an innings of 141 which, following his positive 88 in the Lord's final, seemed to indicate that he was in the right frame of mind for the Edgbaston Test.

On Friday, the day the selectors met, Warwickshire started a three-day game, also at Portsmouth, and, although Robin Smith played, I heard that he considered himself unlikely to be fit enough for the following week's Test match. As told to me, the sequence of events is as follows.

On that Friday, Smith informed the selectors that it would be wiser not to pick him, but he was told that it was too early to rule himself out of the fourth Test. He said that if they named him in a squad of at least 13, then he would report for a fitness test, but stressed that he did not think the finger would stand up to a five-day game.

In that knowledge, Dexter, Stewart and Gooch decided not to release the names until Sunday morning, so that another check could be made after Saturday's play in the current round of three-day games. On that day, Smith dropped down to number seven in Hampshire's second innings after leaving the field earlier, following another knock on the finger. He also withdrew from the following day's Refuge game – the clearest possible indication that the view expressed the previous day to Stewart was now confirmed in the most ominous manner.

Despite the Sunday press giving wide coverage to the Smith situation, when the Press Association representative, David Lloyd, contacted Peter Smith for the squad details, he was given 12 names, including Smith. Only when Lloyd referred to the events at Portsmouth did the selectors decide, over the telepone, to name Hugh Morris as stand-by. It is remarkable that they were unaware of the up-to-date situation, having delayed the announcement of the XII for that very reason.

Even worse, the advice of the Warwickshire captain had been ignored, with Lawrence and Illingworth in a squad which contained neither Botham nor Reeve nor any other front-line seamer to support DeFreitas and Pringle other than the erratic Lewis. Which meant that the original XII included a batsman who, as was proved the following Thursday morning, was never likely to play, and two bowlers, Lawrence and Illingworth, from whom Gooch would have to choose one.

The selectors knew that, like those at Headingley, the conditions were likely to be so peculiar that they needed to pursue a 'horses for courses' strategy. Yet they denied Gooch the option, on the day, of fielding the sort of four-pronged seam attack which, arguably, would have won the game. Instead, he was committed to choosing Illingworth or Lawrence, with the inclusion of the latter in the squad a complete waste of a precious place.

MONDAY 22 JULY

What was easily the worst weekend of the summer for the selectors, had a deplorable foot-note on Monday morning, when Morris felt obliged to contact Lord's from Cheltenham, where Glamorgan were playing Gloucestershire, for confirmation that he should report that evening to Birmingham. Similarly, Lewis refused to give an interview at Hove about his selection, because he had received no official confirmation of his selection. And all of this after the longest gap of the summer between the end of one Test and the selection for the next.

It was an embarrassing mixture of crass selection and poor public relations, compounded by the undignified attempt to persuade Smith to play, which made the position of poor Morris an impossible one. Any Test debutant needs proper mental preparation, and not one riddled with uncertainty about his selection for at least three days before taking guard. The performance of the selectors made a mockery of Gooch's remarks to Tony in an interview immediately after the Trent Bridge game: 'We've got two weeks now to get ourselves ready for Edgbaston.'

The selectors might have imposed a bigger handicap on the team, but it is difficult to see how. With the series all square, they sent a side in to the game which included three batsmen and two bowlers whose form made their selection a risk. The choice of Hick, Lamb and Atherton, irrespective of the fourth combined failure to come, was a justifiable gamble. That of Illingworth and Lewis, with Lawrence as the only alternative, was most definitely not.

THURSDAY 25 JULY

The England track record at Edgbaston is easily the best of any home ground – 15 wins from 27 Tests, and only two losses: against Australia in 1975, and the West Indies in 1984. Richards was determined that, having squared the series at Trent Bridge, he would go flat-out for the win that would maintain his record of never having captained his country in a losing series. Although the previous 46 games since he took over from Clive Lloyd in the home series against New Zealand in 1984-85 included 29 wins and only five defeats, those five losses included two against England in the last 17 months.

Patterson replaced Allen, which gave Richards a full hand to play against an England batting order that was now the most lopsided in history. Atherton, Hick and Lamb, now three, four and five following Smith's withdrawal, came into the game with a combined total of 158 from 15 innings. Morris replaced Smith and Lewis came back for Lawrence. Apart from the two newcomers and Illingworth, the other eight players had played in all three previous games, with ten of the West Indies side also playing in every Test.

The umpires were David Shepherd and Barry Dudleston, who was standing in his first Test match. The former Leicestershire and Gloucestershire batsman had stood in the four-day game at Northampton the previous year when Ambrose was the centre of controversy following the bowling of three beamers in two overs at Reeve. Not only that, he was at square leg 26 days before this game, when Smith hit the same bowler for three fours and a six before he received the waist-high full toss which damaged a finger and now kept him out of the fourth Test.

In the same game, Kevin Shine also hit Ambrose for six and got the same sort of lethal delivery. Lance Gibbs, who I have known since his Warwickshire days between 1968 and 1973, insisted to me they were not deliberately bowled. All I can say is that, having seen the incident at Northampton, and listened to the views of Hampshire players in their three-day game at Southampton, I know of no reason to change my opinion that Ambrose never bowls such a ball after a wicket-maiden. It happens only after punishment, and the sooner the authorities give umpires the powers to take action against, not only head-high full tosses, but those at chest level as well, the sooner the game will be rid of this evil.

Richards won his third toss of the series and his decision to field first should have paid the biggest dividend of all – a wicket off the first ball of the game, the start of which was delayed for 75 minutes because of early morning rain. Gooch edged a short ball from Ambrose to Hooper at second slip, but the head-high two-handed chance went down.

It took West Indies just 11 more deliveries to forget the mistake, with Patterson angling one across Morris to induce an outside edge from the left-hander to Dujon. The ball pitched middle and did not move all that much. Tom Graveney said: 'When he sees that he'll decide he shouldn't have played at it.' But that is easier said than done when you are facing your ninth delivery in Test cricket.

Gooch and Atherton found sufficient gaps in the attacking field placings to hit five fours, and a lunchtime score of 43 for one from 10 overs reflected their positive approach, with the captain's 24 coming off 25 balls. Raymond thought that 'Viv's toss decision was influenced by the appearance of the pitch when the covers came off ... there was every appearance of more moisture than was there. There are a lot of cracks, it is very dry and the variability of bounce is bound to get worse.' Which meant that, if England could score 250, Richards' decision to field first might rebound.

The score was 53 when Atherton got one from Walsh which pitched six inches outside off stump and cut back a long way to strike the left pad. Umpire Shepherd thought about it, before deciding that the ball would not have missed leg stump. Hick thus came in to yet another crisis situation, and Tony commented that 'although he has been successful for Worcestershire between Tests, different questions are now asked about his technique.'

Ray noticed that Hick was moving onto the front foot before the ball was bowled. 'A lot of people say the back foot should be moved across first, but if you wait forward, you can still move the back foot quickly.' Maybe, but the best players are those who move least before the ball is bowled. It is not just coincidence that not one of the West Indies top six stands with his bat in the air, and few of them commit themselves a great deal before the ball is bowled.

Tom said: 'The astonishing thing is, since he started, Hick has never had a bad patch – I've never known any player go that long before. But whatever ball game you play, you must keep your eye on the ball – yet he gets hit by not watching it.' And so, when Hick was tested with a short one from Ambrose, Tom was quick to spot that 'he went back on leg stump again. His back foot takes him away from the line of ball, yet the whole secret of playing quicks is to get your head behind the line of ball.'

It was not until the 23rd over that Marshall came on, and immediately started to swing the ball in to the right-handers. Raymond spotted Richards and Haynes have a chat with their senior bowler and noted that 'since then he has started to swing it the other way. He's at his best when he gets the outer going with the occasional inner, because when he only moves it back in, too many go down leg side.'

As usual, prophetic words, with Gooch completely bamboozled by a big inswinger which followed two that went the other way. He was bowled for 45 out of 88 for three, with Raymond commenting that 'his feet were nowhere. He tried to force it, but you can't attack with both feet together.' I thought it was a mesmerising piece of bowling skill, and wrote for the next day's *Post*: 'Harsh critics might criticise Gooch's footwork. I prefer to give full credit to a thinking man's wicket that was well planned and brilliantly executed. Bowling at its best.'

A crowd of around 14,000 watched Hick and Lamb struggle, with Hick escaping from a low edge to Hooper off Marshall. Tom thought that 'it barely carried, and it's unfair to call it a chance – Hooper did well to stop it.' Richie stuck a little pin into that kindly theory: 'Malcolm looks as thought he's calling it one.'

Bowling from the City end, Marshall was still able to bend his inswinger against the cross-breeze, proving again that a correct hand action is the only thing that matters. Lamb flung himself at a loosener from Patterson – but to no avail, and he stood there, champing gum behind his grill, with his square chest bristling like a streetfighter determined to avoid the last sunset. He had been batting for 40 minutes when he was well beaten by another inswinger from Marshall and umpire Dudleston gave his first LBW decision in Test cricket. Lamb's expression indicated he did not think it was plumb, but the replay showed it was not too high, nor did he get his leg outside the line of off stump.

With tea not taken until 4.10pm because of the use of the extra hour following the morning rain, the BBC2 news was delayed for 20 minutes, by which time England were an uneasy 117 for four from 41 overs. The final session was no better, with Marshall and Ambrose sharing five wickets, and Walsh extending Ramprakash's run of scores in the 20s.

Hick never looked comfortable and, after twice fencing outside the off stump, paid the penalty against Ambrose, for the fifth time in six innings, when he again withdrew his back foot to give Richards a fast catch at first slip. The worrying thing about the Worcestershire man was that, even after facing 103 balls for his 19 runs, he still did not look 'in' as a top-four Test batsman surely should after batting for two and a half hours.

Ramprakash and Russell dug in as best they could on the untrustworthy pitch, and caused the biggest cheer of the day when the scoreboard ran amok as the 150 was passed. The slot for the first digit skipped the figure '1' and so had to flip through all the others to growing applause, with the unlikely score of 951 for five drawing from Tony: 'Just the stuff of which dreams are made.'

The dream soon turned into a familiar nightmare, with three wickets going for four runs in 26 balls to leave DeFreitas and Lewis to rescue what they could from the wreckage. I got Russell's dismissal wrong when I complimented him on the way he had fended off a short delivery from Ambrose with: 'That was well bowled and well played. Oh no it wasn't! He's out,' after Richardson took the easy, lobbed catch.

That was 159 for six, with the crowd stunned as the West Indies poured through the gap. Pringle got one from Ambrose which left him and would have been good enough at normal height. To complicate matters, having seen Russell defend his throat, Pringle then watched his hit the off stump no more than half-way up. Under no circumstances could this pitch be called satisfactory for the first day of a five-day Test match.

The next ball was the first in Walsh's third spell, and a rare misjudgement from Ramprakash resulted in a mis-hooked catch to Logie, and the England supporters were probably pleased that the slow over-rate of the West Indies would not allow the full ration of overs. It is a curious view of the Test & County Cricket Board that play shall not continue past 7pm, even if the minimum number of overs has not been bowled. The theory is that spectators do not want to stay after 7pm, but most of the Edgbaston crowd did not leave their seats until the players left the field because of bad light.

Had play run its course, at 7pm there would still have been five or six overs to bowl and, although in this case the slow over-rate did not favour the West Indies, a fielding side should not be able to exploit a possible tactical advantage allowed by the TCCB ruling.

The ninth wicket to fall was that of Lewis, LBW to Marshall for 13 to complete a day for West Indies which left them well on top. Ambrose's second spell of 12-4-22-3 incorporated everything from the top drawer of pace, hostility and accuracy. At the end of play, Tom summarised England's batting thus:

'Three or four got in, yet England could not get on top. Atherton's did quite a lot, and Gooch got into a tangle against a wonderful piece of bowling from Marshall. Lamb was caught playing across his crease ... so many of our batsmen are only getting half way, neither forward nor back. Hick played the short ball better, but his slight change of stance to open up the left leg didn't help his footwork. As for Ramprakash, he would have been better cutting than hooking, and it bounced a bit as well.'

What the first day showed, was the difference the return of Patterson made to the West Indies attack. His presence allowed Richards to revert to the well-tried formula of rotating his four fast bowlers, almost by numbers. The inclusion of the inexperienced Allen in the second and third Tests weakened the policy, and forced Richards into permutating any two from Ambrose, Walsh and Marshall, for longer periods than were ideal.

As for the England batting, Atherton, Hick and Lamb were unlucky that they had to battle to save their immediate England careers on such a sub-standard pitch, and with the selection of the bowlers flying in the face of local expert opinion, the day was, arguably, the most damaging to England in the series so far.

FRIDAY 26 JULY

A capacity crowd of 18,500 saw England have a bad day, during which their poor bowling was not helped by a fickle performance from Lady Luck. As usual, DeFreitas and Pringle must be exempt from criticism, but the support bowling was wayward and expensive. As I wrote in my match report at the end of the day for the *Post*: 'The England bowling was, for the fourth Test in succession, a two-man affair, with their best bowlers, DeFreitas and Pringle, producing combined figures of 38·3-18-65-2, while the rest managed 48·3-11-181-2. *The original selection was poor, and the price is about to be paid.*'

Such a disproportionate ratio was the inevitable result of a selection that defied logic and understanding. When the XII was announced the previous Sunday, several Warwickshire and Hampshire players referred to it as 'a bad joke', and none could understand the omission of all three Warwickshire seamers.

At the start of play, it took 11 deliveries to wind up the innings. DeFreitas edged a useful ball from Marshall low to the right of Richardson at slip, to give the Barbadian a deserved fourth wicket, and to leave Gooch with an inadequate-looking total of 188 to defend.

England badly needed early wickets, but luck ran against them, with Haynes and Simmons repeatedly beaten outside off stump by DeFreitas. Even though Raymond's point in the previous Test about the natural length of DeFreitas being marginally too short was validated, it was a travesty that West Indies lost only Simmons in 25 overs of play before lunch. He fell to a good slip catch by Hick off one from DeFreitas which bounced and was edged sharply to the left of Hick at second slip. The way he took the hip-high catch two-handed made it even more a matter of regret that his batting no longer warranted a place in the side.

The opening stand was worth 52 off 85 balls, with Richardson, like Haynes, bearing a charmed life either side of lunch. The opener watched a ball from DeFreitas bounce back on to his stumps without dislodging a bail, with the bails equally firmly in place after the opener deposited a thankful kiss on them. DeFreitas beat Richardson at least six times in as many minutes, but finally got a belated reward with the wicket of Haynes. The second-wicket pair, despite living so dangerously, had added 41 at four runs per over when the Lancashire bowler seamed one away from Haynes, with the resultant edge just carrying to Russell.

Gooch was already in trouble, and forced by the nature of the pitch to perm his three seam bowlers for longer than he would have liked. Raymond said: 'He just can't keep going with his three pace bowlers – he has to gamble with spin. Otherwise, even if he gets a wicket or two, his three seamers are going to be too tired to keep going.' It was to prove another accurate prophecy, with DeFreitas having to leave the field later with cramp, thus further weakening the attack.

With a high level of humidity to contend with, the selection policy was already exposed – savagely so when Illingworth was first brought on with the score 111 for two. As usual it was DeFreitas and Pringle first with 26 overs for 32 runs and the rest – in this case Lewis – nowhere, with 65 runs having been hit from 17 overs. What would Gooch have given for a fourth front-line seam bowler – yet he had been party to the original selection, so he must share the blame. Finally forced to choose between his spinner and Lawrence, he made the right choice, but he should never have been in that position.

I asked Raymond to explain the difference between this pitch and the one at Headingley: 'This one is slower and balls are keeping low here – they didn't at Headingley. Also there was more grass there and that allowed more seam movement. It was cold there – here it is warm, which has allowed more swing.'

Richie was in rare critical mood, particularly about the field-setting for Illingworth. 'I would do away with that bat-pad man close in on the off side. I would take him away and put a man at short mid-on and keep a long-on. Have a man either side of the wicket for the mis-timed drive – surely a bowler wants to encourage that. But it seems to me to be a different world of field placings these days.'

Tom thought it certain that, 'with DeFreitas off the field, it seems to me that the West Indies will have a dart at Illingworth – and that would really cause problems for Gooch.' And so it proved. The slow left-arm bowler's first five overs cost 25, but he struck back with the wicket of Hooper off the last ball before tea. The score was 148, and 55 elegant runs had come from the third-wicket pair when Hooper tried to sweep, and helped the ball back on to leg stump.

The 96 runs for the second and third wickets had come from 34 overs, and England were in danger of being rushed out of a Test match which still had well over three days left. Especially when Richards came out to accelerate an already healthy run-rate with three fours and a three off the first ten balls he received from Illingworth. Richardson reached 50 off 101 deliveries, and promptly thumped Pringle through the covers for his eighth four.

The final difference between the first innings totals was emphasised by the boundary count, with England managing 15 fours out of 198, compared with the West Indies' 40 out of 292. For a side to concede over half its runs in boundaries was unforgivably poor bowling. What disappointed Raymond most of all was that, when Richards hit Illingworth over mid-off for four, 'he didn't really get to it, and with any spin he'd have holed out in the covers. He really should be turning it.'

With the spinner's first eight overs costing 41, what should have been a real batting battle of attrition was becoming embarrassingly one-sided. With 31 overs from his two Mister Steadies costing 41 compared with 118 from the other 27, Gooch was forced to turn again to DeFreitas, but he could not finish his first over and limped off with figures of 16·3-9-22-1. He must have passed the outside of the bat 20 times, but conditions were such that, providing bowlers at both ends got the ball into the right area enough times, wickets would inevitably fall.

With 25 overs left, West Indies were 176 for three and, as Raymond said: 'With DeFreitas off, Illingworth not turning it and Lewis, apart from a good opening spell, not looking penetrative, they could take this game right away from England by the close of play.'

Richards, unusually, did let the home side off part of the hook, holing out to Lewis at mid-off in trying to hit Pringle over the top. It was a good catch, with the fielder flipping his cap off and taking the head-high catch with both hands reversed, Australian fashion. The total was then 194 for four and what should have been a grim Test match was becoming a Caribbean Calypso.

Illingworth came back for his fourth spell, and was immediately hit through the covers by Logie. Tony pointed out the obligatory bat-pad man on the off side, and Tom agreed: 'It puts too much pressure on the bowler and it is giving runs away when England's tactics surely should be to keep things tight.' A theory to which I am sure Gooch would subscribe, except the lesson of the folly in selection was now being brutally rammed home.

Illingworth looked unlucky when an appeal against Richardson, then 73 out of 215, was turned down, as Raymond pointed out: 'It pitched on and straightened. Richardson was lucky to get away with that from umpire Dudleston.' Richie thought that it may have spun too much and missed off stump, but I thought Raymond got it right.

With the Illingworth analysis now reading 11-1-57-1, Richie noted the bowler talking to Russell. 'Keepers can be a tremendous help. A bowler might think he's bowling normally, but a keeper can spot little differences – angle of the arm perhaps, or body action.' Illingworth immediately switched to over the wicket, with Raymond agreeing because 'there is a bare part of the pitch around leg stump, so providing he doesn't bowl too wide, I wouldn't argue.' His field was a three-six split favouring the leg side, but so nimble was Richardson's footwork to play several straight-bat strokes wide of mid-on, that the spinner reverted to round the wicket after three overs. Richardson immediately square cut another four, to prompt from Tom: 'All he has to do is to wait for the bad ball which, unfortunately for Illingworth, is coming every over.'

Just before the close of play, Richardson crowned a great day for his side by reaching his 13th Test century, and his first in England. He had then hit 13 fours and faced 201 balls. I commented: 'What an innings in a match where, at the end of the second day, no other batsman has got to 50.' It had been a magnificent innings, but too much had been given to him too easily.

The close of play score of 253 for four gave the West Indies a lead of 65, with 36 fours already hit, 15 off Lewis. He might have been able to do a better job as one of four seamers, but he was one of only three, and his style of bowling made him too big a selection risk. His sensational bowling spell the following morning can be compared to one of Greg Norman's charges of a 65 in the final round of a major when he is not in contention. It got him some stripes back, but by then the damage had been done.

SATURDAY 27 JULY

Another capacity crowd were enthralled by a pre-lunch session which crackled along to provide eight wickets and a paltry 43 runs. Most of the morning belonged to England and Lewis who, with the second new ball, took five for 16 in 11 overs. If only ... Had he produced that sort of form the previous day, England would still have been in the match, although Raymond thought that one contributory factor in his two widely contrasting performances could have been avoided: 'I know Lewis never settled yesterday when he changed ends. I'm a great believer if a bowler settles in not changing him.' I agree with that and, even though there is no slope to contend with at either end at Edgbaston, in my 20 years with Warwickshire, I always felt more comfortable bowling from the Pavilion end.

Lewis's golden run began with a slice of the sort of luck which England did not enjoy the day before. Logie went for a square cut off a short delivery, only for Atherton to take a good catch in the gully to end an attractive partnership of 63 from 22 overs. I was behind the microphone and said: 'Lewis is the sort of bowler to whom confidence is so important. He tends to look a diffident sort of cricketer, and who knows ... that wicket might give him just the boost he needs.'

It certainly did. Richardson was the next to go, LBW to one that ran in a little from around off stump. The Antiguan never looked like recapturing his form of Friday, although it must be said that the quality of bowling was now much higher. The score was 258 for six, and although England had got off to a magnificent start, the lead of 70 already looked enough, assuming that the West Indies four fast bowlers did their stuff on a pitch which had already caused much argument.

Groundsman Andy Atkinson was reported as saying that 'if someone gets a hundred, it cannot be too bad, and it certainly was not a 188 all-out pitch.'

Raymond said that 'somewhere between the two lies the truth. I said 250 would be a good score and if someone bowls well, any side would struggle to get past there.' I asked him about the cracks which Andy Lloyd warned me about two weeks earlier.

Raymond had done his usual early morning inspection of the square. 'I could push my key down some of them. The pitch will definitely take spin as well, but any decent seamer will do the job quicker, because of the big variability of bounce. A lot of pitches have cracks close together, but some of these are like dinner-plates and about 18 inches apart, while others are much closer — that is why it is so much up and down. Test pitches should definitely not be like that. You can put up with sideways movement, but not up and down.' The basic problem of the Warwickshire square is that it is so devoid of pace that attempts to create it can produce an unacceptable inconsistency of bounce.

DeFreitas beat Dujon with a delivery that moved extravagantly off the pitch like a leg break, but again it was from the wrong length. A now-exasperated Raymond said: 'Just look where it pitched — around half way. It was too short and by the time it gets to the bat it is doing too much.'

He had repeatedly made the same point earlier in the series, and that morning's *Daily Mail* contained an interesting breakdown of the bowling of Ambrose and DeFreitas in the first two days of the match. An analysis of 140 deliveries bowled by Ambrose revealed that only 27 balls were short, and there were three yorkers and one half-volley. In vivid contrast, 45 of 99 balls from DeFreitas were short and there were no yorkers or half-volleys. On such a slow pitch, and with DeFreitas slower through the air than Ambrose, those figures go some way towards explaining why England appeared to be so unlucky on the second day.

A different sort of luck came England's way with the dismissal of Dujon, who appeared unlucky to be given out LBW by umpire Dudleston. The batsman got in a good forward stride of three feet, and was beaten by a ball which moved back sharply after pitching just outside off stump. As is usually the case with DeFreitas, the ball was delivered from the outer half of the return crease, and it was difficult to avoid the conclusion that, with seven feet still to travel after the ball struck Dujon's pad, it would have missed leg stump. A few minutes before that incident, I related to the viewers a conversation I had the previous evening with both umpires. 'They said how much more taxing it is for them on this sort of pitch, where movement and variable bounce means they are called on for decisions much more often.'

Ambrose lasted five balls before Lewis had him well caught, waist high, by Hick at second slip and a score of 267 for eight meant that the now wildly excited crowd had seen the West Indies lose four wickets for 14 runs in 55 minutes. If the crowd was in need of further entertainment, then Walsh was the man to provide it. He began with a series of defensive missed pushes which were more extravagantly executed than the occasional stroke which made contact.

An amused Tony said: 'This really should be put to music. I'm not sure he's not a case for the men in the white coats. What worries me is that the comedy of his batting and the extreme seriousness of his bowling don't seem to come out of the same person. Also what is cabaret time for the crowd is not quite that for England, with every run crucial.'

What prompted these remarks was the finish after every defensive stroke, with Walsh completely chest on towards the bowler, the right hand off the bat, and the elbow 90 degrees akimbo – all accompanied by a shuffle of the feet which owed much to the old music-hall sand dance act of Wilson, Kepple and Betty.

His partner, Marshall, could not get the ball away, and seemed just as mesmerised as everyone else by Walsh's antics. So much so, that he did not score any of the 18 added for the ninth wicket, before Lewis showed what a magnificent and safe fielder he is by making a difficult, swirling catch offered by Walsh look relatively easy. The bowler had to turn and chase the ball back towards the pavilion, and it was probably just as much a chance for mid-off and mid-on as the bowler.

Walsh walked off to a big ovation from a good-humoured crowd, who may not have realised they had just seen another of several valuable batting contributions from the lanky, batting comedian. He faced 32 out of 52 balls in the stand, and his 52 runs in the series had come out of 95 added while he batted at number ten in the first four Tests.

A camera tour of the Warwickshire committee balcony revealed John Major between Dennis Amiss and Bob Woolmer, and their smiles became even wider when Lewis completed a wonderful spell by bowling Patterson – the very next ball – after Tom put the mouth on him by saying: 'Courtney swung the bat to good effect, and if Patrick does it in the same fashion he might be just as successful.'

In 20·3 overs, the West Indies lost their last six wickets for 39 and, even if the lead of 104 looked a match-winning one, at least the door was still open for England to sneak back into the match – always providing they could bat well and long enough. My broadcast tribute to Lewis said: 'It speaks highly of his temperament to come back after such a mauling yesterday. He's brought England back . . . not into the game in any realistic way, but at least on to the fringe of it.'

In vision with Tony, Raymond agreed: 'It shows if England had had any luck yesterday, they could even have got a lead. The luck changed today, but they also bowled better.' Commenting on the use of a third man compared with long periods the day before when too many runs went to that boundary, Raymond said: 'Yesterday we gave too many away. When you've got nothing to bowl at you can't afford over 30 runs like that – I would always risk doing away with a fourth slip instead.'

The euphoria of the England supporters lasted 11 balls, by which time the lunchtime smoked salmon must have tasted like sawdust. Patterson bowled the second over of the innings, and the third and fifth deliveries accounted for Morris and Atherton. Gooch's 21st opening partner for England got a good one, which pitched around middle stump and straightened back to make the LBW decision from Dudleston a formality.

Gooch stared at the clock, showing five minutes to one, with time seeming to stand still when Atherton was caught by Hooper at second slip off a ball which straightened and bounced after pitching just outside off stump. Hooper expertly took the catch two-handed to his left, knee high, and although Gooch survived the next over from Ambrose, it could so easily have been four for three, with a vicious away swinger and a shooter missing everything.

Tom was scathing about the pitch. 'I don't know how you bat on things like this. Batting becomes a lottery' – a view with which eight batsmen that morning would not disagree.

Hick's final innings of the series was a nightmare. He edged his first ball just short of Richards at first slip, with Richie commenting that 'Dujon could have dived for that, and it would have been a chance.' Hick's back foot movement to that ball was a tell-tale one. It was back and outside leg stump, with only the impetus of the missed stroke pulling it back to where it originally should have gone. He was again beaten outside off stump, and the agonised crowd could scarcely watch the final act of execution. It came off his eighth delivery, and only the 29th of the innings. His suspect method had already been criticised by Raymond. 'The face of his bat is so open when he plays at Ambrose on off stump.' Correct, but it was the faulty withdrawal of the back foot which caused the open face, because the attempted stroke was played so far away from his body.

He paid the inevitable penalty when he was bowled by one from Ambrose which, according to Raymond, 'came back and kept a touch low ... but the bat was not straight.' There is no hiding-place in modern Test cricket, with endless replays pinpointing a player's faults, but Hick can only benefit from a study of that dismissal, which reveals a gap between crooked bat and pad of nine inches. Also his front foot went no more than 12 inches towards the ball. A stride of two feet and a straight bat would have saved him.

Patterson incurred the attention of Dudleston for running straight down the pitch, and also the wrath of Raymond for the absence of an official warning. 'I just do not believe how the umpires keep treading it down and saying nothing officially. After about half a dozen friendly chats, a patch starts to appear. I really believe they should warn them and make them go wider or get back.'

Lamb's first ball from the patch kept low and he did well to dig it out for two runs. Raymond again made the point that 'the ball was straight. I reckon the England bowlers' line of mostly outside off stump was wrong. On a pitch like this, you give the bowler an extra man leg-side and bowl straight. With such uneven bounce, they can't keep hitting through mid-wicket.'

Gooch soldiered on and, after Keith screened his sequence of scores in the series – 34, 154*, 37, 68, 13 and 45 – I added: 'That record represents a massive effort. You need courage anyway against the West Indies, but when you play against them so many times and you know the relentless battering waiting, it must be rather like a full back under a series of up-and-unders from the All Blacks.'

Dudleston finally warned Patterson officially at 30 for three, and the next ball was such a ferocious no ball, bowled from much wider, that Tom said: 'It seemed twice as quick, a temper ball. He went over a long way, almost a deliberate no ball.'

Occasionally in the commentary box, a remark is made into the microphone which creases even the most experienced and hard-bitten commentators. They are few and far between, which is why they are cherished by everyone – except the commentator, whose life tends to flash in front of him as soon as the unreclaimable phrase hits the airwaves. We do not have an award for the Remark of the Season, but the one from Tom, following a fearsome bouncer from Ambrose to Gooch, was gold-medal class: 'It's nice to know the big fella can still get it up when he wants to.'

Tony, alongside Tom and on air, exploded. Malcolm dissolved into giggles for most of the afternoon, while Richie's double-take from the corner of the box was a collector's item. The scanner crew's response was neither quiet nor short of laughter, while Tom gamely struggled on.

Lamb was clearly determined to get forward as often as possible and Raymond said: 'I was chatting last night with Mike Procter, and he said how hard Lamb has been practising to get well forward.' The defiance of the fourth-wicket pair could only be admired, with hardly a ball failing to move, squat or leap. An amazing delivery from Walsh pitched two feet outside off stump, angled back to hit Lamb on the right hip and was deflected back over middle and off. But for that, it would have missed leg stump by at least a foot.

Another also cut back and glanced his mid-riff, to be followed by one that scuttled along the ground, with Lamb battling to keep his England career alive under impossible conditions. Finally, with the score at 71 and the fourth-wicket partnership worth 66 from 23 overs, yet another unplayable delivery from

Walsh forced a catch to Dujon. As Richie commented over the replay: 'That was a fast leg break. I'm not sure how you play that. Lamb didn't do too much wrong, but he's gone to a superb delivery.'

Tom agreed: 'That's one of the best deliveries I've ever seen. In many ways Lamb was unlucky to be good enough to touch it.' Another replay from the reverse angle showed the ball, bowled from wide of the return crease, pitching six inches outside off stump and then bouncing waist high as it held from leg to off. To get such a ball at any time was bad enough, but just before the tea interval was particularly cruel. I thought that was Lamb's best innings of the series and should have been good enough to take him to the Oval.

Richie greeted Ramprakash by saying: 'This young fella doesn't know yet there are some easy runs in Test cricket. Not all that easy ... but occasionally. His only experience so far has been against these four quicks, and he has shown he is a determined and skilful player.'

At 74 for four, England were still 30 behind, and Sunday's ticket-holders could hardly have been counting on much play – a view that was reinforced when Gooch was bowled by Patterson ten minutes after the resumption. Raymond said: 'It was a straightforward full-length ball he was trying to whip through mid-wicket. It didn't do much except get him out.' In fact, a study of the replay showed that the ball nipped back from outside off stump to take leg stump.

The wicket earned the bowler a kiss from Simmons, which fired him to an exchange of high fives which were sledge-hammer-like in their force. Throughout the series, I had noted with interest the unusual back-foot drag of Patterson, and arranged, via the 'lazy mike', for his delivery stride to be recorded from main and reverse cameras. It was then replayed in slow motion, and I was able to draw attention to the terrific strain placed on his right foot and ankle, with the drag-plated toe turned inwards to face cover point, as the extended ankle was forced to face the leg side.

The Jamaican fast bowler quickly followed up with the wicket of Russell, whose ninth ball was edged to Dujon to make England 96 for six and, seemingly, down and out. Patterson's figures were then 10-1-27-4, which prompted me to say how they underlined his importance to the West Indies. 'He brings another dimension to their bowling – he's the quickest. Curtly camouflaged a few cracks at Trent Bridge, but they are really lost without him.'

Walsh was now off the field, with ice packed around sore shins, but Richards could not have been worried, so on top were his other three bowlers. Pringle helped Ramprakash to take England into the lead and then on to 127, when Marshall got the Middlesex batsman out for 25, the second time in the match he was out in the 20s and the sixth time in the series. As Richie said:

'One thing is for sure. He won't throw away too many innings in the future after this baptism of fire. When runs are there for the taking – he'll take them.'

Pringle was surprisingly put down by Logie, five yards away from the bat at short leg, off a simple chance off Hooper, but Richards looked happy and relaxed when Patterson completed his fifth haul of five wickets in a Test innings by bowling DeFreitas through the gate. That was 144 for eight, and the game could have been settled had Lewis been run out when he was five yards from safety at the bowler's end after the calling for a start-stop single which prompted Raymond to say that 'the last call was probably "help!".'

Play finished at 6.43pm, with England's 156 for eight giving them a token lead of 52. The bowling of Lewis underlined what might have been had he performed better on the second day, but the devastating reply, either side of lunch, when the first three England wickets went for five runs, was a hammer blow. For the third day in succession, the West Indies outplayed England, with the gutsy resistance of Ramprakash showing what might have been had the rest of the middle order functioned more effectively. For the second successive Test match, the West Indies looked unstoppable.

SUNDAY 28 JULY

Thousands of optimistic ticket-holders must have wondered how long the match would last, but a contest that could have been all over by lunchtime, was still going strong at 5pm, thanks to a rearguard action between Lewis and Pringle that ranks with anything seen in modern Test cricket. Not just the runs scored, but because of the context of the match and the difficult batting conditions.

The morning, for the second successive day, belonged to Lewis. The skies were overcast and Raymond's pre-match pitch inspection was filmed. It revealed, when shown to the public, that Patterson's follow-through had created rough on leg stump on a good length.

Richards started with one slip and a gully, believing that edges were unlikely to carry. My experience of Edgbaston told me that whatever happened for the quicker bowlers, would do so much slower today than earlier in the game. First indication of the excitement to come was a flailing, flat-bat stroke by Lewis for four over cover point off Patterson. A no ball was pulled for another four, and then Dudleston's second look at the Jamaican's follow-through showed that his first left-foot stride after the delivery stride was just as close to leg stump as the previous right-foot stride, whereas most bowlers pull away from the stumps at that moment.

Raymond, commenting on the bowler's drag-plate on the right foot, said: 'There aren't many draggers now, because bowlers are mostly square on, compared with former draggers like Fred Trueman who got sideways on.' He might have added that those old-time draggers did so to gain advantage forward of the bowling crease from the back-line law which obtained then. Now, there is no point.

Lewis then set about Ambrose, with a leg-side pick-up described by Richie as 'a brilliant stroke. The man back there ... 15 yards in, Clayton Lambert would have needed to be on the ropes.' With Walsh still off the field, Richards brought on Hooper, but a cover drive followed of such pedigree that Richie called it 'as classic a stroke as you could ever see'.

The crowd, now visibly growing as the news spread, cheered the 50 stand, by which time the dependable Pringle had batted for 190 minutes. Tony asked Raymond to think of an explanation why the pitch now seemed easier. 'Both Pringle and Lewis have worked out that you struggle to get batsmen out on the front foot. I played on a similar pitch in 1983 and Warwickshire won the game by getting the biggest score of the match on the last day. It always seemed to get lower and slower here, but the new ball is going to be crucial.'

Lewis was now in full flow, and a magnificent sight it was, with clean hitting on both sides of the wicket, off front and back foot. Marshall was hit for 13 in one over, which took the crowd to the edge of hysteria. The lead was now over 100, but Tony made a valid counter-point: 'We must keep things in perspective. If Lewis and Pringle can do it, so can Haynes, Richardson and Richards.'

The Leicestershire all-rounder crowned two dream-like days with his first 50 for England. He had then faced only 75 balls and hit eight fours, and a pleasing acknowledgement of the sustained applause was that he removed his helmet and waved his bat all round the ground, including his own dressing-room, but not pointedly beginning with it. Does the modern player really believe that he must show a successful bat to his team first? It is a gesture which might not be intentionally lacking in grace, but certainly gives that impression.

In the 85th over of the innings, Marshall seamed one away from him, but he went through with the stroke and hit it high over mid-on for four. The score was 217 for eight, making the ninth-wicket stand of 90 a ground record against the West Indies, replacing the previous best in 1963 between Sharpe and Lock, in a game in which Trueman's 12 wickets were well supported by five from Dexter.

The crowd willed the ninth-wicket pair to survive until lunch, but it was not to be. Rightly, Lewis was still going for his shots, but he checked a cover drive off Ambrose, and substitute Lambert swooped to take a fine catch as he dived forwards. His 65 off 94 balls came out of 92 for the partnership, and he and Pringle batted for two and a quarter hours to give England a slim chance of victory.

The unexpected fight-back made the morning session worth 82 off 27 overs, with the crowd, now over 10,000, happy in the knowledge that they would still be watching cricket at tea. The lead of 134 was extended to 151 before Pringle's wonderful effort of concentration ended when Logie caught him low at mid-wicket off Marshall for 45. He faced 237 balls and batted for five hours and five minutes – further evidence of his growing stature as a Test player. Only Gooch at Headingley and Smith at Lord's had played longer innings. His batting time in the series was now over 12 hours, and he resisted in this innings throughout partnerships for the last four wickets of 31, 17, 92 and 19 – a total of 159, which was in direct contrast to the 96 scrambled from the first six wickets.

West Indies had 14 overs to negotiate before tea, and what a mess they made of things! Sides needing low totals to win a game often get into trouble and, although Haynes and Simmons safely negotiated the first six overs, the seventh from DeFreitas created a roaring reaction from the crowd that seemed to reduce the West Indies batsmen to panic.

With the score 23, Haynes got a good one which bounced and left him, and the safe hands of Hick at second slip did the rest. Richardson, on whom much now rested, aimed a wild slash at his second ball, and again Hick obliged with a catch which went much quicker and higher. Only a quick-reacting, natural slip fielder would have reversed his hands to take the flying ball, and our wide-angle camera's coverage was superb. Richie shrewdly commented that 'the main thing for the England bowlers now is not to get too excited. They must bowl with common sense as well as enthusiasm . . . now they need a disciplined performance.'

DeFreitas had created the opening, and he it was who widened it with his third wicket in 13 balls. He brought one back to hit Simmons half-way up the pad, with the batsman pinned only inches in front of the batting crease after reversing his initial forward movement. At 24 for three, with the shrieking crowd making it difficult to hear ourselves talk in the box, I heard Richie say: 'I assure you that what you see is on this ground where all the excitement is taking place.' Keith had given him a cutaway of a horizontal lady, boots off and fast asleep in front of the hospitality chalets behind the terrace at the City end.

Now it was down to Richards. The fury of his gum-champing exercises rises and falls according to the degree of crisis, and he came in to bat giving the gum some fearful punishment. Another wicket, especially if it was his, could give England their most unexpected win since Botham's Headingley Test in 1981, but I got the feeling he got hold of Hooper and threatened him with disbarment – or something worse – if he got out.

Slowly, the foundering Caribbean clipper was righted as it became a game of patience, with Richards holding the master card as Gooch went for broke with his three seamers. Lewis bowled two bouncers to Richards, the avoidance of one of which removed his cap. Referring to the new ICC rule to restrict a bowler to one bouncer per batsman per over, Richie said: 'He won't be able to do that next year' ... a pause, then drily: 'Vivian will be disappointed at that.'

The tea interval, with the score 34 for three, was always more likely to benefit the batting side, unless the bowlers could re-establish their momentum, but they could not, and even though Richards took 31 balls to reach double figures, the tension had visibly eased. I doubt whether he had applied himself so rigorously for several years and, although he survived a good appeal for LBW from Pringle, Tony drew on his experience as Glamorgan chairman to read the tea-leaves correctly. 'He is a player of some moods. He can sometimes just decide to succeed, and today he's playing straight and well forward. I saw him last year for Glamorgan do it so many times.'

Tom thought that the time was long overdue for the introduction of Illingworth, but Gooch's decision to persevere with seam until the game was more or less won and lost, at 108 for three, reflected a lack of faith in his spinner which was really a tacit admission of the error in the original selection.

Raymond made two criticisms of the England captain: 'He's changed his seamers around at different ends – and it rarely works. You've only got to be a bit out with the footholds and the line goes. I think he should have tried spin before now from the City end – when the score was about 70. It should turn from that end and if Gooch hasn't got the confidence to bowl the spinner, he shouldn't be playing.'

The 100 came in the 32nd over, with the second 50 coming off 77 balls, and the acceleration continued at an even greater pace. Richards reached 50 off 73 balls, with that obligatory first salute to the dressing-room indicating he was close to delivering a Test victory to his colleagues. Hooper also got to 50, with a lobbed inside edge to backward short leg off Pringle unpunished because, by now, the fielders were well scattered elsewhere.

The third 50 of the innings came off 40 balls, and now the only question to be resolved was whether Richards would hit the winning run. Facing Ill-ingworth with a single needed, he smashed a six of such height and power off the fourth ball that he turned away in triumph before the boundary was cleared. The mighty man punched the air in joy as he ran off the field into the welcoming arms of his team-mates. They met him half way, and carried him off like a triumphant emperor – which is just what he was.

Hooper sneaked off the field, almost unnoticed, but his half-century was further proof of his growing maturity, and our cameras showed the prized souvenir stump he had grabbed when the winning six was hit. He and his captain won the match with their stand of 133 in 32 overs – the first half of which were played with an over-my-dead-body attitude which showed the steel in the modern West Indian cricketer, compared with his equivalent 20 years ago.

Thousands of spectators gathered in front of the pavilion for the awards. BBC Radio's Champagne Moment was the winning six, although it gave Illingworth the doubtful possibility of being remembered for taking a wicket with his first ball in Test cricket and being hit for six off his last.

The crowd, who took the game's aggregate of spectators to over 60,000, deserved a great day, and they got it. Edgbaston has staged many fascinating Test matches, but none more than this one. Richardson's 104 won him the Man of the Match award. What a shame that he was helped, predictably, by too much wayward bowling when the match was still in the balance. Sometimes, selectors escape the full price for their mistakes. Not on this occasion.

ENGLAND v WEST INDIES
at Edgbaston on 25, 26, 27, 28 July 1991

ENGLAND		Runs	Balls	Mins		Runs	Balls	Mins
* G. A. Gooch	b Marshall	45	79	132	b Patterson	40	91	149
H. Morris	c Dujon b Patterson	3	9	8	lbw b Patterson	1	6	6
M. A. Atherton	lbw b Walsh	16	48	62	c Hooper b Patterson	1	2	3
G. A. Hick	c Richards b Ambrose	19	104	149	b Ambrose	1	8	10
A. J. Lamb	lbw b Marshall	9	29	40	c Dujon b Walsh	25	74	106
M. R. Ramprakash	c Logie b Walsh	29	84	110	c Dujon b Marshall	25	74	102
†R. C. Russell	c Richardson b Ambrose	12	28	42	c Dujon b Patterson	0	9	13
D. R. Pringle	b Ambrose	2	11	16	c Logie b Marshall	45	237	305
P. A. J. DeFreitas	c Richardson b Marshall	10	32	46	b Patterson	7	20	27
C. C. Lewis	lbw b Marshall	13	24	37	c sub (Lambert) b Ambrose	65	94	135
R. K. Illingworth	not out	0	2	10	not out	5	40	58
Extras	(b 4,lb 3,nb 23)	30			(b 5,lb 21,nb 14)	40		
TOTAL	(70.4 overs, 333 mins)	188			(105.4 overs; 468 mins)	255		

WEST INDIES		Runs	Balls	Mins		Runs	Balls	Mins
P. V. Simmons	c Hick b Lewis	28	62	85	lbw b DeFreitas	16	23	34
D. L. Haynes	c Russell b DeFreitas	32	109	150	c Hick b DeFreitas	8	22	26
R. B. Richardson	lbw b Lewis	104	229	273	c Hick b DeFreitas	0	2	2
C. L. Hooper	b Illingworth	31	64	74	not out	55	101	146
* I. V. A. Richards	c Lewis b Pringle	22	26	42	not out	73	97	137
A. L. Logie	c Atherton b Lewis	28	54	78				
†P. J. L. Dujon	lbw b DeFreitas	6	17	30				
M. D. Marshall	not out	6	43	78				
C. E. L. Ambrose	c Hick b Lewis	1	2	5				
C. A. Walsh	c & b Lewis	18	32	37				
B. P. Patterson	b Lewis	3	16	17				
Extras	(lb 7,nb 6)	13			(lb 4,nb 1)	5		
TOTAL	(107.3 overs; 440 mins)	292			(40.4 overs; 173 mins)	157	(for 3 wkts)	

WEST INDIES	O	M	R	W	O	M	R	W
Ambrose	23	6	64	3	33	16	42	2
Patterson	11	2	39	1	31	6	81	5
Walsh	21	6	43	2	7	1	20	1
Marshall	12.4	1	33	4	19.4	3	53	2
Hooper	3	2	2	0	12	3	26	0
Simmons					3	0	7	0

ENGLAND	O	M	R	W	O	M	R	W
DeFreitas	25.3	9	40	2	13	2	54	3
Lewis	35	10	111	6	16	7	45	0
Pringle	23	9	48	1	7	1	31	0
Illingworth	17	2	75	1	4.4	0	23	0
Gooch	6	1	11	0				
Hick	1	1	0	0				

FALL OF WICKETS

	ENG	WI	ENG	WI
1st	6	52	2	23
2nd	53	93	4	23
3rd	88	148	5	24
4th	108	194	71	
5th	129	257	94	
6th	159	258	96	
7th	163	266	127	
8th	163	267	144	
9th	184	285	236	
10th	188	292	255	

Toss: West Indies
Umpires: B. Dudleston & D. R. Shepherd
Man of the Match: R. B. Richardson
RESULT: WEST INDIES WON BY 7 WICKETS

CHAPTER SEVEN

THE CLIMAX

THE OVAL TEST
8–12 AUGUST

SELECTION SUNDAY 4 AUGUST

Faced with the daunting task of beating the West Indies on what was likely to be the truest pitch of the series, the England selectors went for broke. Not only did they bring back Botham and Tufnell to give Gooch an attack which was, numerically, the strongest of the summer and the most varied, they preferred Stewart to Russell in what Gooch admitted was a 'high risk' selection. Not given to over-statement, that comment from the England captain was like Guy Fawkes admitting to hiding a couple of sparklers in the House.

The relative merits of the two glove-men was not the only point of argument, although Alan Knott's high opinion of the Surrey man's ability weakens the argument of those, myself included, who believed that the gulf was too wide to risk in a five-day game. A half-chance can win a Test. As the selectors told Russell, his omission was no reflection on his ability – more on the failure of specialist batsmen to score runs earlier in the series.

The strongest criticism levelled at the selectors about Stewart was that he had not kept wicket for Surrey in 1991 in any first-class cricket. No matter that he wore the gloves in limited-overs cricket – the difference in demands of technique and concentration are enormous, particularly as he would be keeping to England's best attacking spinner.

Charges of nepotism can be dismissed—if anything, the father-son relationship between the England manager and the Surrey cricketer has worked against the player. The XII announced included only six of the victorious team in the first Test match—Gooch, Atherton, DeFreitas, Pringle, Ramprakash and Smith, back after missing the Edgbaston game. Morris was retained for a second opinion, with Botham, Tufnell and Lawrence bringing welcome new blood to an attack which, in the first four Tests, only ever operated on half power.

The one stroke of fortune the selectors enjoyed was that, in spite of the bowling selection policy which was too stubbornly loyal by far, they were still in a position to pick a side for the fifth Test to square the series. No matter how the figures are analysed, the fact that England arrived at the Oval only 2–1 down, with no more than half an effective side against the strongest side in the world, will go into the history books as one of the inexplicable miracles of cricket.

The omission of Hick was predictable, but that of Lamb was less so, as was the inclusion of Atherton. The retention of the Lancashire batsman and Morris in front of Lamb and Gower was hardly in line with the 'high risk' policy. If it really was a one-off pick, then to omit two of the only four England-qualified players who average over 30 against the West Indies—Gooch and Smith were the other two — made little sense. There are certain areas in sport where few people go — and scoring a Test hundred against the West Indies is high on the list. Only 13 three-figure scores had been achieved by current England-qualified batsmen, so whether or not Lamb and Gower were in form should not have counted against them. The high-risk factor in picking either, or both, of them was surely more likely to pay off than the choice of other batsmen ahead of them.

Any journalist with positive views needs, occasionally, to slip on the hair shirt, and I am no exception. Having voiced the strongest possible criticism of the selectors before the Edgbaston Test, I will balance the books by reprinting this part of my article on Monday 5 August in the *Birmingham Post*:

> High risk? It is something more than that when the most specialised place in the side — that of wicket-keeper — goes to a man whose only first-class wicket-keeping duties for Surrey in the last two seasons were in the final five games of 1990, just before the side was picked to go to Australia. Even if Stewart gets runs, the unquantifiable factor is the cost of the half-chances which a part-time keeper is likely to miss.
>
> It is not exactly a good deal if your batsman-longstop scores 50 which, incidentally, Stewart has managed three times in 23 Test innings, if he then misses Richie Richardson or Viv Richards, who goes on to hit a big hundred. Not that

Stewart even qualifies as a part-timer. The mental and physical demands of a wicket-keeper are enormous in Test cricket, and yet a man is picked to stand behind the stumps for, possibly, at least a day and a half, when his previous longest spell keeping wicket this summer is three and a half hours. An even greater illogicality is that, in Tufnell, the selectors have chosen an attacking spin bowler for whom the best wicket-keeper is a must.

The dropping of Russell is an insult, not only to him, but to at least half a dozen county wicket-keepers, including Steve Rhodes, Colin Metson and Steve Marsh, all of whom share a pugnacious approach with the bat as well as being technically sound glove-men.

Verdict: the top of the order is not right. The bowling is as good a mix as is available. But that wicket-keeping decision is easily the worst of several this year. England have done well to be only 2–1 down in the series, but that position is in spite, and not because, of the selection policies.

What sometimes we so-called pundits lose sight of – and it is a salutary lesson when we are reminded – is that our sides never have to play . . . those of the selectors *always* do.

Of Botham who, to his dying day, will believe he should have played in the fourth Test – Tuesday 16 July at Portsmouth notwithstanding – I wrote: 'He is worth a gamble. Now it is up to him because whatever won't be on offer to him as a bowler on the best pitch of the series, will as a batsman. His previous eight caps as a Worcestershire player comprise five against Pakistan in 1987, and three against Australia two years later. Injuries have held him back, and it is ironic that he is included together with all-rounders like Lewis, DeFreitas and Pringle – all of whom have been preferred to him in the past year or so, much to his public disgust.' Regarding the previous Test, the tragedy is [sorry Keith] that if Botham had played at Edgbaston instead of Illingworth, England might well have won the game.

THURSDAY 8 AUGUST

Walking into the historic Oval at 9.15am, I met Lance Gibbs, who told me that Logie had a knee injury and Lambert would make his debut. I have always been keyed up before a Test match, even in my first days in the press box in the early 1980s before I combined writing with broadcasting, but I felt a greater sense of anticipation about this one than usual.

Perhaps it was because Richards was playing in his last Test in England, with the normal over-the-top tabloid hype spiced by the return of his great friend and former Somerset colleague. Perhaps it was because of the ante-post voucher, burning a hole in my file, promising me a good pay-day if West Indies won the series. If the England selection was a 'high risk' affair, then the downside of my gamble was such a 'low risk' that it would be sheer lunacy to hedge my stake by accepting the niggardly odds of 6–1 against an England victory. The possibility of England taking 20 wickets on a good pitch, with the West Indies needing only a draw to take the series and win my bet was as faint as ... Stewart having an exemplary match with gloves and bat, for instance.

Our small commentary box seemed crowded, even at that early hour, because Keith had invited Gordon Greenidge to be our third summariser, with Raymond and Geoffrey, and I spent a few minutes chatting to him about basic disciplines – such as avoiding talking at the same time as the commentator, by leaving his microphone face down until, by placing his hand on it, I would know he wanted to speak. And impressing on him the need to listen through his earpiece to Keith and Alan in the scanner van. Little of what they would say would affect him, but talk-back between them and us during play about possible themes to develop would help him to avoid starting a different topic. I did my homework on the Cornhill information bundle, and noted with interest the comparison drawn between Bradman and Richards, both 39 when they appeared in the final Test at the Oval. Also, both men were captains on their last two tours of England, and both scored Test double hundreds on their first appearance on the ground.

A big section on Botham highlighted his magnificent England record, with the final paragraph emphasising the importance of this, his 98th Test, to him. It said: 'His record against the West Indies is mediocre. His batting average against them is 21·02 and his wickets have cost 35·84, compared with his overall Test record of 34·35 batting and 28·27 bowling.' The comparison would have revealed an even bigger difference, if the overall record included only countries other than the West Indies.

The package had a final word of comfort for my bank manager: 'West Indies have won four of the last five Tests here.' Sit back, enjoy it, and plan how to spend the winnings ... those were my contented thoughts as we prepared for the start of play.

Although it seemed likely that Pringle, despite his invaluable all-round contributions in the first four Tests, would be left out of the 'high risk' XII, he reported unwell to save Gooch the unpleasant task of telling his Essex colleague that he was not wanted on voyage. And what a voyage it promised to be, after the England captain won his second toss of the series and, as at Trent Bridge, decided to bat first.

The match was a sell-out for the first four days, and around 12,000 were in their seats, basking in hot sunshine, when Gooch took guard in that schoolboy fashion of his, with only the right hand holding the bat. The first over of any Test match is always scrutinised for clues about pace and bounce of the pitch, which is why Ambrose's second delivery looked ominous. It was short – but nowhere near bouncer length – and forced Dujon to take it overhead, with hands reversed. Raymond revealed that the pitch was flooded six days earlier by a storm, 'unusually late for a Test pitch'. The next ball slipped and arrived slowly at third slip, but the best bowler of the series soon settled down and should have dismissed Morris in his second over when the opener could only splice a gentle catch to Marshall in the gully. But it went down to give Morris the reprieve denied him in the fourth Test.

There was life and lift for Patterson as well, although he was soon in 'unofficial' trouble with umpire Kitchen about his follow-through. Yet again, despite a posse of slips, Richards posted a fine leg, but no third man and, yet again, the batsmen were helped on their way with several edged boundaries. A bowler deserves to concede a boundary off ill-directed leg-side deliveries, but I cannot sympathise with him when an edged boundary past the slips produces a theatrical gesture of frustration. The modern bowler seems prepared to concede a four off the edge off a good ball, but not one to fine leg off a bad delivery.

Geoffrey agreed, but for a different reason: 'When I played, they had a third man and fine leg, but no mid-off ... and that encouraged you to drive, which is what the bowler surely wants. Anyway, Curtly is not going to get driven too often, and I wonder how many runs mid-off saves off him in a day. Not too many.'

Morris continued to have a torrid time – one bouncer from Ambrose hit him on the side of the face as he instinctively jumped with the bounce, instead of ducking. While Morris recovered, Richie took the viewers on a conducted tour of the splendid new Oval ground, with its new stands providing a nostalgic circular roll-call of famous former Surrey cricketers.

Ambrose was still firing his rockets – another hostile delivery hit Morris's bat-handle, with both his feet off the ground. Gooch got one which disappeared over him and Dujon for four byes, and with such high-quality fast bowling posing problems, England's progress to only their second half-century opening stand of the series was far from tranquil, as Tony emphasised, thanks to a sheet of facts and figures from Malcolm: 'Together with the 108 at Trent Bridge, this is the only opening stand of over 22 for England, and four of them have been under ten.'

Gordon Greenidge was interesting to listen to about Richards: 'This is his 50th Test as captain, and he has never lost any of the 12 series involved. A lot of people look for changes in a man, which is why they have criticised him for not being the man they want him to be. It is to his credit he's always stayed the same, and you've got to respect a man for always being true to himself and refusing to change just because other people think he should.

Another entry by Morris into the high-jump competition brought this from Geoffrey: 'It would have been much better to have left it. You can't control the ball with both feet off the ground . . . he's lucky he fended that one off Walsh short of gully.' Rock-solid advice which, nevertheless, is easier to give than receive. An opener's first instinct is to try to fend down the rising ball, which is why a short man like Morris could not naturally drop his hands when a short delivery began to climb.

The extra pace of the pitch enabled Marshall to force a mis-hook from Gooch for four over Dujon's head, and it was a relieved opening pair who went off at lunch with 82 on the board from 27 overs bowled. After the break, several short singles were picked up and, as Raymond said: 'The quick single has two advantages. Apart from keeping the scoreboard ticking over, it brings the fielders in, and then pushes can get through the ring for twos and threes.'

Ambrose was now at his menacing best. A wicked delivery cut back to Gooch, who could only fend it just short of Lambert at short leg. Raymond thought that 'Logie fields closer than that, and might have caught it – it was in the air a long time'. A study of the replay confirmed that view, with the ball pitching five yards in front of the stumps and three feet wide of the cut part of the pitch.

In his next over, Ambrose did his best to cut Gooch in half with one that pitched 12 inches outside off stump, before it ducked back and bounced so sharply that Dujon took it two feet outside leg stump. As the late Eric Morecambe used to say: 'There's no answer to that.' The bowler was like a hunter, closing fast for the kill of a weakening prey. Another bouncer brought an uncharacteristic and ineffectual jab from the home captain into the vacant short square leg area, before Patterson caused similar problems in the next over.

A miscued leg-side lob was all Gooch could offer at bowling which might have been short, but was straight and fast. Gordon was full of praise for both batsmen: 'They both deserve full credit. They've got into some strange positions against the rising ball, but they've coped well and done a good job for England.'

The first three hours of the day produced the stiffest possible examination of temperament and courage, as well as of technique, and, but for their successful negotiation of that period, it is unlikely that England would have gone on to win the game. The pummelling, if anything, increased in intensity, with Ambrose posting two short legs – one in front and one behind square – to Morris, prompting Tony to say that 'I think Curtly fancies him if he digs it in around chest height.' Still Morris was, like a leaping salmon, rising to the short-pitched bait, and it was no great surprise when he was hit on the side of the helmet, and needed attention from Lawrie Brown before he faced up to his 130th and final ball.

Geoffrey had repeated his criticism that Morris was making more trouble for himself than necessary by jumping with the short delivery, and stressed the different approach required at the Oval: 'This pitch is like no other in England. It's so much bouncier. You have got to discipline yourself to leave much more alone.' In loped Ambrose to dig another one in short of a length, and he finally got his reward as Morris could only push a defensive stroke to Lambert at short leg. I said: 'That was a fearful delivery, and there's no disgrace in getting out. If ever a man has worked for a wicket, it is Ambrose.' Geoffrey agreed: 'Morris has fought hard with lots of courage and determination, but he's been got out by a fine bowler who, to be honest, deserved the wicket.'

Both Geoffrey and I received letters from viewers complaining about our praise of Ambrose's hostility, which the writers thought should have been condemned as intimidatory. Why I disagree is that Ambrose did not overdo the bouncer in this instance. He is not averse to expressing his frustration with an unacceptable succession of bouncers, but not this time. He simply exploited the ability, given to him by Mother Nature, to make the ball lift chest-high off a fuller length than most other bowlers, on the quickest pitch of the series. It was hostile bowling of the highest quality.

Morris retired to count his bruises and runs, which numbered 44 out of the opening partnership of 112, while Gooch wondered if the splendid start was to be wasted, as happened at Trent Bridge. I heard myself say: 'Somehow Gooch has got to get his side through the next half-hour with no further loss. Batsmen all over the world know to their cost that one wicket leads to two or three.'

Within 20 deliveries, the nightmare scenario became reality. Poor Atherton lasted four balls before he got what I described as: 'High-class fast bowling and who knows what the answer is? To think he waited for three hours for that.' The ball from Walsh bounced and went straight for Atherton's chest before it hit his left glove on its way to Hooper at slip.

In came Smith, finally promoted to the position he might have filled after Headingley, and, after he avoided a bouncer from Ambrose, a close-up of head and shoulders showed a form of exhortation to himself which contained a couple of remarks that did not need an expert lip-reader to interpret.

The Antiguan fast bowler sometimes seems irresistible, and he swept Gooch aside with a fine delivery which came back from six inches outside off stump to hit the left pad on the line of middle stump. The ball pitched about ten feet short of the batting crease and, having already moved ten inches in ten feet, it needed to do no more than four more inches in the remaining four feet between Gooch's pad and the leg stump. Our high-square camera showed it was all right for height, and Ambrose's 27th wicket of the series had rushed England from 112 without loss to 120 for three in 21 balls.

Ramprakash came in for what Raymond described as 'another test of character and ability' at yet another time of crisis and was then hit by Ambrose. Richie observed: 'That's certainly a pretty good test of character – he didn't even bother to rub it . . . just gave Curtly a long, hard look. If you look at the theory of the game – which incidentally has never won anything in all the years I played – you could say that Ramprakash could find it easier to play his strokes on this firm pitch. Against that, the West Indies quicks can get more bounce, but at least it's even.'

The Middlesex batsman was then hit on the left wrist and, while he received treatment, Richie added: 'We know two things about him: he's never reached 30 and he has a ton of courage. In all the innings he's played, he has stood up to the West Indies fast bowlers all through and never taken a backwards step.'

Play stopped for five minutes, which allowed Alan to organise a pan around the ground, which included a close-up of our commentary box, with Richie and Raymond in residence. Richie contented himself with one remark: 'That's the air-conditioned commentary box. Old-fashioned air-conditioning mind you . . . just the breeze from one side to the other.'

The fourth-wicket pair hung on, like a boxer on the ropes waiting for the bell, until tea when the score was 129 for three, with the West Indies having taken an overwhelming points lead in an afternoon session which produced 47 runs for three wickets from 23 overs. Even allowing for the stoppages for treatment for Morris and Ramprakash, a total of 50 overs in the first two two-hour sessions was an appalling rate.

Richie had, for a long time, favoured a rule which made it mandatory for a fielding side to bowl a minimum of 30 overs per session, before they could have their break. Applying that to this day's play, lunch would have been at 1.12pm and tea at 4.25pm, and during the series, lunch would only have been taken before 1.10pm once, and tea before 4pm once. The new penalties contained in the International Cricket Council's code of conduct came into existence last winter, and the fines are so swingeing that it is doubtful if a problem that has bedevilled Test cricket for the last decade will continue to bother spectators, administrators and commentators. The basis for fining players is a five percent deduction for every over a side falls short of its minimum quota in a five-day Test. After allowances for wickets are deducted, the West Indies would have forfeited 85 percent of their match fee, and England 70 percent in this final Test – and that with 95 overs of spin bowled.

An interesting comparison throughout the series shows that the deductions from the West Indies players' fees would have been: 70 percent at Headingley, 25 percent at Lord's, 45 percent at Trent Bridge, 70 percent at Edgbaston and 85 percent at the Oval. England were much better, as they should have been with DeFreitas and Pringle operating off shorter run-ups, and Malcolm and Lawrence much brisker than the West Indies fast bowlers in getting back to their marks. They would have escaped a fine in the first, second and fourth Tests, but would have forfeited 45 percent of their match fee, which is over £2,000, at Nottingham and 70 percent at the Oval. A contributory factor is the difference in the number of no balls bowled in the series. The West Indies transgressed 173 times, with Marshall the chief offender with 60, while England over-stepped the mark 103 times, with Pringle (46) and Lawrence (36) the chief culprits.

Before the final session began, I asked Gordon to list his side's fast bowlers in order of sheer pace. 'Ian Bishop is now the quickest, then Ambrose and then Patterson.' An interesting view, with most people believing that Patterson is at least second.

Ramprakash gave a difficult, low chance to Lambert at short leg, which brought this little exchange between Tony and Geoffrey, who said: 'That is a nasty place to field.'

'Did they ever get you there?'

'Just once in one of my early games for Yorkshire. They put me there – a ball whistled past my right ear and I said: "Thank you very much – that's my lot".'

As Smith and Ramprakash soldiered on – and it really was the cricketing equivalent of trench warfare – Geoffrey outlined their problems with an incisive analysis that only a former front-line soldier could give:

'They bowl 75 balls an hour – you get half. Of those, half a dozen will be bouncers and at least another dozen will be whacked in so short you try to leave them alone. That leaves fewer than 20 to play, most of which you are trying to avoid getting out to. It's a big enough problem stepping up from county cricket to Test level, but there is another step-up from Test cricket to Test cricket against the West Indies. It needs enormous concentration with not only so few hittable balls, but so few balls anyway.'

Hooper was now on, and the change brough the wicket of Ramprakash – an inside edge from bat to pad to Lambert at short leg, although the batsman had to be given out after not walking immediately. Raymond took the viewers through the replay, spotting that 'his top hand is not behind the handle, it's on the side. He doesn't push far enough forward, hence the inside edge to one that turned a bit. Also, one of the reasons the edge went on to the pad and in the air, was because the knee of the left leg is behind the foot. The left knee should be bent right forward to get the balance right – that way the pad might have killed the edge.'

That is the sort of faultless analysis that conveys more to youngsters in 45 seconds than 50 pages of any coaching manual. The fourth-wicket stand was worth 68 in 24 overs, with Ramprakash's 25 including two fours off 78 balls faced. The partnership was crucial in that, not only did it push back the tide, it did a lot for the morale of an England dressing-room which, when those three quick wickets went after lunch, must have feared that another sound position would be wasted.

Stewart joined Smith with 22 overs to be bowled, and under extra pressure because Botham was unlikely to be able to bat because of a reported stomach upset. First night nerves? The official diagnosis said otherwise, but even the biggest names are not immune. I asked Keith to run Stewart's Test record and world ratings, to emphasise that his selection was a double gamble in the batting department as well as behind the stumps.

His aggregate of 541 runs at an average of 24·59 explained his 50th position in the Coopers Deloitte rating list, and the most controversial selection of the summer could hardly have been under greater pressure when he walked to the crease on his home ground. Ambrose left the field for 31 minutes with a slight groin strain, but the fifth-wicket pair eschewed all risks as they played for stumps. Smith was then 54 off 131 balls while Stewart, after staying on one run for 35 balls, ended the day with 19 off 85 balls.

A score of 231 for four represented a good day for the home side, especially after the loss of three quick wickets in the middle of the day. Marshall had a quiet day, but so threatening was the hostility of Ambrose, Patterson and Walsh, that West Indies could easily have ended the day with a crucial advantage. Instead it was honours even – just.

FRIDAY 9 AUGUST

Another even day, with Smith underpinning an England total which was good, if not commanding. Richie took the first half-hour and, just to prove he is human, began with a couple of errors. Smith got a brute of a ball from Ambrose, which he managed to fend down just short of Simmons in the gully. The fielder was deeper than usual, but Smith helped to make his own luck by the power of his square-cutting, which persuaded Richards to post his gully deeper.

Richie noticed Smith taking his hand off the bat during the reflex jab, pointing out that 'if the ball had been caught, the umpire would have had to judge whether the hand was on the bat when the ball was hit.' Except, when I saw the replay much later, it was Smith's right hand which left the bat-handle, but the ball struck the *left* hand.

His second mistake was pursued with the sort of dead-pan, self mockery that characterises the most effective sporting commentator in British television. In a few sentences, he gave a lesson to us all about how to come clean with the public, with a minimum of fuss and a maximum of understated humour. He told the public that Alec Stewart had received an eye injury in pre-match practice, which necessitated the insertion of two stitches. When Geoffrey conveyed the news to us that it was Lawrence, Richie immediately threw his hands up and confessed thus:

'I wish I hadn't opened my mouth about the England practice. It seems that it wasn't Stewart who was hit, it was Lawrence. They're so similar in build and everything else, we made an understandable mistake.'

Gordon, slightly heavier-handed, added what Richie had left to the imagination of the viewers: 'And of similar complexion as well.' Richie restored the balance: 'Indeed – you can never tell about these things in the big city. Collectors of further trivia might like to know the reason why we know it was Lawrence and not Stewart. It is because Geoffrey Boycott was called in at nets to hand over his handkerchief to staunch the flow of blood. He's now reduced to using tissues . . . like the rest of us.'

He then closed the chapter, as Keith screened the scoreboard, with 'England are now 239 for four . . . and that is one thing I can guarantee is correct.' All done with great style, as he switched to an explanation of his remarks, made the previous day, about the lush state of the Oval outfield.

'A letter in the post today from Leaky Pipes System explains it perfectly. They have installed a new drainage system here in October 1990 – thin porous piping – 16 miles of it, two feet apart and eight inches down. It cost £23,000 and it has worked brilliantly.'

Smith twice square-cut Ambrose for four, bringing from Gordon an admiring comment: 'There is such terrific power in his square-cutting.' That, coming from one of the most ferocious square-cutters in modern cricket, was rather like Placido Domingo praising Pavarotti for singing in tune.

Stewart had played with such restraint that it was a shock when he wafted a wide delivery from Patterson to Richardson in the covers to end a good partnership of 75 in just under two hours. Geoffrey was critical: 'A little bit sloppy. He's done that too often for England. He shouldn't get caught off the middle of the bat at cover after doing the hard work.'

The crowd's disappointed groan at the loss of an England wicket soon turned into a roar as Botham strode to the crease, back on the Test scene for the first time since Trent Bridge in 1989. As he took guard, I asked Keith to get a wide-angle close-up which showed the special padding he was wearing. I told the viewers: 'What you see there, around the back and shoulders as well as elsewhere, is what he ordered specially from his Worcestershire chairman, Duncan Fearnley, last March.' I repeated the conversation I had with Fearnley at the time that 'it proved to me how serious he was about playing for England again, because he said he would need the extra protection against the West Indies fast bowlers.'

Little of Botham's on-field involvement with play is short of drama, and his first four balls from Ambrose included two bouncers and a yorker. Richards posted two men out for the hook, but the bait was ignored as the umpires concerned themselves about the woeful over-rate, as well as the follow-through of Patterson, which earned him an official warning from umpire Kitchen. In a two-hour session which produced 24 overs, Kitchen had a word with Walsh about his tempo – or lack of it – between deliveries. A now irate Raymond said: 'I've just clocked Courtney sauntering back to his mark as 39 seconds. A lot of the time he stands at the end of his follow-through for 20 seconds . . . if he went about things properly, he could save at least two minutes an hour.

There is little argument that the length of run-ups is not a big factor in slow over-rates. After all, I watched Vic Marks and Nick Cook slow down to six overs in 32 minutes in Lahore under Gower's captaincy in 1984. More important is the speed with which bowlers get back to their marks, as well as desisting from playing statues at the end of their follow-through, when they are out of the game.

Botham played with such care that his double-figure score comprised ten singles, and Smith passed 2000 runs for England in his 50th innings on the way to the safe negotiation of another session, when he was 92 out of 310 for five. The capacity crowd had seen England prosper with 79 runs for the loss of Stewart, but off only 24 overs. Shameful.

Often a batsman gets stuck in the so-called 'nervous nineties', but Smith sprinted into three figures with a four and a three off Marshall, to earn from Geoffrey: 'This has been a fabulous innings – at least as good as the one he played at Lord's.'

Marshall was the first bowler to swing the ball on the second day, and he brought one back a long way to win the LBW decision against Smith, to make the score 336 for six. The delivery pitched six inches outside off stump and moved back a lot, with Raymond reading the dismissal this way: 'He played a little bit across the line, with the bat coming down from second slip towards mid-wicket. As a result he got a bit too far over. But it's been a marvellous innings – positive and he's taken the fight to the West Indies.'

I have heard comments from players and press that Raymond and Geoffrey are too critical of players, and forget that they used to make mistakes. I disagree. They are employed to spot the tiniest of technical faults, and, in Smith's case, it was not nit-picking to highlight a flaw, more a case of explaining to the viewers why a well-set batsman with 109 runs to his name, missed a good ball and got out.

Of Smith's innings, I wrote for *Post* readers: 'His exhibition of concentration and sound technique, against the most searching examiners in Test cricket, brought him 256 balls to face, from which he hit 13 fours, and his time of 352 minutes took his occupancy of the crease this summer in six innings (two not outs) to 19 hours and eight minutes.

'Think of it. Three whole cricketing days spent taking a battering from traffic which keeps coming round and round – just like being marooned in the fast lane of the M25 throughout a succession of peak rush-hours.'

Richie, who misses so little, spotted that the attention of Richards was elsewhere when the ball struck Smith's pad. 'He was feeling his right knee – perhaps it clicked or seized up.'

The West Indies captain immediately left the field for what turned out to be treatment for a bee sting, which Richie relayed thus: 'He'd have been better up here in the commentary box – there aren't any wasps or bees. Ray Illingworth has swatted them all. All wasp lovers please write to Mr Illingworth.'

Botham reached 20 after two hours of unblinking concentration which was particularly stern against Marshall, whose dismissal of Smith took his Test total of wickets to 375 – one behind Botham. However many times you hear a Test player say he is unaware of a particular landmark, take no notice. The best are usually aware of the situation – and so they should be.

The arrival of Lewis brought a change of approach from the Worcestershire man. Richie thought: 'It might be my imagination, but I have a feeling that Botham has set himself to have a bit of a dash at Ambrose.' Raymond added: 'Yes, he's now starting to try to hit the ball on the bounce. He's not going to get many half-volleys, so you've got to make something for yourself, which is why he's trying to drive the ball on the up.'

It was fatal, as my written accounted showed. 'Richards, sting attended to and back in charge, spotted the signs and immediately brought back Ambrose, and it worked. After 131 minutes at the crease, and with 19 singles out of 31, Ambrose banged one in short, and Botham unwisely went for the hook. With his eye in, any of the other West Indies fast bowlers might be hookable, but not Man Mountain.

'It was too quick and straight and, even though he made some sort of contact to deflect the ball away from his stumps, his attempt to write a new Oval ballet sequence was unsuccessful. As he overbalanced towards the stumps and tried to straddle them, he got his left leg out of the way, but not the right which disturbed the leg bail. Lady Luck being the perfidious woman she is, his hit-wicket dismissal was his first in 155 innings for England.'

At least it earned Brian Johnston and Jon Agnew a place in the radio archives for their giggling reaction on Test Match Special to the new correspondent's close-of-play summary, in which he rued Botham's inability 'to get his leg over'.

A now much more confident Lewis took charge of the tail, with his unbeaten 47 off 90 balls taking England to a total of 419, which Raymond said was 'a good score with spin in the pitch'. DeFreitas, Lawrence and Tufnell managed 20 of 68 added for the last three wickets, two of which went to Walsh and one to Patterson.

DeFreitas got a Walsh special, one angled in from wide out, to pitch 12 inches outside off stump and then hold up to take the outside edge on its way to Dujon. The latest Battle of the Gloucesters was won by Walsh, after a furious exchange of bouncers, hooks and drives, with Lawrence nicely caught at slip by Richards before Tufnell was caught by Haynes at the fourth juggling attempt off Patterson.

Extras totalled 54, including 39 no balls, and West Indies were left 26 overs to negotiate before the close. Lawrence, whose follow-through soon attracted the attention of Kitchen, and DeFreitas pressed too hard in the early overs, and 24 came from the first four overs and 39 from the first ten. Geoffrey understood their problem: 'It happens sometimes after a dressing-room pep-talk that bowlers get wound up and lose their natural rhythm. They've got to settle down and try not to rush everything.'

I spoke about the pressure on Stewart behind the stumps. Geoffrey slipped in a statistic that, for once, did not originate with Malcolm: 'I didn't realise he shares the world record of 11 catches for a keeper, at Leicester in 1989. I didn't know until half an hour ago – his Mum told me.' Long, Marsh, Bairstow and Hegg are the others, though Pooley, Tallon and Taber all had 12 victims in a match, including stumpings.

Gordon was surprised when Gooch brought on Tufnell ahead of Botham and Lewis: 'I suppose he noticed what Hooper did, which showed the pitch will take spin.' The left-arm spinner immediately turned one to Haynes, and a lofted mis-hit just evaded Atherton in the covers.

Lawrence switched to the Vauxhall end and soon struck with the LBW dismissal of Simmons, whose technique at the end of his first full series showed little signs of adapting to the demands of five-day Test cricket. The delivery from Lawrence was straight, of full length and slanted back in a touch – but not enough to beat a class opener who would have gone further forward.

Richie has never been sold on the attraction of the Mexican Wave, and one prompted this acid comment: 'While all that was happening, I've seen one of the more brainless things you could ever see at a cricket match with that ridiculous Mexican Wave – the spectators in that mid-wicket area tossed all their rubbish in the air – it's blowing across the ground and will hold up play.' And so it did 20 minutes later, with the same mindless spectators booing Richardson when the latter's refusal to continue until the distracting pieces of litter were cleared caused a ten-minute delay while 30 stewards tidied things up.

Tufnell is an interesting bowler. There are many ball-changes in cricket – bowlers who start their run-up with the ball not in the bowling hand – but they are mostly fast bowlers. Abdul Qadir is one slow bowler who tosses the ball from left to right hand, but Tufnell takes that one move further. As he takes his first stride and hops on to his left foot, the ball is spun from left hand to right and then back into the bowling hand. He has an aggressive action, with plenty of 'body', and although he has a nice loop, batsmen find it difficult to get down the pitch to attack him.

Another Lawrence no ball was caught by Smith at long leg off Richardson. An unhappy final two hours for England also included a drop of Haynes by Gooch at slip off Botham's fourth ball of the innings. It was low and sharp, but no more difficult than several taken earlier in the series by the England captain. As a final gesture, Richardson hit Tufnell for a straight six and, at 90 for one at the close, the West Indies had clawed back some of the ground lost earlier.

England could look back on solid partnerships for five of the middle-lower order wickets, while Richards could reflect that an overnight deficit of 329, with nine wickets in hand was a better position than, at one time, seemed likely when Smith and Botham were together. As I closed my Tandy at 7.45pm that night, I thought of the mere 130 runs which were needed to avoid the follow-on, and that ante-post voucher on West Indies winning the series began to glow even brighter.

SATURDAY 10 AUGUST

Somewhere in the history of Test cricket, a team may have tossed away a near-unassailable position in a five-match series with as abject a batting approach as that of the West Indies in their first innings . . . but I doubt it. A third successive capacity crowd, in what was already an enthralling Test match, could hardly believe their eyes as, like lemmings over the cliff, Richards and his players slogged their way to defeat – and all in 49 minutes of batting madness, either side of lunch.

As a performance, it was a throw-back to the brittle days of the 1950s and early 1960s, only worse bearing in mind that the series was there to be clinched with a draw. As I wrote my Monday morning match report for the *Birmingham Post* at the end of the day, I tried to forget my bet – and one day, possibly, I will, although I doubt it. The first paragraph read thus:

The West Indies had one hour of sheer lunacy on Saturday, either side of which they scored 220 for four off 78 overs. Nearly a good day? Not when, in the other ten overs, they lost six wickets for 18 runs and went most of the way towards losing the match, and thus giving England a freakish chance to square the series. Phil Tufnell wove such a suicidal spell in a post-lunch spell of 2.3-1-2-4 that an incredulous crowd watched wickets tossed away like confetti, while poor Haynes gave his impression of the boy who stood on the burning deck.

The morning session started quietly enough, with Haynes reaching 50 for the 52nd time in his 102nd Test match. Raymond disagreed with Gooch's choice of Botham and DeFreitas to share the attack: 'Looking at the surface before play, it is starting to wear and dust at the Vauxhall end because of a follow-through from Pringle in the NatWest quarter-final here ten days ago. That's why I would have definitely opened with Tufnell. Not just because of the wear, but it's better for a spinner to start against batsmen still playing themselves in. When he does come on, I'm sure this Pavilion end is the end for him.' Clairvoyance at its best.

In over 40 years' association with the first-class game, I rate Raymond as possessing one of the two shrewdest all-round cricketing brains I have known – my first Warwickshire captain, the late Tom Dollery, had the other. His next comment, about Botham's field-placing, is a good example: 'That silly mid-off really shouldn't be there – he's stopping Richardson pushing through the ball, although that's what Botham wants him to do. Put him in the slips and encourage the drive instead if it's swinging.'

Such exploration of cricket's minutiae is a constant reminder of how few tricks the former England, Yorkshire and Leicestershire captain has ever missed. I am still not sure how I managed to edge him 5–3 in dismissals of each other in county cricket – perhaps because Fred left him with so few opportunities to bowl at me.

The sun-soaked crowd wanted three things – Botham to take a wicket, their own Stewart to take a catch and Richards to walk in to bat. It took ten deliveries from Botham to grant them their first two wishes, with Richardson edging his fourth ball of the morning to Stewart as he tried to cut. Raymond covered the replay with: 'It was shorter, wider and it swung. I've said all summer that anyone moving it away from Richardson has a chance.'

The catch to Stewart was straightforward – unlike one which he took at the other end four balls later to put the first thoughts into people's minds that the follow-on target of 220 might not be simple. DeFreitas made one bounce and the edge from Hooper arrived at the sort of awkward height to Stewart which could have caused a problem, but did not.

With the score 98 for three, the scene was set for Richards to take centre stage, but Lambert was next in, because of the indisposition of his captain. The switch fooled our captions department, who flashed up the name of Richards – albeit for a split-second only as they heard Tony announce the arrival of Lambert.

The left-hander is a compulsive hooker and cutter, with an unorthodox stance, based on a guard of leg stump. An unusual positioning of his feet has him standing at least 12 inches wide of the stumps. Raymond said: 'That is strange because, with the ball going across them, left-handers need to cover their off stump. He does move into line as the ball is bowled, but it means he has to move a lot around the crease.'

DeFreitas's figures were now 10-4-28-1 – quite a recovery after his first two overs cost 22. I replaced Tony and immediately launched another Colemanballs entry into *Private Eye* across the air waves. Botham clearly fancied Lambert so much that, after one close call and a staring match, I heard myself say: 'Just look at Botham. He expects a ball with every wicket.' What a showcase he would need. Keith helped me through the next minute with a list of the world's top catchers in Test cricket, which showed the England man with 112 catches in fifth place behind Border, Greg Chappell, Richards and Cowdrey.

Lambert is a rare animal in that he refuses to compromise his natural game, even when playing for his country for the first time. He wound up DeFreitas so much that the Lancashire man received a warning from Kitchen for overdoing the bouncer – three in one over. Another one in his next over was followed by two flashing fours through the covers, and a hooked six off Botham which everyone on the ground and field seemed to find entertaining – except the bowler.

Richie pressed for the introduction of Tufnell, and Geoffrey agreed. He used the telestrator to circle the patches of rough outside the left-hander's off stump, and also the worn area just outside the off stump of Haynes. The telestrator first became available in our commentary box in 1990, but I am still not sure that we maximise its use – with the exception of Geoffrey. It is partly a matter of confidence in using the pen slowly enough, and also asking the producer to make it available at the right time. It is an extra technical discipline, but one well worth mastering because of the extra knowledge that can be imparted to the viewers. In particular, it is useful to pinpoint changes in the field which we may well talk about but, from a normal camera shot, are difficult to spot from a distance.

Richie remarked on a three-way conversation between Botham, Gooch and Lawrence: 'With three slips and a gully, one assumes that the attack will be directed outside off stump.' After the next ball, which went for a leg-side single, he took his punishment like a man: 'And we all know what assumption is.'

Geoffrey was more scathing. 'In my opinion England have bowled badly at Lambert – he's raced to 36 and it's no good putting seven on the off side if you don't bowl there. It is great stuff for the crowd, but Gooch must be thinking England are losing their initiative. He must bowl the spinner.' I replaced Richie as Gooch finally brought his spinner on, after 90 minutes' play and with the score now 158 for three, just 62 short of the follow-on target.

Despite Lambert having had less than half the strike – 48 of the 106 balls in the fourth-wicket partnership with Haynes – he had scored 39 out of 60 when Tufnell tossed up his first ball of the day. The left-hander's ears went back with his bat, and a one-handed heave sent a high catch to Ramprakash to start a sequence of rash strokes and wickets that still defies analysis.

Dujon is exempt from criticism, LBW on the shuffle across the crease to Lawrence. He should have played forward, but at least it was a defensive stroke to a full-length delivery. Still no Richards, but as Marshall joined Haynes, a remarkable discussion between Gooch and the umpires took place. It was remarkable in that, with our cameras elsewhere, we gave it only one mention, and the Sunday cricket correspondents all, to a man, missed the significance of what, otherwise, would have made their headlines next day.

I told the viewers: 'They've just had a word with Gooch about the ball. They are entitled to do that if they think the ball has been maintained in any irregular fashion. Things they look for are the raising of the seam and, in an effort to increase swing, roughing up one side. Cleaning the seam is acceptable – it's just a matter of striking the right balance.' Raymond reminded viewers of 'a couple of years in the 1970s when only the bowler was allowed to shine the ball.'

Holder and Kitchen had inspected the ball, and were so dissatisfied with its state, with one side having been apparently artificially roughened, that they asked Gooch for his comments. Normally a captain will defend his players, but it seems that on this occasion, there had been such a clear transgression of Law 42 (5) that the conversation was a short one. The relevant part of the law says: 'No-one shall rub the ball on the ground or use any artificial substance *or take any other action* to alter the condition of the ball.'

It also seems that the umpires expected mention of the incident to be included in a statement from the Test & County Cricket Board at the end of the day about gestures made by Tufnell earlier in the day. The absence of any reference to an incident which was a tabloid correspondent's dream explains why the remarkable incident has escaped public comment until now. Such a roughening of one side of the ball, by a fingernail or a bottle-top, is done to obtain extra swing, and cannot be done in two minutes.

The fact that the umpires did not, as the law allows, change the ball for one of similar wear prior to the contravention, shows that their vigilance prevented an incident which nobody, in or out of the press box, would have failed to notice. I often wonder what sort of reports would appear if there were no television monitors available in press boxes. At Trent Bridge and Lord's, where the press are seated well off-line, I can understand the dependence upon the replays, but not at the behind-the-arm sites at Edgbaston, Old Trafford, Headingley and the Oval.

I often amuse myself by organising an imaginary mischievous contest in which the national correspondents have to watch a day's play in a sound-proof room, with no access to television. I then award handicaps based on a tough golfing par of 72 and, in the last seven years, I reckon only three writers would have beaten par, with two others capable of equalling it. This is not a dog-eat-dog exercise, but simply my comment on the sort of correspondent most newspapers now prefer to use – hence the use of so many former Test player-experts nowadays.

An already incident-packed session lacked one thing for the expectant crowd – the appearance of Richards, so Marshall kindly organised it for them with a back-foot slash off Tufnell which was beautifully caught, two-handed in front of his right knee, by Botham at slip.

Richards finally decided the nonsense had to stop, and came in to face two balls before the break to a huge reception of warmth and affection that washed around the Oval throughout the whole of his walk to the crease. He touched his cap and was clearly moved by applause which, although not of party-conference duration, still lasted for 63 seconds.

West Indies had now lost three wickets for three runs in 28 balls, with poor Haynes paddling along for 24 in the two-hour session from 91 balls. He was then 70, and must have believed that the lunch break would be used by his captain to drill some badly-needed discipline into his remaining troops, with 59 still needed to avoid the follow-on.

What happened next took only a little longer than the section of 'A Question of Sport' which bears the same name. Richards kept Haynes company for 19 deliveries, before his high body temperature triggererd a batting hot flush that raged through the remaining batsmen like an uncontrollable fever. He danced down the pitch to Tufnell before, realising he could not drive the ball, he turned and got a lifting outside edge which was brilliantly taken by Stewart, high to his right. Richards walked past Haynes and the incoming Ambrose, whose clear responsibility was to play for his vice-captain. He did . . . for one ball, before he drove at the next and was snapped up by a jubilant Botham at slip.

If Haynes was dumbstruck at the fall of his captain, he must have been close to a coronary when Ambrose studiously avoided any eye contact as he went off, to be replaced by Walsh. Tufnell's feet had scarcely touched the ground since lunch, and a delirious crowd, like the England players, noisily bayed their approval as they scented blood.

Even Richie, who has seen most things in cricket and is rarely surprised by what he has not, was take aback two balls later when Walsh, like Ambrose, batting by numbers, followed one perfunctory block with a fatal slog. This one found Gooch at mid-off with Richie saying: 'You wouldn't believe it. You'll forgive me Gordon if I raise an eyebrow. What's going on out there?' Gordon Greenidge swallowed at least as hard as his partner, Haynes, who was over 100 yards away. 'It beats me. I just don't know what's happening.'

The scoreboard told him that, from 172 for six, his team had skidded, apparently completely out of control, to 172 for nine – all in five balls and, unforgiveably, all to wild slogging strokes with a powerless Haynes watching in horror from the other end.

As Walsh and Haynes had instinctively crossed before the catch was taken, Richie drily pointed out that 'Desmond has at last got the strike ... and he'll regard that as something of a bonus – even though it's only one ball.' Patterson waved airily at his first ball from Lawrence and, just to complete a ruinous period of 43 minutes of self-destruction which, in racing would have certainly precipitated a stewards' inquiry, the number eleven casually took a single off the last ball of the same over, without ever sharing Haynes's appreciation of the urgent need for a second run.

He lasted three more balls, before edging an attempted drive off Tufnell to Botham at slip to complete a run of seven wickets for 18 in 65 balls, with six of the seven wickets tossed away. Tufnell took the last four wickets in nine balls against batsmen whose approach was inexplicable. The only sensible thing Patterson did was to lag discreetly behind Haynes as the players left the field, with the opener carrying his bat for the second time in Test cricket. His 75 off 198 balls out of 359 bowled in the innings was a typical effort of solid technique and application on a pitch which still favoured the bat.

What the collapse did prove was, as Raymond was quick to point out: 'It is quite remarkable that Gooch took so long to bring Tufnell on.' During the break, he and Tony detailed the nine wickets to fall in the day for 81 in 26 overs, with only Hooper and Dujon not out to wild strokes, Tufnell's astonishing figures for the day were 5·3-2-4-6.

Raymond praised the spinner: 'He deserved his figures, because he induced the false strokes by turning the ball past the bat. As a result, he got them hitting across the line and in the air.' Tony asked him about the second innings. 'I would definitely bring him on in the first ten overs before the batsmen settle in. That way helps him and enables the four fast bowlers to switch around and not get tired.'

The temperature was 80 degrees – probably slightly less than that in the visitors' dressing-room – and Gooch did as Raymond suggested by bringing Tufnell on for the ninth over of the innings. Simmons hit him for a huge six on to the top of the pavilion, but our former England all-rounder was unimpressed. 'It pitched just outside off stump and he hit it over long-on – it only had to turn a bit.'

Our cameras showed the broken slate on top of the roof, with the massive hit apparently discouraging Tufnell from pitching it up, and Simmons and Haynes reduced the first innings deficit of 243 by 48 in 18 overs by the tea interval, when there were still 38 overs to bowl.

Whether by design, to give Haynes a breather, Simmons took such a large slice of the strike that, when he was out for 36 to Botham, he had faced 83 balls compared with 56 for Haynes. His dismissal was as predicted by Geoffrey, who believed the opener to be vulnerable in the gully area. 'It was a sliced drive and it was super captaincy, super bowling and super fielding by Lewis. They've had a man there for him all through this game, and it's always satisfying to get a planned wicket.' Lewis's brilliant full-length catch enhanced a fast-growing reputation as one of the world's best fielders.

Richardson was now suffering from a high temperature, so one dasher was replaced by another, with the combustible Lambert somehow winning promotion over his Guyanese compatriot, Hooper. There might be the odd match situation which is suited to Lambert's flailing approach, but arrears of 190, with well over two days to go, was not one of them, and Botham soon underlined the value of his carefully crafted medium-pace method with his second wicket in 20 minutes. Lambert went for a hook, the ball hit the top of his left pad as he was through the stroke too soon, which gave umpire Kitchen one problem to solve—height. Kitchen is not an umpire who fires people out instantly, and he certainly thought about it before he ruled against the batsman.

My view was that it was so marginal that Lambert could consider himself unlucky, but at 71 for two, England were well on their way, with Richardson now forced to come in with 26 overs remaining. He began in tremendous style, with two fours off Botham through the covers and, although he was dropped by Lawrence off his own bowling when 20, he went for his shots so well that the 50 stand came up off 80 balls.

Haynes had been on the field for every ball of the match so far, although in this second innings he was naturally happy to give the strike away. I had given the odd thought during the day to a certain bet that was now in danger but, such was my disregard of the commentator's superstition that the best way to ensure a wicket is to say something to the contrary, that I drew attention to the chances of Haynes completing three full days on the field.

'If Haynes does survive the last 50 minutes today, his colleagues will be grateful for how he's batted all day while 11 have come and gone at the other end.' That was good enough. The next ball from Lawrence nipped back to strike him on the left knee-roll, and, two feet forward, he was given out LBW for 43 out of 125 for three. His 114 balls received were out of 262 bowled, and had he received even half-decent support during the day, the West Indies would not have been in such a desperate situation.

With DeFreitas feeling unwell and off the field, Geoffrey was full of praise for Lawrence, who worried Hooper in particular. 'He really has got up a head of steam. Gooch will have asked him for one burst and he's putting everything into it. It's a tremendous effort.'

At close of play, West Indies were 152 for three, and still 91 adrift at the end of the most remarkable day's play of the series. All credit to England for their bowling and catching, but it was the totally irresponsible approach, either side of lunch, of the West Indies batsmen, which gave Tufnell an analysis I doubt he will better in the rest of his Test career.

SUNDAY 11 AUGUST

This was the day which persuaded me of two things: Sunday Test cricket has a future in England, and I no longer consider a rest day in a Test match to be essential. A fourth successive capacity crowd proved the public demand, given the right match situation, and I also believe that the size of the crowd engendered an atmosphere to which the West Indies batsmen responded in a different manner than might have been the case before a typically sparse Monday, fourth-day crowd.

The fact that the Monday crowd was to be another capacity one was because the public came along to see the finale of a gripping contest which could end in any of the four possible results. My reservations about the abolition of rest days mainly concerned the extra mental and physical demands this could place on players, but a short conversation with Geoffrey persuaded me differently. He felt that aspect was exaggerated, and this final Test convinced me that continuity of play can add to the entertainment.

In any case, the rewards for Test players are so good that they must be prepared to make the odd sacrifice. The weather was overcast as Raymond named Tufnell as the key bowler: 'I thought he bowled a little too quickly yesterday, because there is plenty in this pitch for him, bowling from the Pavilion end.' How would the West Indies tackle the danger man? Slog or block? It did not take much working out, remembering how they went after Illingworth at Trent Bridge and Edgbaston, but the mental scar-tissue from their first innings was a prime inhibiting factor. Or was it?

Hooper could not have made a more positive start, with a violent, premeditated attack that would have won him any audition for the bugler at Balaklava. The first over went into Malcolm's scoresheet thus: 2-6 (over long-off)-1-·-1-3. Raymond immediately recommended a change in the field placings. 'They're obviously after him. I would drop mid-on right back, leave the gap and encourage them to try to play through there against the spin.'

Tony said: 'It wasn't a bad over – just excellent batting. I just caught sight of Botham going out of his way to have a quick word with Tufnell. That's what senior players should do . . . encourage and settle young players in situations like this.'

The two former England captains were adamant that the one fielder Tufnell did not need was the obligatory bat-pad man at silly mid-off, but it took another five balls of further mayhem before he retreated. Richardson took a single off the first ball of Tufnell's next over to bring Hooper back on strike. His ears went back and so did the ball, back over the bowler's head – this time over long-on for a six from what was a more desperate stroke, with Hooper never to the pitch of the spinning ball. A three and two singles made the first two overs of spin worth 25, and then Hooper launched himself at Lawrence.

A hook for six was described by Tony as 'brutal and beautiful', although nothing seems to deter the Gloucestershire fast bowler, and he made Hooper hop about with another bouncer in the same over. Occasionally, a brilliant innings appears from nowhere in Test cricket, and this was one of them. Having dropped anchor the previous evening, with 11 off 48 balls, the full-speed-ahead order he received that morning from the bridge was carried out so effectively that he hit 34 off the first 23 balls he received.

Tufnell and Lawrence were hit for 44 from their first seven overs, and when the 200 came up in the 64th over, the last 50 had come off 49 balls, compared with 125, 106 and 105 for the first three. It was exciting stuff, with the Sunday crowd swept up in the mood created by a counter-attack which, if sustained for another hour, would cause considerable damage to England's winning chances. I described Hooper's 50 off 82 balls, including three sixes and three fours as 'as exciting a half-century as we've seen in this series, with the last 39 coming off 34 balls.'

Still Gooch kept faith with Tufnell, and he got his reward when Hooper went to the well once too often. This time, he checked an off-drive and Gooch took the catch at short extra cover to produce extreme reactions from the England players. These varied from the acceptable joy of Gooch, Stewart, Botham and other fielders, to the unacceptable mouthings and gestures of the bowler. The sooner that cricketers like Tufnell realise that punishment and failure are not a personal slight on their ability, but part and parcel of the game, the better chance they have of maximising the use of their considerable talents.

Botham – you know, that quiet, even-tempered cricketer who rarely raises an eyebrow – waded in to quieten the young bowler down, as Hooper walked off, having scored 43 out of 53 off the bat in 50 minutes, to an ovation which continued, then increased, with the appearance of Richards. Piquantly, like

Bradman, he also needed a few runs to retire from Test cricket with a distinctive career average. The unique Australian walked the same path 43 years earlier, needing four runs to retire with a Test average of 100. On a lower, but still special, level, Richards needed 20 to maintain an average for the West Indies of over 50.

The West Indies captain's last of his 24 Test hundreds was his 110 against India in Kingston 27 months previously, and his last century against England – coincidentally also 110 – was in Antigua in April 1986, when he hit the fastest hundred in Test history. I was privileged to witness that innings, and if anyone doubts my statement that, in the tiny press box, we were still scanning the record books about the speed of his 50, when a roar told us he was now 100, this breakdown of the latter part of his staggering innings proves my point. He reached 53 with his second six off his 35th ball, after which he went:

2, 4, 4, 4, 1, 1, 2, ·, ·, 6, 6, 4, 6, 1, 2, ·, ·, 2, 1, ·, 4.

He and Richardson took their side into the lead just before lunch, although Richardson had two escapes. He played a ball from Tufnell on to Smith's shin at silly mid-off – a desperately difficult chance. But an even greater slice of luck came the Antiguan's way when he was given not out by umpire Kitchen after offering no stroke to one from Lewis which seemed to fulfil all the requirements of the LBW law. Gordon Greenidge admitted: 'I think Richie was a bit fortunate not to be given out.' Our high-square camera showed that the ball was not passing over the stumps, but again I emphasise that my comments are not a reflection on the umpiring abilities of a man who I firmly believe is among the top three umpires in English cricket.

He must be sure in his mind before he gives a batsman out, and whether or not our replays prove him right is not the point. We have hindsight and he does not. A cliche maybe, but a man who never made a mistake never made anything. Lewis bowled better than at any time in the match, with Botham emphasising his total integration into the side with a couple of pieces of advice and encouragement. Those critics who doubted his ability to fit into the Gooch regime were answered in the most comprehensive manner in this match, with responsible runs, intelligent bowling, splendid catching, and a visible on-field involvement with his captain and young bowlers.

Raymond drew on his experience with Leicestershire to assess Lewis: 'His strength, like Paddy Clift, is that he has plenty of variation of pace, with a whippy arm and hand action. He is not an out-and-out quick bowler, but he's capable of the occasional genuinely fast ball.'

Just before lunch, Richards drove Tufnell through mid-on and sprinted four runs which accomplished two things: the runs wiped out the first innings arrears, and also took Richards past 20, and earned him the guarantee of a retiring Test average of over 50. At lunch, the score was 249 for four, with

Richardson now 65, Richards 23, and the crowd still in a daze after two hours of attacking Test cricket at its best in which 97 runs came off 29 overs.

Lewis continued his best spell yet for England of 15 overs for 16 runs, and with DeFreitas also bowling well, the first hour of the afternoon session was a dog-fight. The new ball was due but, with the old one swinging so much, Gooch did not take it for ten overs.

It did the trick, albeit not in the orthodox manner. Richards, now 60, was starting to cut loose and, with the score 305 and the lead 62, the balance of the match was tilting back to parity – always assuming that the fifth-wicket partnership, now worth 97, could survive until tea.

Lawrence had been hammered off the back foot through mid-off for four, before Richards decided he wanted a drink, half an hour before the interval. He might deny his concentration suffered, but the next ball from Lawrence was his last. Lawrence had posted one man – Morris – at wide mid-on to guard the entire acreage in front of square on the leg side, only for Richards' final stroke in Test cricket to be drilled straight into the chest of his Glamorgan colleague.

The ball disappeared into safe hands and so, disgusted with himself, did Richards into the pavilion, with Keith cleverly pinpointing a boundary banner which read: 'Thanks Viv. We'll miss you.' His 60 included nine fours and 11 singles – evidence enough of his application and concentration which relaxed, fatally, just once. As Richards walked off, cap in one hand and the bat held high in the other to acknowledge the warm affection of the applause, Raymond said: 'One false stroke and Viv ruined all his hard work to give his side a chance of saving the match and perhaps even winning it.'

Dujon had a troubled 14 minutes at the crease in which he faced 13 out of 16 balls, including one sumptuous four through the covers before he too, like his captain a few minutes earlier, suffered a fatal break in concentration, although this time, the batsman was blameless.

A persistent pigeon had his eye and beak on a re-seeded part of the square, close to the pitch, which looked particularly fruitful, and defied efforts to shift him by Dujon and the England fielders for 93 seconds. That is a long time, especially when, twice, the batsman has vainly taken guard and prepared to face his next ball from Lawrence. When it was finally bowled, it was short and wide, but Dujon was drawn into a poor stroke, which edged a catch shoulder-high to the right of Stewart, who took it well. Richie was straight in: 'Caught pigeon, bowled Lawrence. He's been fiddling and fussing with that bird on the pitch and now he's gone.' Now why should that have sent Malcolm retreating into his private world of giggles?

At 311 for six, with the lead only 68, England were right on top but, if they needed a reminder, there was still Richardson to deal with. When Dujon was out, he had scored only 45 out of 159 since the start of play, but he raced to 99 with a hooked six and two fours through mid-on and the covers off Lawrence. Having already been out twice in Test matches for 99, the superstitious among us feared the worst when Malcolm mischievously revealed he had faced 222 balls, but a single, two balls later, secured his 14th Test hundred and his fourth against England.

He had then batted for nearly six hours and, while he was there, nothing could be taken for granted. Especially when, after nine overs of the final session had been bowled, four lights gleaming on the indicator beside the scoreboard were evidence enough of the poor light which brought an end to the day's play, with 27 overs still to be bowled.

The score was 356 for six, Richardson was 108 and Marshall 17, with the seventh-wicket partnership already worth 45. The truncated day was a good one for the West Indies – worth 204 runs for the loss of three wickets. The lead was 113, and overnight sums suggested that, with a minimum of 95 overs to be bowled on the final day, if West Indies could bat for at least 35 of them, England's victory target would pose twin difficulties regarding the total required and the run-rate.

Lawrence's two wickets in 12 deliveries were the bowling highlight of the day, although the performance of Lewis was encouraging, following his spirited come-back with the ball in the previous Edgbaston Test. Stewart's alert catch off Dujon was vindication of the selectors' decision to gamble with him, with his concentration and effectiveness undiminished during an innings which had already lasted for 119 overs.

MONDAY 12 AUGUST

The Glorious Twelfth took on a patriotic cricketing connotation within one minute of the start of the final day's play. DeFreitas bowled the first over from the Vauxhall end and thought he had Marshall first ball, LBW playing no stroke to one which the replays seemed to offer overwhelming support to the bowler. No matter, the next ball nipped back through an obliging 'gate' and the large crowd whooped their delight as the middle stump was taken out of the ground.

Possibly unnoticed by the crowd, but not by our camera crew and Keith, Botham quickly took the bowler away from his happy colleagues and had a quick and quiet word – presumably to quieten the obvious agitation about the first-ball decision, which was still bothering DeFreitas. The importance of an early wicket to the morale of both sides was considerable, so the impact made by a second one, two balls later, was a shattering one for the West Indies.

Ambrose was LBW to, arguably, the plumbest decision of the series, to complete a pair of two-ball ducks and provide DeFreitas with his 22nd wicket of the series. The two wickets in three deliveries eased my betting conscience a little because, after gritting my teeth during the first four days, at the end of which the West Indies were in their best position in the match, I had cravenly backed England before the start of play at what I thought were generous odds of 4–6. Other quotations of 2–5 were more realistic because, even without those two early wickets, England would expect to win more than six games out of ten from the overnight position.

Richardson now had the problem of trying to husband the strike, as well as score the minimum of 50 runs his bowlers needed to make a game of it, but a blow on the right little finger from a delivery in DeFreitas's second over, which went through the surface of the pitch and lifted nastily, made his task even more difficult and he twice needed treatment. Meanwhile, the antics of his partner might have amused the England players and the large crowd, but did little for Richardson's concentration. Walsh had come in in such a rush after the dramas of the first five balls of the day, that he had to return to the dressing-room for his box, and then make a second re-visit because he emerged, boxed up, but with only one batting glove.

The nearest thing to a Stewart error came with the score 368 for eight, when Walsh edged a ball from DeFreitas low to the right of the wicket-keeper, with the ball barely carrying at catchable height. With Richardson completely out of touch, it was left to Walsh to manufacture 14 of the 22 runs which accrued for the ninth wicket, before Lawrence gave himself some controversial ammunition for the Gloucestershire dressing-room in 1992, by getting his county colleague LBW to an inswinger which hit his back leg in line with leg stump.

Richardson was 'boxed' by DeFreitas, which brought from Gordon this explanation of the stages of pain a batsman goes through amid unfailing laughter from his partner and the fielders. 'It is very painful. You don't feel much to begin with ... then a warm feeling goes through your whole body. Your knees go weak and all you can do is fall to the ground.' Malcolm, already in danger of a convulsion, gave up the unequal struggle when, after attention to the unfortunate batsman, I volunteered to the viewers:'Three balls left.' I never did find out who muttered behind me, 'Must be badly swollen then.'

Lawrence took the last wicket – that of Richardson, who finally tried a lofted on-drive, only to see Gooch bring down a good catch, high and two-handed to his left. It was not a lucky wicket, because the ball swung in to take the stroke wider than intended and earn Lawrence his first five-wicket bag for England. Not only that, but a now fully-recovered Malcolm slipped the information to me that it was the first time the Gloucestershire bowler had taken more than two wickets in an innings for his country.

Without Richardson's innings of seven hours and 40 minutes, the game would already have been England's, but now they had to score 143 to square the series – in a minimum of 80 overs if you please. Richardson faced 44 of the 84 deliveries on the last day, but managed only 12 of the 29 runs added. It was a battling, rather than fluent, innings, as is shown by the fact that his 121 runs came out of 314 while he was at the crease.

During the break between innings, Tony asked Geoffrey his view of Richards. 'I think it's very simple. It has been a privilege to have played against him. My big regret is I never played with him – he makes batting so easy for his partner. He has been a dominant personality and a dominant player ... a truly great cricketer. That word is often misused by people but he's been one of the two finest batsmen I have ever seen – Sobers was the other. At his peak, he was so outstanding with hand and eye co-ordination ... he could see the ball so quickly and get into position a fraction quicker than everybody else. He was also such a violent striker of the ball, he could play some amazing strokes, and I'm glad he finished with an average of over 50.'

As Gooch and Morris walked out to bat, Tony related a chat he had had with Richards after the first day's play. 'Viv said that at five feet eight inches, Hugh should be trying to get under the bounce, and he'd have a better chance if he anchored his feet to the ground.'

In Patterson's first over, the point was emphasised by Geoffrey, following a rising ball to the left-hander. 'Morris has simply got to work out what to leave. Chest high you play it – half a yard shorter, it bounces shoulder or neck high, and that's the one that got him in trouble from Ambrose in the first innings. It is a very difficult one to play defensively, and he should be leaving it alone.'

The next ball came through throat high, and Morris reflexively jumped and gloved it high above the head of Dujon, who leapt to take a splendid catch – fittingly enough the one which took him past the figure of 269 Test victims of Alan Knott. The catch was his 272nd victim, but two of those were taken in the field.

Atherton came in to try to rescue something from the series, and ran positively with Gooch to take the score to 40 in the last over before lunch, before he was out with three balls to go. He did not get forward to a ball which Raymond said was of forward length, and Hooper took a fast-travelling catch off Patterson to make the home dressing-room a great deal more reflective than otherwise might have been the case.

Richards called on his best bowler, Ambrose, for a final effort but, for the first time in the series, there was no fire in the furnace. Smith and Gooch square-cut long-hops for four, and when the home captain hooked Ambrose for another four, his first six overs had cost 34. The crowd, easily the largest on the final day of a Test match in England for over 30 years, cheered the onslaught, and when Smith pulled Patterson for four, the scoreboard showed 75 for two off 12 overs, with the game all but won and lost.

The first four overs after lunch were hammered for 35, and the arrival of Marshall into the attack brought two things in his second over: a discussion between Tony and Gordon about the fast bowler's retirement, and a wicket next ball. Gooch played around a ball which came back to qualify for one of those hotly debated 'leg-stumpish' decisions which bowlers think themselves hard done by when the appeal is refused, and batsmen the same when it is upheld.

The rumbustious third-wicket stand was worth 40 from 45 deliveries, but much more than that in the switch of the psychological balance of the match . . . until, that is, Smith holed out four balls later to Patterson at mid-on off Walsh. His 26 included five fours off only 32 balls but, with two young men on nought, and 63 still needed to win, the relaxed atmosphere among the crowd was now wound up to an unbearable tension.

Another wicket then, and Richards must have fancied his chances, with Geoffrey almost drooling alongside me: 'This is Test-match cricket at its best. It's lovely. It is now a test of character as much as of ability and technique. Anyone who loves cricket wants to see fast bowlers tearing in, straining every sinew and nerve, and the batsmen fighting them off.' Anyone, that is, with the possible exception of Ramprakash and Stewart, and probably Botham and company as well.

The fifth-wicket pair braced themselves for the kitchen-sink treatment, with the crowd gasping with every tension-charged delivery. Stewart edged Walsh just short of Dujon, and Tony and Geoffrey both criticised Richards for posting a silly mid-off for the Surrey man, yet having no second slip on a pitch which still offered generous pace and bounce.

A sprinting Marshall beat Stewart on the outside with successive deliveries to bring from Raymond: 'I don't imagine the England dressing-room is too noisy right now . . . Ian Botham won't be waving his water-pistol around. A wicket now and the game will be wide open.'

What a time for two of the younger brigade to stand together on the bridge. In one sense, Stewart had been there before, because he was at the wicket with Larkins in Kingston on 1 March 1990 when the winning runs were hit, but this was a much tougher situation. Richie said: 'I wonder whether Mark Ramprakash realised when he made his debut on 6 June that, nine weeks later, on the last day of the last Test in the second session, he would be batting at the Oval with the hopes of his side squaring the series resting squarely on his shoulders. That's the sort of thing a young fellow dreams about.'

The runs dried to a trickle – three in four overs as Marshall wove a spell of 4-3-1-1, but Stewart refused to compromise his normal attacking game which, at Test level, had proved to be both his strength and weakness. He hammered Marshall for four through the covers, with Richie noting that 'he's the sort of player you've got to be prepared to take a bit of the cold with the hot.'

Ramprakash took 19 balls to score his first run, with Richards deciding that Ambrose had so far been too bad to be true. Back he came, to be greeted by two more cleanly struck strokes for four by Stewart – the cover drive was especially praised by Richie. It brought up the 100 in the 23rd over, with Malcolm finishing the series with a piece of real trivia. With England now back on course for victory, and Ambrose about to leave the field, wicketless for the first time in the series, our scorer revealed that the fast bowler's pair was the fifth by a West Indian at the Oval, following Everton Weekes, Herman Griffiths, Gerry Alexander and Jackie Hendriks. Now there is one for the Trivial Pursuit board.

Back came Patterson, but a 'Nelson' score of 111 for four proved unlucky for the bowler, with 17 streaming off his first two overs, thanks to leg-side fours from both batsmen helping bring up the 50 partnership, and encouraging the crowd to start singing. Echoing their celebratory mood, I paid this tribute to the selectors: 'They must be pleased with themselves. Any time they pick a side and it wins a Test is good, but when it is to square a series and they've chosen what they describe as a "high risk" team, and Stewart has been in the thick of it all through, then it really is a triumph.'

With one run needed, Richards brought on Lambert – perhaps as punishment for starting the downhill toboggan crash two days earlier. Ramprakash, who had earned the right to drive in the last nail, instead avoided finishing in the 20s for the eighth time in nine innings in the worst possible way. He pulled at and missed a straight one, to set up the sort of fairy-tale finish that has so many times been a feature of the career of Ian Terence Botham.

Never having played in a winning England side against the West Indies, here he was, striding to the middle, with helmet, and ample padding, a part-time bowler on, one run needed and 49 overs left. His appearance provided the perfect finish for the now wildly excited crowd, and he did it with the ultimate flourish – a four to fine leg off the only ball he faced. Stewart's forceful 38 included five fours off 51 balls faced, and the home win laid several statistical ghosts to rest.

The series was the first in eight between the two countries since 1973 which England had not lost, and also the first time since 1957 that they had won two games in a five-match series. A large number of the delighted crowd gathered in front of the pavilion for the awards ceremony, with the adjudicator, our Raymond, telling the throng that he had narrowed his award down to three men: Robin Smith, Phil Tufnell and Richie *Robinson*. We all do it, you see.

He gave it, rightly, to Smith, and the two managers made their reverse awards for the Man of the Series to Gooch and Ambrose. Of Gooch, Lance Gibbs said, 'I give it to him for leadership, superb batting and for making this summer a happy and memorable one.' Stewart praised Ambrose for 'high-quality pace bowling in each Test, and for usually following a bouncer with a beaming smile.'

Richards held on to the Wisden Trophy, and said to Tony: 'It is a little sad to lose, but we can't feel that way because we have to give credit to England for the way they've played and it has been a sporting series. It's a draw but cricket was the winner. Thanks to Graham for the spirit in which it has been played, and I think we've put to rest a few bad vibes.' He then made an oblique reference to his team's recent series against Australia: 'I hope this extends to other sides in the future.'

Gooch contented himself with saying: 'It has been a tremendously hard-fought series, and I am pleased with the way we hung on when things went against us.'

I wrote in Tuesday's *Birmingham Post*:

The England selection committee is entitled to stick out its collective chest after yesterday's marvellous win at the Oval. Alec Stewart is one of nature's truculent and abrasive characters, and I bet he got huge pleasure in stuffing a few thousand words down the throats of a few correspondents, including this one. He kept wicket adequately, missed nothing and took a fine catch off Tufnell to dismiss Richards.

West Indies had the maddest hour imaginable on Saturday and paid the penalty. England's performance throughout a bruising summer, which was still played in the best spirit of any of the previous six series in the 1980s, was one of guts and resilience. That is what the West Indies were short of on Saturday, and that is why the series ended all square.

Farewell to Richards and hello to Botham. Excitement, entertainment, cour-age, nostalgia – and the right result. The perfect Test match.

From 6 June to 12 August – fittingly Deliverance Day to the Glorious Twelfth – the series was a pleasure to commentate upon. Except for a certain ante-post voucher!

ENGLAND v WEST INDIES
at the Oval on 8, 9, 10, 11, 12 August 1991

ENGLAND		Runs	Balls	Mins		Runs	Balls	Mins
* G. A. Gooch	lbw b Ambrose	60	132	207	lbw b Marshall	29	43	76
H. Morris	c Lambert b Ambrose	44	130	187	c Dujon b Patterson	2	5	8
M. A. Atherton	c Hooper b Walsh	0	4	6	c Hooper b Patterson	13	17	32
R. A. Smith	lbw b Marshall	109	256	352	c Patterson b Walsh	26	32	40
M. R. Ramprakash	c Lambert b Hooper	25	78	109	lbw b Lambert	19	58	89
†A. J. Stewart	c Richardson b Patterson	31	106	118	not out	38	51	86
I. T. Botham	hit wicket b Ambrose	31	82	131	not out	4	1	1
C. C. Lewis	not out	47	90	112				
P. A. J. DeFreitas	c Dujon b Walsh	7	29	40				
D. V. Lawrence	c Richards b Walsh	9	34	35				
P. C. R. Tufnell	c Haynes b Patterson	2	16	13				
Extras	(b 8,lb 10,w 1,nb 35)	54			(b 4,w 1,nb 10)	15		
TOTAL	(151.1 overs; 661 mins)	419			(31.4 overs; 169 mins)	146 (for 5 wkts)		

WEST INDIES		Runs	Balls	Mins		Runs	Balls	Mins
D. L. Haynes	not out	75	198	282	lbw b Lawrence	43	114	170
P. V. Simmons	lbw b Lawrence	15	36	66	c Lewis b Botham	36	83	89
R. B. Richardson	c Stewart b Botham	20	47	71	(4) c Gooch b Lawrence	121	312	460
C. L. Hooper	c Stewart b DeFreitas	3	4	4	(5) c Gooch b Tufnell	54	88	94
C. B. Lambert	c Ramprakash b Tufnell	39	49	79	(3) lbw b Botham	14	25	22
†P. J. L. Dujon	lbw b Lawrence	0	1	6	(7) c Stewart b Lawrence	5	14	14
M. D. Marshall	c Botham b Tufnell	0	6	13	(8) b DeFreitas	17	28	52
* I. V. A. Richards	c Stewart b Tufnell	2	7	17	(6) c Morris b Lawrence	60	105	165
C. E. L. Ambrose	c Botham b Tufnell	0	2	2	lbw b DeFreitas	0	2	2
C. A. Walsh	c Gooch b Tufnell	0	2	2	lbw b Lawrence	14	29	48
B. P. Patterson	c Botham b Tufnell	2	7	9	not out	1	7	13
Extras	(lb 9,nb 11)	20			(b 7,lb 5,w 2,nb 6)	20		
TOTAL	(57.3 overs; 282 mins)	176			(132.5 overs; 572 mins)	385		

WEST INDIES	O	M	R	W	O	M	R	W
Ambrose	36	8	83	0	8	0	48	0
Patterson	25.1	3	87	2	9	0	63	2
Walsh	32	5	91	3	9	3	18	1
Marshall	24	5	62	1	5	3	9	1
Hooper	34	1	78	1				
Lambert					0.4	0	4	1

ENGLAND	O	M	R	W	O	M	R	W
DeFreitas	13	6	38	1	20	9	42	2
Lawrence	16	1	67	2	25.5	4	106	5
Tufnell	14.3	3	25	6	46	6	150	1
Botham	11	4	27	1	16	4	40	2
Lewis	3	1	10	0	25	12	35	0

FALL OF WICKETS				
	ENG	WI	WI	ENG
1st	112	52	53	3
2nd	114	95	71	40
3rd	120	98	125	80
4th	188	158	208	80
5th	263	160	305	142
6th	336	161	311	
7th	351	172	356	
8th	386	172	356	
9th	411	172	378	
10th	419	176	385	

Toss: England
Umpires: J. W. Holder & M. J. Kitchen
Man of the Match: R. A. Smith
RESULT: ENGLAND WON BY 5 WICKETS

ENGLAND v WEST INDIES

ENGLAND
BATTING AVERAGES - Including fielding

Name	Matches	Inns	NO	Runs	HS	Avge	100s	50s	Ct/St
R. A. Smith	4	7	2	416	148*	83.20	2	2	2
C. C. Lewis	2	3	1	125	65	62.50	-	1	3
G. A. Gooch	5	9	1	480	154*	60.00	1	2	6
M. R. Ramprakash	5	9	0	210	29	23.33	-	-	4
P. A. J. DeFreitas	5	8	1	134	55*	19.14	-	1	1
D. R. Pringle	4	7	0	128	45	18.28	-	-	1
D. V. Lawrence	2	3	0	47	34	15.66	-	-	-
R. K. Illingworth	2	4	2	31	13	15.50	-	-	1
A. J. Lamb	4	7	0	88	29	12.57	-	-	7
H. Morris	2	4	0	50	44	12.50	-	-	1
G. A. Hick	4	7	0	75	43	10.71	-	-	8
R. C. Russell	4	7	0	73	46	10.42	-	-	5
M. A. Atherton	5	9	0	79	32	8.77	-	-	3
D. E. Malcolm	2	3	1	9	5*	4.50	-	-	1
S. L. Watkin	2	3	0	8	6	2.66	-	-	-

Played in one Test: I. T. Botham 31, 4* (3 ct); A. J. Stewart 31, 38* (4 ct); P. C. R. Tufnell 2.

BOWLING AVERAGES

Name	Overs	Mdns	Runs	Wkts	Avge	Best	5wI	10woM
P. A. J. DeFreitas	185.5	55	457	22	20.77	4-34	-	-
P. C. R. Tufnell	60.3	9	175	7	25.00	6-25	1	-
D. R. Pringle	128.1	33	322	12	26.83	5-100	1	-
S. L. Watkin	36	4	153	5	30.60	3-38	-	-
C. C. Lewis	79	30	201	6	33.50	6-111	1	-
D. V. Lawrence	78.1	7	350	10	35.00	5-106	1	-
R. K. Illingworth	56.4	10	213	4	53.25	3-110	-	-

Also bowled: I. T. Botham 27-8-67-3; G. A. Gooch 8-1-14-0; G. A. Hick 24-5-95-2; D. E. Malcolm 42.3-3-180-3.

WEST INDIES
BATTING AVERAGES - Including fielding

Name	Matches	Inns	NO	Runs	HS	Avge	100s	50s	Ct/St
R. B. Richardson	5	10	1	495	121	55.00	2	3	4
I. V. A. Richards	5	8	1	376	80	53.71	-	5	4
D. L. Haynes	5	10	3	323	75*	46.14	-	3	2
C. L. Hooper	5	9	2	271	111	38.71	1	2	9
A. L. Logie	4	5	0	120	78	24.00	-	1	4
M. D. Marshall	5	7	1	116	67	19.33	-	1	-
P. V. Simmons	5	10	0	181	38	18.10	-	-	4
P. J. L. Dujon	5	7	0	89	33	12.71	-	-	17
C. A. Walsh	5	7	0	66	18	9.42	-	-	-
B. P. Patterson	3	5	3	11	5*	5.50	-	-	1
C. E. L. Ambrose	5	7	0	37	17	5.28	-	-	-
I. B. A. Allen	2	2	2	5	4*	-	-	-	1

Played in one Test: C. B. Lambert 39, 14 (2 ct).

BOWLING AVERAGES

Name	Overs	Mdns	Runs	Wkts	Avge	Best	5wI	10woM
C. E. L. Ambrose	249	68	560	28	20.00	6-52	2	-
M. D. Marshall	172.1	36	442	20	22.10	4-33	-	-
B. P. Patterson	117.3	20	389	13	29.92	5-81	1	-
C. A. Walsh	187	42	493	15	32.86	4-64	-	-
I. B. A. Allen	47	4	180	5	36.00	2-69	-	-

Also bowled: C. L. Hooper 64-13-137-2; C. B. Lambert 0.4-0-4-1; I. V.A. Richards 5-1-6-0; P. V. Simmons 3-0-7-0.

CHAPTER EIGHT

THE
WINNING
HABIT

ENGLAND v SRI LANKA LORD'S
22–27 AUGUST

THURSDAY 22 AUGUST

With Atherton shortly to enter hospital for a back operation, the England selectors had a simple job to pick a side for the third-ever Test match in England against Sri Lanka. As promised to him, they brought Russell back to keep wicket, with Stewart promoted to number three, following his two valuable innings at the Oval. Pringle was omitted but, with Botham batting at number six, Gooch could still field a five-man attack.

With the touring parties for New Zealand, the World Cup and the 'A' tour of West Indies to be chosen on 9 September, there was little chance of the sixth Test match of the summer becoming an anti-climax – certainly not as far as the England players were concerned. Nor for the public after the first day, when England limped their way to 229 for six off 74 overs before they were glad to take the offer of light with 16 overs remaining, although it started to rain ten minutes later.

Of the chosen XI, only Gooch, Smith, Russell, Lewis, Ramprakash, DeFreitas and Tufnell could be considered near-automatic selections for the senior tour, which the critics of the 'guarantee' contracts to seven named players four months earlier could claim as proof of what they believed to be a flawed scheme. Of the seven, Atherton and Fraser were both awaiting serious operations to try to cure long-standing injuries to back and hip respectively, while the form of Lamb and Malcolm had declined so sharply that they both failed to survive the series against the West Indies.

Dexter made a counterpoint that the two injured players could concentrate fully on regaining fitness, unworried about the financial shortfall if they failed, while Lamb and Malcolm could similarly play themselves back into contention in county cricket, free of worry about their short-term future. Raymond said: 'I think £140,000 is too much money to pay out so far in advance. If players want to go on tours that the Board disapprove of, then they should be told they won't get picked. After all, there are plenty of players who want to play for England above all else, and the top players are well paid by their counties anyway.'

When Gooch won the toss, the crowd of 7000 settled down in warm sunshine to watch the home batsmen enjoy themselves, but the lively medium-pace outswing of Ratnayake posed so many problems in the pre-lunch session that a score of 94 for one represented one of the biggest cricketing injustices of the summer. Bowling from the Pavilion end, which encourages more movement into the right-hander than the other way, in his first 14 balls he had two desperately close LBW decisions go against him, beat the outside edge six times and was also edged for four. Gooch was the main sufferer, with two deliveries that beat the outside edge, moving at least six inches against the slope after pitching.

As for the LBW rulings, neither Gooch nor Morris played a stroke at deliveries which came back a lot, and the bowler will have decisions in his favour which look less plumb. Morris was the first England batsman to come under the microscope, with his wish to play his natural game tempered by the high stakes on offer. Raymond asked Keith for a high-square view of his stance. 'He has quite a wide spread, which is why he finds it difficult to get on to the balls of his feet against the quicks.'

Gooch became so frustrated at his inability to hit the ball properly that it was unsurprising when he gave a waist-high return catch to Ramanayake, to be out for 38 in the 21st over, with the score now 70 for one. Stewart and Morris added 44, albeit with no great conviction, before Ratnayake got the wicket he deserved. He moved one back to Morris and, this time, Hampshire gave him the LBW decision. The dismissal left the Glamorgan opener still in no-man's land with the selectors, with his winter plans now largely dependent upon his second innings.

Cricket being the peculiar game it is, the Sri Lankans began to take the wickets they earlier deserved, even though the movement had diminished, and took three good wickets in 23 balls for six runs. Smith, who must have found it difficult to wind up his concentration against bowling which was, relatively speaking, powder-puff stuff compared with that of the well-known demolition squad of Ambrose and company, was out to his eighth ball and Ramprakash to his fifth.

For two batsmen who, between them, had stood up to the West Indies fast bowling for 36½ hours to be knocked over in 13 minutes was the equivalent of surviving 15 rounds with Mike Tyson at his best, and then being flattened by a featherweight with one hand tied behind his back.

Smith got a nice outswinger from which he just failed to withdraw, and wicket-keeper Tillekaratne took a good low catch. Ramprakash was turned too chest-on by an outswinger from Hathurusinghe for the forcing off-side stroke he tried, and Mahanama held on to a fast-travelling catch at second slip to give the bowler his first Test wicket.

Identification and pronunciation of the Sri Lankans posed more problems than usual in the commentary box, with Raymond hoping before the game that the real tongue-twisters would either have nick-names or would not play. Tony, mischievously, said of Ramprakash's dismissal: 'I didn't quite see who caught that Raymond, did you?' The unabashed reply was: 'No, and neither did I.'

A score of 120 for four was not quite a crisis for Botham, but it gave him ample opportunity to play the sort of innings which would give him back his number six spot for the foreseeable future. Stewart had his luck, especially when he hooked a bouncer from Ratnayake to Kapila Wije-gunawardene at long leg, only for the catch to go down. If only the fielder had kept his hands together for as long as it took Raymond to pronounce his name . . .

Botham, sans helmet, hit four fours in a bright innings of 22 off 33 balls, but an off-stump bouncer from Ramanayake induced a mis-hooked top edge to Mahanama in the slips with the score now 160 for five. Stewart reached his fourth half-century for England, with the help of a comedy of footwork errors by two fielders on the square-leg boundary which they could rehearse for a week and still never repeat.

Skipper Aravinda de Silva did not turn to spin for 61 overs, but Don Anurasiri dismissed Lewis with his first ball – a wide delivery which turned to take the edge and give de Silva a smart catch. Russell joined Stewart, who was now starting to sniff that elusive first Test hundred, and the two England wicket-keepers improved the score to 229 for six when bad light intervened to end a day which surprised England, the crowd and, probably, Sri Lanka as well.

FRIDAY 23 AUGUST

Rain so badly interfered with the second day's play that only 35 overs were bowled, and Stewart had to wait for over four hours on 96, before Lawrence safely sprinted a near-suicidal single to give him his hundred. Russell and DeFreitas were both bowled by this time, but it was Stewart's day. He scored 37 of England's 53 runs and, as his figures of 240 balls faced in 308 minutes show, his innings showed welcome patience and concentration.

Stewart now needs to build on that innings – at county as well as at international level. It is a poor reflection on his ability to make better use of his talents that it was only his 18th first-class hundred in 300 innings, but he can look at his side's first innings scorecard, and reflect that, without his innings, the result of the game would have been different.

Ratnayake cleaned up the tail to finish with good figures of 27-4-69-5 – the fifth time in 19 Tests he has secured a five-wicket haul. Only medium pace, he hits the seam and swings the ball from a good line. By build and method he is a good support bowler, and it is to his credit that he gets such good results.

The last hour of the day offered some of the best entertainment of the summer, with de Silva hitting seven fours in a marvellous exhibition of slashing strokeplay, which brought him 42 off 30 balls out of his side's 75 for two in 14 overs. With DeFreitas taking both wickets in consecutive overs, the tourists were in serious trouble at 22 for two – until the arrival of de Silva, who waded into Lawrence and Lewis so violently that 47 came off their seven overs.

SATURDAY 24 AUGUST

Main interest overnight concerned the winter plans of Botham, with doubts expressed about his availability for the entire senior trip of three months to New Zealand and Australia. By chance, I gave him a lift back to his hotel that evening and our conversation, then off the record, led me to believe he would go if allowed to join the party towards the end of January. The popular view in the national press was that the selectors should insist on all or nothing, but a perfectly reasonable compromise was announced two weeks later.

The Saturday crowd was the biggest of the match – 13,000 – and it saw Gooch take a firm grip of the game, with a rapid, unbeaten 60 out of the close-of-play score of 100 for one, increasing the overall lead to 158. The England captain was at his most majestic after DeFreitas's best bowling performance of 26-8-70-7 proved too much for every batsman except Hathurusinghe and Ratnayake.

The Lancashire bowler was helped by two stunning catches in the gully by Lewis and Smith in the first hour of play, and when Lawrence had Tillekeratne caught by Morris at short leg off bat and pad, the score was 139 for six, and the contest becoming ominously one-sided. Ratnayake is a remarkably uncomplicated batsman who blocks anything that is not of full length, and wallops what is. The crowd loved it, as did they the earnest entreaties from his partner to 'cool it' after each uninhibited swing of the bat. Ratnayake would nod, then simply give the same treatment to the next ball if it was pitched up, and he followed this recipe so successfully that he scored 52 out of 74, the biggest partnership of the innings, before he was softened up and yorked by DeFreitas.

The all-rounder's runs came off 55 balls and he hit seven fours in a performance that earned him applause as he walked off that was a well-earned recognition of an authentic Test-match counter-attacking innings. The problem facing Sri Lanka is, at present, apparently insuperable. They cannot sustain a competitive effort in five-day Tests without much more experience, which is denied them by other countries because they have no strength in depth.

MONDAY 26 AUGUST

This Test would have been a better one with no rest day, if only because a much larger crowd on Sunday, compared with Monday, would have enjoyed the sight of Gooch at his best. He reached his 15th hundred for England – six of them at Lord's – off 173 balls, and destroyed an attack which conceded 264 runs before tea at over five runs per over. He even paraded a series of reverse sweeps when the left-arm slow bowler, Anurasiri, bowled over the wicket to six fielders on the leg side, and on one occasion turned round to attempt an authentic left-handed pull.

When Stewart was caught at point for 43 out of 136 added for the second-wicket partnership, Gooch stepped up another gear, hitting his last 74 runs off 79 balls and, with Smith helping himself to 63 off 90 balls, Gooch declared half an hour before tea, leaving Sri Lanka 423 to win. His tour-de-force was the seventh time he has passed 150 in Test cricket, and, although he was probably unaware of it, he had then passed the aggregate of Hutton and Bradman on his way to becoming the 13th man to score 7000 Test runs, with every chance of overtaking Cowdrey's 7624 by the end of the 1992 English season, and thus becoming the third heaviest English run-scorer behind Boycott and Gower.

Lewis and Tufnell dismissed the Sri Lankan openers in the final session to leave the tourists on 79 for two, with victory a mathematical possibility, but not much more. Until they find a way of producing cricketers who are capable of influencing a Test match — and that is difficult without extensive international experience — Sri Lanka can only wait in the wings for the sort of walk-on parts which might entertain, but are of little assistance to their ambition for meatier roles.

TUESDAY 27 AUGUST

Tufnell took four and Lawrence two of the eight wickets to fall in 66 overs by teatime. Russell and Lawrence made their debut in this same fixture in 1988, and it was therefore fitting when, in their 25th and fourth appearance for England respectively, they combined to dismiss the dangerous de Silva, who gloved a leg-sided catch, to make the score 119 for four, and give Tufnell ample scope to work his way through the middle-lower order.

Jayasuriya hit cleanly for 66 from 70 balls, but the only other noteworthy feature was a clutch of dropped catches, including one to Gooch and three much harder ones to Lewis. Ten batsmen reached double figures — more evidence of a potential that will remain unfulfilled until the International Cricket Council resolves their Catch-22 situation. Tufnell bowled his first 27 overs of the day without a break and showed that, on this evidence, he has much more variety than any other slow bowler in English cricket. If he can harness his fast bowler's temperament, he should enjoy a productive Test career.

Botham's two slip catches took his total for England to 117, three behind the top England catcher, Cowdrey, and his two-match return to the England side was successful, albeit without a whiff of the fireworks which illuminated many of his previous 97 Tests. Unfortunately, his presence at the Oval and Lord's did little to solve the seemingly eternal problem of balance for Gooch and Stewart. His bowling is useful, but only worth a fifth bowling place unless conditions are helpful, as they were at Headingley and Edgbaston. The nettle must be grasped by batting him at number six, with a specialist wicket-keeper behind him, and Stewart taking his chance as a front-line batsman.

Records mean little to Gooch, but the fact that England had now won two consecutive Tests for only the third time in 63 games (the other instances were against Australia at Edgbaston and the Oval in 1985, and against New Zealand at Edgbaston and India at Lord's in 1990), pleased him. 'We are now pulling together as a side and we are believing in ourselves once again. Our general attitude was not up to standard in Australia, but that has improved and the players this summer got their rewards. At this level, nothing short of 100 percent effort and commitment is good enough, and we must keep that spirit going for the winter.'

Gooch has many strengths as a man, not least of which is a matter-of-fact approach to cricket which has a calming effect on his side. When he describes innings like his 333 against India in 1990, and his 154 against the West Indies at Headingley as 'OK. Satisfying, a great thrill' and the win at the Oval as 'a good effort', he does much to even out the mental highs and lows which can destabilise a Test dressing-room. The metamorphosis, from the man who resigned the Essex captaincy in 1987 because of its effect on his batting, into the most inspirational captain of England since Brearley, is a remarkable one, and a tribute to one of the most selfless cricketers in the modern game.

Who better than Richie to pay a final tribute to Gooch? 'Graham Gooch produced a remarkable turnabout in captaincy success during the season. As a side issue, he led Essex to the Championship, and in the Test arena he was tremendous. Rarely have I seen a team so demoralised by defeat [against Australia] make such a brilliant comeback so quickly. It was a great performance, and it was because of Gooch's wonderful leadership that it happened.'

ENGLAND v SRI LANKA
at Lord's on 22, 23, 24, 26, 27 August 1991

ENGLAND		*Runs*	*Balls*	*Mins*		*Runs*	*Balls*	*Mins*
* G. A. Gooch	c & b Ramanayake	38	70	88	b Anurasiri	174	253	327
H. Morris	lbw b Ratnayake	42	97	160	c Mahanama b Anurasiri	23	71	105
A. J. Stewart	not out	113	240	304	c De Silva b Anurasiri	43	100	137
R. A. Smith	c Tillekaratne b Ratnayake	4	8	9	not out	63	90	111
M. R. Ramprakash	c Mahanama b Hathurusinghe	0	5	5				
I. T. Botham	c Mahanama b Ramanayake	22	33	42				
C. C. Lewis	c De Silva b Anurasiri	11	25	34				
† R. C. Russell	b Anurasiri	17	50	64	(5) not out	12	11	27
P. A. J. DeFreitas	b Ratnayake	1	33	32				
D. V. Lawrence	c & b Ratnayake	3	18	25				
P. C. R. Tufnell	lbw b Ratnayake	0	4	8				
Extras	(b 9,lb 8,nb 14)	31			(b 15,lb 23,w 1,nb 10)	49		
TOTAL	(95 overs; 394 mins)	282			364 (3 wkts dec)			

SRI LANKA		*Runs*	*Balls*	*Mins*		*Runs*	*Balls*	*Mins*
D. S. B. P. Kuruppu	b DeFreitas	5	11	12	lbw b Lewis	21	76	103
U. C. Hathurusinghe	c Tufnell b DeFreitas	66	201	281	c Morris b Tufnell	25	77	109
A. P. Gurusinha	lbw b DeFreitas	4	8	15	b Tufnell	34	74	97
* P. A. De Silva	c Lewis b DeFreitas	42	32	33	c Russell b Lawrence	18	91	116
R. S. Mahanama	c Russell b Botham	2	11	13	c Botham b Tufnell	15	49	68
S. T. Jayasuriya	c Smith b DeFreitas	11	7	9	c Russell b Lewis	66	70	115
† H. P. Tillekaratne	c Morris b Lawrence	20	52	76	b Tufnell	16	60	62
R. J. Ratnayake	b DeFreitas	52	55	72	c sub (‡) b Lawrence	17	34	36
C. P. H. Ramanayake	lbw b DeFreitas	0	3	5	not out	34	57	93
K. I. W. Wijeguna'ene	not out	6	27	46	c Botham b DeFreitas	4	8	12
S. D. Anurasiri	b Lawrence	1	4	11	lbw b Tufnell	16	29	46
Extras	(lb 15)	15			(b 1,lb 16,nb 2)	19		
TOTAL	(68.1 overs; 295 mins)	224			(103.3 overs; 439 mins)	285		

SRI LANKA	O	M	R	W	O	M	R	W
Ratnayake	27	4	69	5	26	4	91	0
Ramanayake	24	5	75	2	20	2	86	0
Wijegunawardene	10	1	36	0	2	0	13	0
Hathurusinghe	17	6	40	1				
Anurasiri	17	4	45	2	36.1	8	135	3
Jayasuriya					1	0	1	0

ENGLAND	O	M	R	W	O	M	R	W
DeFreitas	26	8	70	7	22	8	45	1
Lawrence	15.1	3	61	2	23	7	83	2
Lewis	10	5	29	0	18	4	31	2
Botham	10	3	26	1	6	2	15	0
Tufnell	7	2	23	0	34.3	14	94	5

FALL OF WICKETS				
	ENG	SRI	ENG	SRI
1st	70	12	78	50
2nd	114	22	217	50
3rd	119	75	322	111
4th	120	86		119
5th	160	105		159
6th	183	139		212
7th	246	213		212
8th	258	213		241
9th	276	220		253
10th	282	224		285

Toss: England
Umpires: H. D. Bird & J. H. Hampshire
Man of the Match: G. A. Gooch
RESULT: ENGLAND WON BY 137 RUNS

‡ (I. D. K. Salisbury)

CHAPTER NINE

THE

WIND-UP

This was the day when the lively bubbling, daily brew concocted by Keith in the scanner van, and served by Tony on air, finally boiled over, with our presenter uttering the F-word to about four million viewers, when he mistakenly thought he was off-air. The ultimate nightmare for any broadcaster — to have a live microphone when he thinks it is dead — thus became a reality during the lunch interval of Warwickshire's home NatWest Trophy semi-final against Hampshire, with the private airwaves between Edgbaston and the BBC studios in London immediately as blue as were the public ones minutes earlier.

The scanner van is really an autoclave on wheels and, having worked extensively for South African television, I never cease to marvel at the relative peace and quiet in which Keith and Alan organise the sharp end of our commentary work. Even so, the odd raised voice 'beneath stairs' is not unusual, with the on-duty producer at full stretch to co-ordinate the efforts of all departments, including the commentary box, nine cameras, sound, videotape, computer, captions and the London studio. It is an enormously taxing exercise, to which an extra dimension is added when one of us has to hand back to base for news, to Grandstand, or hand over to golf, tennis, or racing.

This time, the fall-guy was Anthony Robert, perched on top of the quaint Edgbaston pavilion, with several minutes to fill before he handed back to London just before 1pm. With him was Geoffrey, one of whose tasks was to draw the winner of BBC television's 'Catch of the Season' competition, for which there were over 70,000 entries. The problems confronting Tony were immediate and several. His monitors, never overly sharp in daylight, were a faint blur in the bright sunshine. His earpiece crackled with instructions to him, as well as two-way talk with London about the hand-over which he found more distracting than usual.

Under the firm impression that time was short and precious, he ushered Geoffrey through the wickets of the morning – invisible on the monitors – and the draw, not made easier by the generous Yorkshireman drawing, not one winner, but a whole handful. Tony smoothed things over, and was all but ready to breast the tape when, having had the hurry-up for most of the chat, suddenly he was told he had nearly a minute to fill. At the end of as traumatic an in-vision piece as he did all summer, he finally wished the viewers 'goodbye' and then fell head-first into the largest minefield of all.

A producer controlling the hand-over back to base can give it a 'slow mix', especially if, as happened this time, the presenter gets out a few seconds early on the final countdown of 15 seconds. The blue touch-paper was thus ignited, with the sun-lit monitor screen providing the fatal combustible ingredient. Unable to see that the screen was still full of Edgbaston, and not the newsroom, Tony believed he was off-air and, as he went to unhook the microphone clipped to his tie, gave vent to his feelings with 'for f***s sake.'

London and Keith spent the break discussing the immediate action to be taken to reassure the viewers that Tony was not a graduate from the Kenneth Tynan school of broadcasting. As a result, he apologised soon after lunch 'for an unguarded and off-the-cuff remark which may have caused offence'.

A full written report from Tony and Keith to Headquarters was required, after which our unwitting offender received sympathetic reassurance from on high that the slip was understandable, if not justifiable, and that was the end of an unfortunate incident which hammered home to us all that the microphone can be the deadliest weapon.

I wrote the following comment in the *Birmingham Post*:

> The exasperated three-word utterance which was heard all over the country came after several minutes of bedlam behind the scenes, to which he had to listen through his earpiece, while the other ear was attuned to Geoffrey Boycott. In addition, the part of his brain that, by this time, was not addled, was desperately

trying to engage gear with his mouth, to convince Mr and Mrs Viewer that they were watching another smooth interval production.

I have done my share of these by-the-seat-of-my-pants exercises with Messrs West and Lewis, and my admiration for their unflappability is unwavering. Occasionally, you can tell that something has gone wrong, but you do not know what, and the only sign is that their eyes glaze as they look through you. Some similar misunderstanding occurred between Lewis and Bannister in 1987 when I used a phrase 'margin for error' which was interpreted as the name of a non-existent player, Martin Ferreira.

All I can tell viewers is that the next time you watch your screen and see your presenter smoothly tell you all about the past, present and future, spare a thought for his mind, ears and mouth, which are trying to listen to and make sense of instructions, suggestions and conversations coming from all directions into his earpiece. The remarkable thing is that it goes wrong so rarely.

The episode was widely covered in Thursday's national press, with Tony ruefully saying, after reading one particular tabloid which rarely falls into the trap of understating anything: 'Now I know I'm famous . . . making Page Three, with my photo between a serial killer and a convicted drug dealer.'

Our other non-Test days – although 'AR' might argue that day provided the biggest test of all – included two trips to Southampton to chart Hampshire's progress to their first 60-over final, with wins over Lancashire and Yorkshire, and both one-day finals, although our Benson & Hedges coverage of Worcestershire's defeat of Lancashire was limited to a highlights package, because the live coverage was handled by Sky Television.

People often wonder on what basis the earlier rounds of the knockout competitions are selected for coverage. As a general rule, the larger Test match grounds, if possible, are avoided, in order to spread the screening of cricket around the country. When we cover both semi-finals, we have two commentators instead of three, because there is less live airtime, with two matches sharing the telecast. Usually we also have two summarisers, although as Raymond will feelingly tell you, he has done the odd game single-handed.

On that blue Edgbaston day, Tony could well have been at the Oval, where the in-vision site is less vulnerable to sunlight but, saying that is akin to the old saying that, if your aunt was differently equipped here and there, she would have been your uncle. By far the most stimulating and, at times, exciting part of Tony's work is the teatime interview, when he comes face-to-face with a broad spectrum of people, mostly from the worlds of cricket and entertainment. Rory Bremner and Tim Rice are regular and popular subjects, and the 1991 summer also brought delightful contributions from Alan Coren and Terry Wogan. The chairman of the Test & County Cricket Board's cricket sub-committee, Ossie Wheatley, made two appearances to debate the merits of four-day cricket earlier in the season and, in August, the serious problems posed to his Board by declining over-rates in one-day cricket which seriously affected two of the season's televised showpiece games.

It is a toss-up in our box who is first to turn puce when a side seemingly does not care if it exceeds the maximum time allowed to bowl its 55 or 60 overs, of 205 or 225 minutes respectively. For some time I have campaigned vigorously for the penalties to be increased substantially from the derisory level of £100 per over not bowled by curfew time. Those waverers at Board level who were still not convinced after the 1991 Benson & Hedges Cup final that the players were prepared to fork out a few hundred pounds, if the tactical reward was big enough, were as appalled as the rest of us at the awful perform-ance of Surrey and Northamptonshire in their NatWest semi-final at the Oval on 14 and 15 August.

An 18,000 crowd was denied their right to the climax of a result on the first day when, despite 34 overs of spin, the game could not be finished because of fading light approaching 7.30pm, with six of the day's 120 overs still to be bowled. After extenuating circumstances were taken into account, Surrey were fined £500 and Northants £100. These amounts, shared between 12 players, are derisory. Richie and I worked out a scale of fines, escalating throughout the competition as the money at stake increases. We reckoned that the minimum fines in those later stages of the competitions should be £1000 per over, and Keith was able to screen our proposals during the discussion between present and past Glamorgan chairmen, Messrs Lewis and Wheatley, during the Sri Lanka Test. Wheatley, one of the more long-sighted administra-tors in cricket, was basically in our corner, which is why the level of fines for the 1992 season was discussed at great length at the winter and spring Board meetings, with every indication they would be somewhere near our suggested scale of penalties.

Cricket might be a changing game, but I cannot stomach the fact that, whereas the early Gillette finals were of 65 overs duration, and finished in good time, players now find it too demanding to bowl 120 overs in seven and a half hours. Whether the modern player believes it or not, captains of the 1960s like Micky Stewart, Mike Smith, Colin Cowdrey and Brian Close, not to mention Ray Illingworth, Jack Bond and Mike Brearley from the 1970s, did actually indulge in the odd tactical consideration, but rarely at the expense of an acceptable over-rate. Whatever the cognoscenti of our commentary box did not achieve in 1991, if we have played any part in the reversal of a decline in over-rates, so insidious that players and public hardly realised what had happened in the last decade, then the game will be better for it – to everyone. Players, umpires, commentators and spectators.

SATURDAY 7 SEPTEMBER

The BBC's final televised day of live cricket in 1991 gave me as much personal pleasure as any of the summer, perhaps because I had gone for broke in my preview in the *Birmingham Post* for a Hampshire win. Only once before had I appeared to have set fire to my boats so comprehensively – also before a Lord's final, as it happened, in which India beat West Indies in the 1983 World Cup. I had a similar overwhelming conviction this time, that the nine letters comprising Hampshire were already etched on the trophy. Even the scepticism of the cruelly winged Mark Nicholas, the evening before when I shared my optimism with him, could not shake me, and I was delighted to commentate on the winning hit by Jonathan Ayling off the fourth ball of the final over.

I was pleased for Hampshire, pleased for Nicholas, and delighted for David Gower, whose 1991 position in international limbo will, I earnestly hope, not be permanent, but fear it might. The refusal by him to compromise his rounded approach to life, and the determination of the selectors not to compromise the Gooch–Stewart devotion-to-duty ethos is, in my view, more their loss than his, although I am sure Gower does not agree with me. Dignity is a rare quality in cricket. As Gower proved on 10 June 1986 at Lord's, when he was relieved of the England captaincy, he has it.

During the day, I sought from Tony and Richie their highlights of the drawn series earlier in the summer, and their considered thoughts are as follows. Tony first:

> I thought the injury to Gordon Greenidge in the Texaco one-day international at Old Trafford to be, arguably, the incident which had the biggest influence on the series. I had watched the West Indies in the Caribbean for three seasons – against India, England and Australia, and could see how vulnerable they were. They were a side creaking and ready to be beaten, with, probably, the greatest remaining pillar in the side the opening batting partnership between Greenidge and Haynes now disrupted. We will never know what would have happened had Greenidge not been injured, but I believe the outcome of the series could have been different.
>
> Graham Gooch was marvellous. Batting through the England innings for 154 at Headingley did most to win the match for England. Seam bowlers had a pitch to bowl on of uneven bounce, and batsmen, in the main, had to apply themselves with straight bats. Surprisingly, when I interviewed Gooch for BBC television after the end of the season, he said the pitch was not too bad. He thought that the reputation of Leeds gets at everyone before they start, but he got into a good frame of mind, especially when his top batsmen, Atherton, Hick and Lamb, disappeared quickly twice in the game; he just battled on ball by ball.
>
> Of Curtly Ambrose, it is rare for such a young bowler to be such a key performer. It is also rare for a strike bowler, on occasions genuinely fast, to

perform as a stock bowler. His 249 overs were 62 ahead of any other West Indian bowler in the five games – Walsh – and 63 more than DeFreitas.

I must mention Ian Botham. When he played in the final Test at the Oval, England looked visibly more confident. They had much more presence, and his influence in the dressing-room was as important as on the field, where he could be seen talking to, and occasionally quietening down, fiery personalities like Tufnell and DeFreitas. He gave England charisma – an ingredient not conspicuous lately in England sides.

I must couple Richards with Botham, if only because when I interviewed them at the Oval, they recalled their Somerset days with such a good mixture of affection and humour, even though they obviously hold little respect for those who they held responsible for their leaving.

As for Viv on his own, it was an unforgettable slice of cricket history to see that the greatest talent of his age could still have a serious effect on the course of a Test series. He was definitely a solid scorer of runs – 376 runs including five fifties at an average of 53·71, even though the bravura performances of old were not possible. He was always in a pleasant mood in the middle before the toss, and he and Gooch chatted easily in a good spirit. Both players obviously had respect for the other, and they were good to interview. When I interviewed Richards at Arundel at the start of the tour and asked him which England player he regarded most highly, he was only prepared to talk about Gooch. 'He is still an important player and he showed in the West Indies that he can lead a side to beat us.'

Richie's sky-high opinion of the stature of Gooch as a man, captain and batsman, has been expressed earlier, but here is his analysis of other players and their influence on a series which he says afforded him considerable pleasure:

Smith's two centuries in the series were testimony that he had recovered from the traumas of Australia. He played wonderfully well, and showed great fight and character, as well as good technique. I just wonder why didn't the West Indies, just once, simulate Bruce Reid by having their pace bowlers come round the wicket to him?

Hick, Atherton and Lamb were disaster areas. Hick, as was the case in Australia when he played Sheffield Shield cricket, found there is a giant leap from county cricket to the next level. He will be back, but flaws in technique were established in the series. Atherton is a good young cricketer with plenty of courage. He certainly suffers at the moment from earmarking him for the captaincy when he is not making enough runs to be in the team. Lamb will be back. He had to fail sometime against the West Indies, and it was remarkable that the series should be squared when this trio hardly made any runs.

Regarding Viv Richards, he needed to make an adjustment to his batting, particularly with Greenidge out of the team. He did this, for the most part, very well indeed, with only the occasional rush of blood. In five Tests he made 73, 63,

80, 73 and 60, and it was his steadiness that allowed the West Indies to make as many runs as they did. His batting change showed what a steely character he is.

The injury to Greenidge was the bad luck of the summer for the West Indies, who had no one to take his place. I have no doubt his absence also had an effect on Desmond Haynes's batting over the five matches. Desmond not only had to worry about his own batting, but try to protect his partner as well.

Carl Hooper is one of the best young cricketers around, but he gives the impression of being slightly diffident. His century at Lord's was an excellent effort, but the one for the future was definitely at Edgbaston, where his unbeaten 55 came at a time when England had a realistic chance of winning. Definitely the player of the future for the West Indies, despite the publicity for some of their other youngsters.

At the end of the Test in Perth at the beginning of this year when England were in disarray, DeFreitas told me he intended to work harder than ever before in his cricketing life to hold down the all-rounder's spot. He did that and was a key man for Gooch. A fine Test match season. In years to come, when people are looking at the scorecards, Derek Pringle's name will not leap to their lips. That will be a pity. He did a tremendous job at Headingley, where he made runs and took wickets, and at Edgbaston, where his common sense allowed England their chance. He had to do the job normally done by Fraser, whose injury was a real body-blow for England. He might have only scored 128 runs at an average of 18·29, and taken 12 wickets at 26·83 apiece, but he gave Gooch most of the control that enabled England to arrive at the Oval with a chance of squaring the series.

It may be that 1991 saw the end of the appalling over-rates that have been one of the greatest problems in cricket over the last 30 years, worsening each year. It will depend on whether the ICC members keep their nerve and put an end to a happening that has been a straight out fraud on the people who pay a great deal of money at the turnstiles. The system mooted of five percent of each player's match-fee being deducted for every over not bowled is brilliantly simple. Good luck to them.

8PM SATURDAY 7 SEPTEMBER

Darkness was about to envelop Lord's. The end of the final always brings mixed feelings to me. There is relief that a long and demanding summer behind the microphone is over, with just the run-in with Warwickshire to the Britannic Assurance County Championship to follow for my newspaper. There is sadness that our 37th and final scheduled day of television coverage has ended and, as I sit in the relatively spacious commentary box, I watch our engineers move in to de-rig the equipment.

Yet again I realised what a big team effort is necessary before we utter one cheep down a microphone. I glanced at the planning schedule for the day, several pages long and listing every minute detail as well as all the equipment necessary for the broadcast: the nine cameras, the slow-motion machinery and so on. It was made available to me by Keith, and I appreciated once more the attention to every single aspect of the programme, which characterises the preparation by the BBC for an outside broadcast.

I watched the unravelling of wires and cables from beneath our working desk, and wondered how we manage to avoid cutting the nation off from our telecast with our sometimes over-vigorous soft-shoe shuffle as we commentate. Geoffrey said his final goodbye and left me to think of how long I had waited before I finally managed to get the last word with him. He was eulogising about Surrey's Graham Thorpe, then on 93, and had just said 'sensible and controlled', when Thorpe slashed a catch to mid-off and, as *The Times* put it, 'Jack Bannister was able to complete Boycott's sentence (did I detect a certain relish?) "... and out".' As Maurice Chevalier once said, but not about cricket, 'Ah yes. I remember it well.'

As I will the summer of 1991. I have occasionally, in the past 40 years, witnessed a set of performances by a cricketer which, single-handedly, dictated the outcome of a game, a competition or a series, but there have been few. Not only do the batting and captaincy contributions of Gooch fall into that category, I place them top of the shop, taking into account three factors:

1. The starting base, following the disastrous tour of Australia.
2. The quality of the opposition, especially the bowlers.
3. The nature of the pitches, with those at Headingley and Edgbaston being among the most helpful that the bowlers of both sides will encounter in their Test careers.

Gooch's batting was inspirational, even though Hick, Atherton and Lamb profited little, and his leadership deserves similar praise. I deliberately split his approach to leading England into two, because there must be reservations, tactically, about his on-field captaincy. For example, his refusal to use Tufnell on the dramatic Saturday morning at the Oval was difficult to understand. Not just because of the immediate success of the spinner, when he first bowled shortly before lunch, but because Raymond voiced the view before the start of play that the pitch was wearing in a way which would be particularly suited to a slow left-arm bowler, and so made his early participation a tactical must.

If the series could be replayed, I doubt whether Smith would bat behind Ramprakash for so many innings — five of them. Gooch's field placings were usually sound, although a natural inclination to attack sometimes meant an absence for too long of a third man, and the bat-pad off-side fielder was used far too often. The usual defence is that, even if few catches go there, the fielder's presence can inhibit the batsman from playing normally on the front foot, but it puts the bowler under extra pressure as well.

These are small criticisms, but a bigger one must concern the part Gooch played in selection. Assuming that he usually gets the XI he wants, the selection of Malcolm, Watkin and Illingworth for two Tests each, is either a reflection on his judgement, or a comment on the undue importance he attached to loyalty, and his unwillingness to drop a bowler after one Test. He and the selectors clearly got it all wrong at Edgbaston where, as I understand the position, a majority of two to one was in favour of playing Illingworth instead of a fourth seamer. Had the vote gone the other way, the alternative choice was Lawrence, illustrating the impossible situation in which Gooch helped to place himself on the morning of the match.

The return of Botham at the Oval – and what a pity he seemingly refused to help himself on that bizarre day at Portsmouth, three days before the squad for Edgbaston was picked – solved one problem, but not the most important one. He must not be fitted into the England side at the expense of a specialist wicket-keeper. Either he plays, under helpful conditions like Headingley and Edgbaston, as one of four bowlers, batting at seven and the keeper at eight, or, on good pitches, he becomes the fifth bowler and bats at six.

The selectors proved their point with Stewart in the final Test, but logic is against the repetition of such a 'high-risk' policy. My eclectic XII supports most of these criticisms, with only four English players certain to be chosen: Gooch, Haynes, Richardson, Smith, Hooper, Richards, Dujon, Marshall, DeFreitas, Ambrose, Patterson, Tufnell.

Which brings me back to Gooch. Only he enabled England to square a series in which, for the first four Tests, they had two and a half batsmen, two bowlers and a wicket-keeper.

By 9pm there are no cables, no wires, no monitors and no microphones. And, finally, no lights. A golden Test summer is over, but the memories remain sharp and clear. Jack in the box slowly leaves the box, already impatient for the next time he hears Booker-T and the MGs bubble away with 'Soul Limbo', followed by the countdown before Keith starts it all over again with 'Cue Tony'.